THE
HOLINESS-
PENTECOSTAL
MOVEMENT
IN THE
UNITED STATES

THE
HOLINESS-
PENTECOSTAL
MOVEMENT
IN THE
UNITED STATES

by

VINSON SYNAN

WILLIAM B. EERDMANS PUBLISHING COMPANY
Grand Rapids, Michigan

To

Bishop and Mrs. Joseph A. Synan

parents whose lives
have portrayed the essence of the
sanctified and Spirit-filled life
before their seven children

PREFACE

An interesting and important development in the recent history of the United States is the rise of numerous holiness and pentecostal denominations in the twentieth century. During the past two decades, the growth of these groups has been apparent even to the casual observer. For many years dismissed as the fanatic fringe of the fundamentalist movement, little interest was shown in the holiness-pentecostal churches by serious scholars beyond passing references to "holy rollers" as interesting relics of the nation's primitive frontier past. Perhaps there was a tendency on the part of traditional Protestantism to ignore these groups because they were an embarrassing reminder of what had been true of themselves a generation or two earlier. One purpose of this work is to show that the ideological and behavioral roots of these movements are deeply grounded in American religious and cultural history.

Recent developments have caused a mounting interest in both perfectionism and pentecostalism by both scholars and the public alike. The phenomenal growth rates of these churches since World War Two, contrasted with declining growth rates among the traditional denominations, has caused some concern in many religious circles. The construction of modern church buildings, accredited colleges, orphanages, and other institutions has demonstrated the rising affluence of these groups. A matter of concern has also been the increasing proportion of middle-class constituents in these churches. Perhaps the greatest interest has been generated by the rapid growth of the "charismatic" movement inside the traditional denominations within the last decade. Practically every major denomination now has its own pentecostal element, including the most recent one, the Roman Catholic Church. Outside the United States, the explosive growth of the indigenous pentecostal churches in such nations as Chile, Brazil, and South Africa has prompted some to predict that the future center of Christianity will lie in all probability in the southern hemisphere and will be non-Caucasian and pentecostal. Because of these implications, we feel that an in-depth study of the movement in its birthplace, the United States, is in order.

Although this volume does not pretend to be all-inclusive, it is an attempt to place the major holiness and pentecostal bodies in America in their proper setting as part of the total social and intellectual history of the United States. Since the author is not a theologian, he has made little effort to speak the jargon of theology. This book is not an apology for either the holiness or pentecostal movements; it is simply an investigation of the ideas that produced these movements and a treatment of what the men and women who deeply believed in them accomplished. I have tried to be as fair as any good historian ought to be in telling the story of some widely differing groups. There will in all probability be something to disturb everyone who reads it, depending on the perspective and background of each reader. As a born pentecostal, trained in the holiness tradition, I have endeavored to be as sympathetic as possible within the bounds of historical objectivity. Both the best and the worst have been shown of the Methodist-holiness-pentecostal tradition. It will be the task of the reader to separate the precious from the vile.

The overriding thesis of this work is that the historical and doctrinal lineage of American pentecostalism is to be found in the Wesleyan tradition. Since the history of both the Methodist and holiness movements has already been well documented, the first part of the work depends more largely on already published sources. The major part of the work, however, is based on primary material gathered during several years of study from the official archives of the denominations treated in the book. Another major aspect of the book is the attempt to interpret the important role played by the Southern pentecostal groups in the development of American pentecostalism. They, above all, have been responsible for maintaining a perfectionist or "holiness" emphasis in the movement at large.

I should like to express gratitude to the many individuals who generously aided the author in preparing this manuscript for publication. At the University of Georgia, Horace Montgomery, my major professor, along with Charles Wynes and Willard Gatewood gave invaluable aid and insight in the writing of the graduate thesis upon which this book is based. In the revisions and further research which followed, much help was freely given by many Wesleyan and pentecostal scholars.

I am also indebted to many other persons who have made my work more pleasant and profitable. Among them are Christine Burroughs, Juanita Walker, Dorothy Poteat, Carolyn Dixon, Debbie Benninghoff, and above all, my wife Carol Lee, who not only assisted with the typing, but with all the stages of effort that produced this work.

—Harold Vinson Synan

Franklin Springs, Georgia

CONTENTS

Chapter One

THE DOUBLE CURE
1766-1866

Be of sin the double cure,
Save from wrath and make me pure.
—Augustus Toplady

John Wesley, the indomitable founder of Methodism, was also the spiritual and intellectual father of the modern holiness and pentecostal movements which have issued from Methodism within the last century. Contained in his *Journal*, which he began in 1735 and ended in 1790, and in his published letters and sermons, is Wesley's theology, which has had and continues to have a profound influence on Protestantism. In a lifetime (1703-1791) which practically spanned the eighteenth century, Wesley had time to develop and refine his ideas on theology, society, and ecclesiology. Partly because of the sheer volume of his writings, there have emerged several John Wesleys to whom different people refer for different reasons. Yet the basic premises on which Methodism rests, along with all the other religious movements with origins in Methodism, were meticulously set down by Wesley during his amazing career.[1]

[1] The best collections of Wesley's works are: Nehemiah Curnock, ed., *The Journal of John Wesley* (London, 1910); John Telford, ed., *The Letters of the Rev. John Wesley* (London, 1931); and E. A. Sugden, ed., *Wesley's Standard Sermons* (Nashville, 1920). A recent reprint of all Wesley's works is Thomas Jackson, ed., *The Works of John Wesley* (Grand Rapids, Michigan, 1959), which is a fourteen-

In arriving at his mature theological convictions, Wesley borrowed from many sources. His doctrines were distilled primarily from the Anglo-Catholic tradition in which he was educated, rather than from the continental Reformed Protestant tradition. Methodism, with its strong Arminian base, was in essence a reaction against the extreme Calvinism which had dominated English social, religious, and political life during much of the seventeenth century. If the Calvinist taught that only the elect could be saved, the Methodist taught that anyone could find salvation. If the Calvinist could never be certain that he was in the elect circle, the Methodist could know from a crisis experience of conversion that he was saved. From the beginning, Methodist theology placed great emphasis on this conscious religious experience. This empirical evidence of salvation is what Wesley and his followers have since offered to the world, and it has been the divergent interpretations of this basic premise that have caused periodic fragmentation within the Methodist fold.

Perhaps the best example of the Methodist quest for evidence of salvation based on conscious religious experience is the case of Wesley himself. The son of an Anglican clergyman, he was educated at Oxford, as were his father and grandfather. After receiving the A.B. and A.M. degrees at Oxford, young Wesley took Anglican orders in 1728 at the insistence of his father. Then as a twenty-five-year-old youth, he began an intensive program of religious reading in order to define his own convictions.[2]

In the devotional reading that Wesley followed were several books that profoundly influenced his religious views. Among these were Jeremy Taylor's *Rule and Exercises of Holy Living and Dying*, and Thomas a Kempis' *Imitation of Christ*, which he read in 1725. The most influential works, however, were William Law's *Treatise on Christian Perfection* and *Serious Call to a Devout and Holy Life*. Reading *Serious Call* in 1726, Wesley adopted much of Law's thought as his own. In this book Law called for a holiness of life in the laity which the church for centuries had reserved only for the

volume photocopy of the authorized edition published by the Wesleyan Conference office in London, England, in 1872.

2 Robert Southey, *The Life of John Wesley* (London, 1820), I, 75.

monastics and clergy. "For there is no reason," wrote Law, "why you should think the highest holiness, the most heavenly tempers, to be the duties and happiness of a bishop, but what is as good a reason why you should think the same tempers to be the duty and happiness of all Christians."[3]

The remainder of Wesley's life was spent in the pursuit of the holiness of heart and life that Taylor, Kempis, and Law upheld in their works. In seeking further light on the subject of holiness and how it could be attained, Wesley sought to clarify his own thinking. Reading late at night and early in the morning, he devoured the writings of Clement of Alexandria, Plotinus, Augustine, The Cambridge Platonists, Molinas, Madam Guyon, François de Sales, Fénelon, and Pascal. "Out of such insights," asserts one writer, "not yet fully comprehended, grew the doctrines of Methodism, and in particular the Wesleyan doctrine of Christian perfection."[4]

It was this pursuit of holiness that led Wesley to leave England for Georgia in 1735 as a missionary to the Indians. In a letter to a friend written before embarking for America, Wesley declared, "My chief motive, to which all the rest are subordinate, is the hope of saving my own soul." When asked of whether his soul could have been saved in England as well as in Georgia, Wesley replied, "I answer, no; neither can I hope to attain the same degree of holiness here which I may there."[5]

Like many travelers to Georgia both before and since 1735, Wesley found little of either salvation or holiness. The Georgia Indians were not the gentle, innocent people, hungry for the gospel, as he had been told; indeed they were savage warriors who engaged in constant warfare during his stay. Most of Wesley's Georgia labors were therefore among the whites in and near Savannah. The Indians he found generally degraded and uninterested in his theology. Even the whites disliked him, accusing him of being too strict, cold, and

[3] William Law, *A Serious Call to a Devout and Holy Life* (New York, 1955 reprint), p. 115. See also John Leland Peters, *Christian Perfection and American Methodism* (New York, 1956), p. 19.

[4] Peters, *Christian Perfection and American Methodism*, p. 20.

[5] Wesley, *Letters of John Wesley*, I, 188-190.

formal. Once in the town of Frederica, Georgia, he was falsely accused and insulted. Eventually he was hailed into court in Savannah for refusal to serve the sacraments to a young lady, and disgraced before the very people he had come to help. In spite of aid from General James Edward Oglethorpe, the founder of the Georgia colony, and the support of Dr. Thomas Bray's London-based "Society for the Propagation of the Gospel in Foreign Parts," Wesley was in general a failure as a missionary to Georgia. Returning to England in February of 1738, he lamented, "I went to America to convert the Indians; but O! who shall convert me?"[6]

It was on Wesley's journey to America that he first made contact with Moravian Pietists from Germany who later greatly influenced his thought. On the stormy sea, Wesley had been impressed with their calm. Sensing that he did not share their assurance of salvation, he became a seeker after their perfectionist beliefs. Back in England, he met both the Moravian Bishop Augustus Gottlieb Spangenberg and Peter Bohler, a Moravian missionary en route to Carolina. Bohler told Wesley that "saving faith brought with it both dominion over sin and true peace of mind—both holiness and happiness." Without having yet gone through this experience of conversion and perfect holiness, Wesley began to preach and to seek it.[7]

Wesley's slow and painful conversion from sacramental Anglicanism to evangelical Methodist Christianity came to a climax on May 24, 1738, while attending a reading of Martin Luther's Preface to Romans at a religious society meeting on Aldersgate Street in London. Entering the service with a "strange indifference, dullness, and coldness" after experiencing months of "unusually frequent lapses into sin," Wesley felt his "heart strangely warmed." This was his famous conversion experience, simultaneously conscious, emotional, and empirical. Yet he did not feel that he had attained his goal of holiness or Christian perfection in this

6 Wesley, *The Works of John Wesley*, I, 74.

7 Peters, *Christian Perfection*, p. 23; Wesley, *Journal of John Wesley*, I, 455.

Aldersgate experience, preferring to believe that for him perfect holiness lay in the future.[8]

Later in 1738, Wesley journeyed to the Moravian settlement at Herrnhut, near Dresden. It was here that he met Count Zinzendorf, the German utopian-evangelical who headed the community. Wesley was impressed by the members of the settlement, for they seemed to be "saved from inward as well as outward sin." Later, while conversing with Zinzendorf, Wesley found that the Count did not share his view of a second, perfecting experience of divine grace. In the century that followed, the views of these two men were to be sharply debated theories in evangelical circles, the followers of Wesley believing in a second crisis experience of sanctification and the followers of Zinzendorf teaching that one was perfected at conversion.[9]

Much controversy has surrounded Wesley's own testimony on his experience of sanctification. Some writers within the present holiness movement regard his experience of January 1, 1739, as the time of his sanctification:

> Mr. Hall, Kinchin, Ingham, Whitefield, Hutchins, and my brother Charles, were present at our love-feast in Fetter-Lane, with about sixty of our brethren. About three in the morning, as we were continuing instant in prayer, the power of God came mightily upon us, inasmuch that many cried out for exceeding joy, and many fell to the ground. As soon as we recovered a little from that awe and amazement at the presence of His Majesty, we broke out with one voice, "We praise thee, O God; we acknowledge thee to be the Lord."[10]

[8] Peters, *Christian Perfection*, p. 27; Wesley, *The Works of John Wesley*, I, 103. For most advocates of the "second blessing" theory of sanctification, this experience of Wesley's was his conversion and not in any sense his experience of sanctification.

[9] M. E. Redford, *The Rise of the Church of the Nazarene* (Kansas City, 1951), p. 34; Wesley, *The Works of John Wesley*, I, 110-158. For all modern holiness people the Zinzendorfian theory of sanctification is still anathema.

[10] Redford, *The Rise of the Church of the Nazarene*, p. 34; Wesley, *The Works of John Wesley*, I, 170. Scholarship of this century has confirmed the contention that Wesley taught sanctification to be a second, definite, instantaneous work of grace. See such works as Harold Lindstrom, *Wesley and Sanctification* (London, 1946), pp. 121-124; M.

From 1739 until 1777, Wesley issued and repeatedly revised a tract entitled "A Plain Account of Christian Perfection as Believed and Taught by the Reverend Mr. John Wesley." This eighty-one-page document has served as a veritable manifesto for all the holiness and perfectionist groups which have separated from Methodism during the past two centuries. In the meticulous, logical style that Wesley mastered as a Lincoln Fellow at Oxford, the founder of Methodism built in this pamphlet the edifice of his doctrine.[11]

By 1740, Wesley's ideas on theology were fairly well cast in the permanent mold that would shape the Methodist movement. Succinctly stated, they involved two separate phases of experience for the believer: the first, conversion, or justification, and the second, Christian perfection, or sanctification. In the first experience the penitent was forgiven for his actual sins of commission, becoming a Christian but retaining a "residue of sin within."[12] This remaining "inbred sin" was the result of Adam's fall and had to be dealt with by a "second blessing, properly so-called." This experience purified the believer of inward sin and gave him "perfect love" toward God and man.

Wesley never taught "sinless perfection" as some have charged. "Imperfect judgment, the physical and mental passions common to men, temptation, and the freedom by which, through willful disobedience, he might fall again into sin, would remain real." The perfection which Wesley taught was a perfection of motives and desires. "Sinless perfection"

E. Gaddis, "Christian Perfectionism in America" (Doctoral dissertation, University of Chicago, 1929); Peters, *Christian Perfection and American Methodism;* and Timothy L. Smith, *Revivalism and Social Reform* (New York, 1957). All maintain that the present holiness denominations are closer to Wesley's actual views than the present Methodist Church. Emory Stevens Bucke, *et al., History of American Methodism,* III, 608, 609, agree that Wesley definitely taught a "second blessing, properly so-called," although never leaving a "completely clear" record of his own attainment of it. See also Newton Flew, *The Idea of Perfection in Christian Theology* (London, 1934), pp. 329-341.

11 Wesley, *The Works of John Wesley,* IX, 366-488. Wesley once referred to his doctrine of entire sanctification as "the grand depositum of Methodism."

12 *Ibid.,* 400.

would come only after death. In the meantime the sanctified soul, through careful self-examination, godly discipline, and methodical devotion and avoidance of worldly pleasures, could live a life of victory over sin. This perfection, Wesley taught, could be attained instantly as a "second work of grace" although it was usually preceded and followed by a gradual "growth in grace."[13]

Wesley did not always find it easy to keep this doctrine paramount within Methodism. The Calvinist branch of the Methodist societies, led by George Whitefield, rejected the "second blessing" theory. In May of 1768, Wesley wrote his brother Charles in distress that, "I am at my wits' end with regard to two things—the church and Christian perfection. Unless both you and I stand in the gap *in good earnest*, the Methodists will drop them both."[14] In his last year of life, Wesley wrote to his friend Adam Clarke, "If we can prove that any of our local preachers . . . speak against it, let him be a local preacher or leader no longer . . . [he] cannot be an honest man."[15] In spite of such infidelity from within and great opposition from without, perfectionism became the distinguishing doctrine of Methodism and thus it became the first great holiness church.

When Methodism was transplanted to America, the doctrine of entire sanctification came along with it. The first Methodist preacher to come to British North America was Captain Thomas Webb, a barracks-master in New York City. In the first recorded Methodist sermon in this nation in 1766 Webb declared:

> The words of the text were written by the Apostles after the act of justification had passed on them. But you see, my friends, this was not enough for them. They must receive the Holy Ghost after this. So must you. You must be sanctified. But you are not.

[13] Bucke, *et al., History of American Methodism,* III, 608, 609; George Allen Turner, *The More Excellent Way: The Scriptural Basis of the Wesleyan Message* (Winona Lake, Indiana, 1951), *passim;* Peters, *Christian Perfection,* pp. 27-31, 39-43, 54-78; Gaddis, "Christian Perfectionism in America," pp. 162ff.; H. C. Sheldon, *History of Christian Doctrine* (New York, 1895), II, 376-377.

[14] Wesley, *The Letters of Wesley,* V, 88.

[15] *Ibid.,* VIII, 249.

You are only Christians in part. You have not received the Holy Ghost. I know it. I can feel your spirits hanging about me like so much dead flesh.[16]

When the American Methodist Church was formally organized at the famous Christmas Conference in Baltimore in 1784, the leaders sent by Wesley to effect the organization were Francis Asbury and Richard Wright. These men led the conference to adopt the commission Wesley had given them before they left England, "We believe that God's design in raising up the preachers called Methodists in America is to reform the continent and spread scriptural holiness over these lands." The first *Discipline* of the Methodist Church (1788) was so thoroughly perfectionistic that it carried a complete printing of Wesley's "Plain Account of Christian Perfection."[17]

Wesley appointed Francis Asbury, indefatigable preacher and traveler, to supervise the American branch of Methodism. Asbury was as firmly committed to the doctrine of holiness as Wesley, claiming to have been "saved" at the age of fifteen and "sanctified" the following year.[18] In 1782 he wrote in his *Journal* that the only preaching that did good was the kind which "presses the use of the means, and urges holiness of heart." Once while ill he wrote, "I have found by secret search that I have not preached sanctification as I should have done. If I am restored, this shall be my theme more pointedly than ever."[19]

The earliest stronghold for Methodism in colonial America was in Brunswick County, Virginia, centering around the Bath Parish of the Reverend Devereaux Jarratt. Although an

16 J. F. Hurst, *The History of Methodism* (New York, 1902), III, 1252.

17 Peters, *Christian Perfection*, p. 88; John J. Tigert, *The Doctrines of the Methodist Episcopal Church in America* (Cincinnati, 1902), II, 3-150. The *Disciplines* carried the "Plain Account" from 1788 to 1808, after which it was not included. For the next century a short statement of Methodist history and holiness doctrine was placed in the prefaces of the *Disciplines*.

18 Peters, *Christian Perfection*, p. 85.

19 Francis Asbury, *The Journal of the Reverend Francis Asbury* (New York, 1821), I, 235-339.

Anglican rector, Jarratt cooperated fully with the Methodist pastor Robert Williams and the Methodist societies which lay within his parish. Williams and Jarratt cooperated in revivalistic services that seem quite similar to later pentecostal worship. In all these meetings the ideal of sanctification was preached. In the *Brief Narrative of the Revival of Religion* that Jarratt wrote describing the Virginia services of 1775, holiness religion was much in evidence. Many were "panting and groaning for pardon" while others were "entreating God, with strong cries and tears to save them from the remains of inbred sin, to sanctify them throughout. . . ." Numbers testified to having been sanctified, "instantaneously, and by simple faith."[20]

At times the emotions of the sanctified Methodists would exceed the limits of control. "Some would be seized with a trembling, and in a few moments drop on the floor as if they were dead; while others were embracing each other with streaming eyes, and all were lost in wonder, love and praise," wrote one observer. Another noted that some wept for grief while others shouted for joy "so that it was hard to distinguish one from the other." At times the congregations would "raise a great shout" that could be heard for miles around. All this the placid Anglican Jarratt observed with some awe, later observing that as the emotional element abated "the work of conviction and conversion abated too."[21]

Despite sharp criticism from the Anglican establishment and the colonial newspapers, the Methodists grew faster in Virginia than anywhere else in America. By 1776 half of all the Methodists in America were in Virginia where much of the drunkenness, cursing, swearing, and fighting which had characterized the colony before the revival of 1773-1776 gave way for a time to "prayer, praise, and conversing about God. . . ." This revivalistic outbreak was the first instance of a pentecostal-like religious revival in the nation, and was a

[20] Devereaux Jarratt, *A Brief Narrative of the Revival of Religion in Virginia, In a Letter to a Friend. . .* (4th edition, London, 1779), pp. 7-12; W. W. Sweet, *Religion in Colonial America* (New York, 1965), pp. 306-311; Peters, *Christian Perfection*, pp. 84, 85; Wesley M. Gewehr, *The Great Awakening in Virginia* (Durham, 1930), pp. 143-148.

[21] Gewehr, *The Great Awakening in Virginia*, pp. 153-155.

direct antecedent of the frontier Kentucky revivals of 1800.[22]

From this stronghold in Virginia, Methodists began their successful growth that was eventually to spread over the entire continent. Essentially, eighteenth-century Methodism was a reaction against a prevailing creedal rigidity, liturgical strictness, and "ironclad institutionalism" that had largely depersonalized religion and had rendered it incapable of serving the needs of the individual. Methodist perfectionism in America was "a swing toward warmth, feeling, experience, and morality" and away from the mechanical, permissive, de-ethicalized, and formal worship of the times. The growth of this "heart religion," as Wesley termed it, became a phenomenon not only of colonial frontier life but of urban life as well. The appeal to the poor and disinherited was almost irresistible. The optimistic idea that one could find perfection seemed to match the general optimism that prevailed throughout American society. In rejecting the political and social norms of England and Europe, the rising Americans rejected simultaneously the religious norms of the old world.[23]

Virginians were largely responsible for carrying the Methodist-holiness flame to the other colonies. Jesse Lee, an enthusiast, brought the message "against great opposition" to the stern Calvinists of New England. One Congregational minister is reported to have commented on the Methodist ways that were gaining converts daily:

> They are constantly mingling with the people, and enter into all their feelings, wishes and wants; and their discourses are on the level with the capacity of their hearers, and addressed to their understanding and feelings, and produce a thrilling effect, while our discourses shoot over their heads and they remain unaffected. . . . They reach a large class of people that we do not. The ignorant, the drunken, the profane, listen to their homespun, but zealous . . . discourses. . . .[24]

22 *Ibid.*, p. 155; Peters, *Christian Perfection*, p. 84; see also the Williamsburg *Virginia Gazettes* for unfavorable public reactions to the Methodists (24 AG 39:12, 18 JL 51:22, P. D. 22 JA 67:23, P. D. 30 JI 72:23).

23 Gaddis, "Christian Perfectionism in America," p. 162.

24 *Ibid.*, p. 237.

While Americans were fighting their Revolutionary War and establishing their independence from England, their churches were fighting for and obtaining their own independence of forms and worship. Leading the way were the fiery Methodists. As the frontier reached further and further into the interior of the continent, it was found that the volatile and emotional worship of the Methodists best fitted the temper of the rude frontiersmen. Circuit riders penetrated every corner of the frontier, preaching a religion of the fire and brimstone variety that is found today mostly in backwoods camp meetings. In most cases, the Methodist circuit riders urged their newly won converts to "go on to perfection." As soon as the penitent had recovered from the ordeal of conversion, he was plunged into the agony of seeking for sanctification. In Ohio, Edward Dromgoole, Benjamin Lakin, and James Gilruth carried the holiness flame. In Maryland, John Hagerty "cried mightily" upon feeling the sanctifying "power" and afterwards promoted the doctrine in his area. In 1805, Edward Dromgoole went to Georgia and found that the "greater part" of the 1,500 to 2,000 Methodists to whom he preached had experienced the second blessing. "There," he reported, "the work of sanctification goes on sweetly and powerfully in the hearts of many." In Illinois, the formidable Peter Cartwright led tough frontiersmen into the experience of holiness through his rough-and-tumble style.[25]

Perhaps the most famous outbreak of enthusiastic, pentecostal-like religion in American history occurred in the great Cane-Ridge camp meeting in Logan County, Kentucky, in 1800. Begun in June 1800 by James McGready, William Hodges, and John Rankin, all Presbyterian ministers, this revival continued for over a year and exhibited most of the emotional phenomena that have characterized certain branches of American Protestantism ever since. A Methodist minister, John McGee, succeeded in sparking the movement when, while preaching, he was overcome by his feelings and "shouted and exhorted with all possible energy." Soon the

[25] W. W. Sweet, *Religion on the American Frontier* (Chicago, 1946), IV, 91, 96, 121, 127, 156-157, 249, 440-443; Smith, *Revivalism and Social Reform*, p. 118.

floor of the Red River Presbyterian Church was "covered with the slain" while "their screams for mercy pierced the heavens." The excitement and curiosity engendered by this service soon mushroomed into a full-scale camp meeting in 1801 at Cane-Ridge in Bourbon County under the leadership of another Presbyterian minister, Barton Stone. It was here that the American camp meeting was born.[26]

Those who attended such camp meetings as Cane-Ridge generally expected their religious experiences to be as vivid as the frontier life around them. Accustomed to "braining bears and battling Indians," they received their religion with great color and excitement. Their "godly hysteria" included such phenomena as falling, jerking, barking like dogs, falling into trances, the "holy laugh," and "such wild dances as David performed before the Ark of the Lord."[27]

In August 1801 the Cane-Ridge revival reached a climax when crowds variously estimated at from 10,000 to 25,000 gathered. In the light of the blazing campfires hundreds of sinners would fall "like dead men in mighty battle." Others would get the "jerks" and shake helplessly in every joint. Peter Cartwright reported that he once saw five hundred jerking at once in one service. The unconverted were as subject to the "jerks" as were the saints. One minister reported that "the wicked are much more afraid of it than of small pox or yellow fever." After "praying through" some would crawl on all fours and bark like dogs, thus "treeing the devil." Others would fall into trances for hours, awakening to claim salvation or sanctification. In some services entire congregations would be seized by the "holy laugh," an ecstasy which could hardly be controlled. A responsible student of these phenomena has estimated that by 1805 over half of all the Christians of Kentucky had exhibited these "motor phenomena."[28]

26 W. W. Sweet, *The Story of Religion in America* (New York, 1950), pp. 228-229; Bernard Weisberger, *They Gathered at the River* (New York, 1958), pp. 20-25; Frederick Morgan Davenport, *Primitive Traits in Religious Revivals, A Study in Mental and Social Evolution* (New York, 1905), pp. 61-78; Archie Robertson, *That Old-Time Religion* (Boston, 1950), pp. 56-57.

27 Weisberger, *They Gathered at the River,* pp. 20-21.

28 Davenport, *Primitive Traits in Religious Revivals,* pp. 78-82. Some called these traits "Methodist fits"; see Robertson, *That*

From Kentucky the revivalistic flame spread over the entire South, reaching into Tennessee, North and South Carolina, Western Virginia, and Georgia. In most places the same phenomena were repeated. In some areas another manifestation was reported in addition to those already described. In the revival that hit the University of Georgia in 1800-1801, students visited nearby campgrounds and were themselves smitten with the "jerks" and "talking in unknown tongues":

> They swooned away and lay for hours in the straw prepared for those "smitten of the Lord," or they started suddenly to flee away and fell prostrate as if shot down by a sniper, or they took suddenly to jerking with apparently every muscle in their body until it seemed they would be torn to pieces or converted into marble, or they shouted and talked in unknown tongues.[29]

From 1800 until the present day such phenomena have accompanied in some degree most major revivals, regardless of denomination or doctrine. Even the Mormon Church experienced much the same motor phenomena that characterized the early Methodists and later pentecostals. Shouting, jerks, and dancing were common in their services, and Brigham Young not only spoke in unknown tongues, but interpreted his own messages to his hearers. Mormon choirs

---

Old-Time Religion, p. 56. Many of these phenomena have been repeated periodically throughout Christian history. They seem confined to no particular time or place. Certainly they are not unique to the American South or to "holy rollers." Scenes similar to Cane-Ridge were seen in England while Wesley and Whitefield preached, in Massachusetts under Jonathan Edwards, and in New York City, Boston, and Richmond. In general they are more often associated with the poorer classes and the underprivileged. The author has seen these demonstrations in the twentieth century not only in the United States, but in such diverse countries as Canada and Chile.

[29] E. Merton Coulter, *College Life in the Old South* (New York, 1928), pp. 194-195; also see Guion Griffis, "Camp Meetings in Ante-Bellum North Carolina," *The North Carolina Historical Review* (January 1933), for a description of speaking in tongues in early North Carolina camp meetings. Throughout the nineteenth century speaking in unknown tongues occurred occasionally in the revivals and camp meetings that dotted the countryside. Perhaps the phenomenon was considered just another of the many evidences that one had been saved or sanctified.

were even known to sing songs in unknown tongues in unison.[30]

Within a decade the Western revival which began at Cane-Ridge in 1800 became more institutionalized, as the camp meeting became a regular part of American religious life. By 1830 the more frenzied aspects of the revival had become little more than a memory, while primary concern switched from religious experience to doctrine. However, the emotional type of religion continued to exist, especially on the frontier and in the South, and always there existed the possibility of fresh revival outbreaks. Indeed, the nineteenth and twentieth centuries were to exhibit periodic awakenings and recessions of revivalistic religion that tended to resemble the ups and downs of the business cycle.[31]

The area in the United States that was most subject to the revival cycle was the well-known "burned-over district" of Western New York, so named because of the numerous revivals that had swept over the area. The man most responsible for reinstituting and refining the revival was Charles G. Finney, born in Connecticut, but brought up in Western New York. While a young man Finney joined the Presbyterian Church, but he soon rebelled against its Calvinism. Following his license to preach in 1824, he made a study of Christian doctrine and by 1836 became convinced that entire sanctification was possible in this life. Soon his spellbinding revival sermons were filled with perfectionist thought. In 1837 he went to Oberlin College where, with President Asa Mahan, he added an element of academic respectability to his evangelistic labors. From 1843 until his death people flocked to barns, schoolhouses, and open air meetings to hear him expound his doctrines. According to Finney, a person could achieve the coveted state of Christian perfection or sanctification by simply exercising free will and cultivating "right intentions." Sin and holiness, he explained, could not exist in the same person. While Finney's "Oberlin theology" differed somewhat from the traditional holiness

---

30 Joseph Smith, *History of the Church of Jesus Christ of Latter-Day Saints* (Salt Lake City, 1902), pp. 296-297, 409, 422.

31 Weisberger, *They Gathered at the River*, p. 21; Smith, *Revivalism and Social Reform*, pp. 16-34.

views of the Wesleyans, such differences as there were came mainly from his Calvinistic background.[32]

An illustration of the radical possibilities inherent in perfectionism is seen in the life and projects of one of Finney's converts, John Humphrey Noyes. A graduate of Dartmouth College, Noyes later studied for the ministry at Andover and Yale. At Yale he professed to be sanctified and completely perfected. In his new state Noyes felt that it was impossible to commit sin. In time his ideas became so peculiar that he was asked to leave Yale, losing at the same time his license to preach. Noyes' perfectionism finally led him to teach that direct divine revelation was superior to the Scriptures, he himself, of course, being the arbiter of the divine will. Eventually he taught that Christ had returned in A.D. 70 with the destruction of Jerusalem and that heaven and the perfect society was now in the earth.[33]

From 1836 to 1879, Noyes attempted to create communities of "Bible Communists" in Putney, Vermont, and Oneida, New York. The Oneida experiment began in 1848 and was one of the few utopian experiments in the United States that proved to be economically successful. Perhaps the most startling innovation at Oneida was Noyes' institution of "complex marriage." Feeling that heaven, where "there is neither marriage nor giving in marriage," had already come and that the sanctified could not commit sin, Noyes began a program of "reconciliation of the sexes" to parallel man's "reconciliation with God." His system was a type of sanctified promiscuity, theoretically under feminine control, and regulated by confession, conditional continence, and mutual criticism.[34]

---

[32] Smith, *Revivalism and Social Reform*, pp. 104, 140; for a firsthand account of Finney's views see *Memoirs of Reverend Charles G. Finney* (New York, 1876), *passim;* other excellent sources are found in Robert S. Fletcher's *A History of Oberlin College from Its Foundation Through the Civil War* (Oberlin, 1943), I, 223-229, and Benjamin B. Warfield, *Perfectionism* (New York, 1931), I, 166-218. The social and historical setting is well treated in Whitney R. Cross, *The Burned-Over District, The Social and Intellectual History of Enthusiastic Religion in Western New York, 1800-1850* (New York, 1965), pp. 158-250.

[33] Warfield, *Perfectionism*, pp. 308-336.

[34] Gaddis, "Christian Perfectionism in America," p. 367; Sweet,

In spite of its emotional extremes, its theological variations, and its utopian visionaries, the perfectionist impulse
grew in America into a great crusade in the two decades
preceding the Civil War. The mood of America during those
years was one of optimism and confidence concerning the
perfectibility of man and his society. Revolts against the
gloomier aspects of the Calvinism that had dominated
American religious thought for a century began to take place.
Transcendentalism and Unitarianism became refuges for a
few romanticist intellectuals, while the Methodist Church
served the common man.

In the Methodist General Conferences of 1824 and 1832
urgent calls were given to the faithful to lay greater stress on
holiness. "If Methodists give up the doctrine of entire
sanctification, or suffer it to become a dead letter, we are a
fallen people," warned the bishops. Soon the tide of
perfectionist thought which flooded the nation in literature
and from the lecture platform caused Methodists to look
anew at their own past and eventually to lay claim to the
distinction of being the first to promote this idea in America.
By 1840 perfectionism was becoming one of the central
themes of American social, intellectual, and religious life.
Resulting from this perfectionistic thought were many
reform movements designed to perfect American life, such as
women's rights, the abolition of slavery, anti-masonry, and
prohibition.

Throughout the nation Methodist pastors and theologians
restudied the writings of Wesley and saw that they could join
in the stream of perfectionist thought and even become
leaders in it without violating their own traditions. This was,
after all, only original Methodism as it had always been
believed and practiced. The decade of the 1840's, therefore,
witnessed a veritable flood of perfectionistic teaching in the
Methodist Church. Leading pastors, bishops, and theologians
led the movement, giving it institutional and intellectual
respectability.[35]

Story of Religion in America, pp. 281-283; Warfield, Perfectionism, II,
219-336; Cross, The Burned-Over District, pp. 322-340. Also see
Gilbert Seldes, The Stammering Century (New York, 1965), pp.
157-197.
    [35] See W. W. Sweet, Methodism in American History (New York,

Among the leading proponents of the new emphasis in Methodism were Mrs. Phoebe Palmer and her physician husband, Dr. Walter Palmer, members of the Allen Street Methodist Church in New York City. These two had been won to the holiness standard by the sister of Mrs. Palmer, Mrs. Sarah A. Lankford, who had begun holding "Tuesday Meetings for the Promotion of Holiness" in her parlor in 1835. By 1839 Mrs. Palmer had not only experienced sanctification, but had become the leader of the meetings. As the "Tuesday Meetings" grew in popularity, hundreds of preachers and laymen from various denominations flocked to her home to hear of the "shorter way" of achieving the perfection and ecstasy that early Christian saints had taken entire lifetimes to acquire. By placing "all on the altar," she taught, one could be instantly sanctified through the baptism of the Holy Ghost. Among those who came and found holiness under the Palmers were leading pastors and bishops of Methodism. She counted among her friends and followers no less than four bishops of the Methodist Church: Bishops Edmund S. Janes, Leonidas L. Hamline, Jesse T. Peck, and Matthew Simpson. For the next thirty years the Palmers were the national leaders of the movement, traversing the United States and Canada numerous times, and addressing camp meetings and leading churches on their theme of holiness and perfect love.[36]

The year 1839 also saw the beginning of the first periodical in America devoted exclusively to holiness doctrine, *The Guide to Christian Perfection*. Founded in Boston by Timothy Merritt, this monthly paper carried testimonies of Phoebe Palmer and her husband. Later the name of the paper was changed to *The Guide to Holiness*. In 1865 *The Guide* was purchased by Dr. and Mrs. Palmer and became quite influential within American Protestantism, and particu-

---

1953), pp. 47-59, and Merle Curti, *Growth of American Thought* (New York, 1965), pp. 298-305. Also see Smith, *Revivalism and Social Reform*, pp. 114-147, and Carl Degler, *Out of Our Past* (New York, 1959), pp. 154-160.

[36] Bucke, *et al.*, *The History of American Methodism*, II, 609-610; Smith, *Revivalism and Social Reform*, pp. 123-124, 144.

larly among Methodists. At its peak, it enjoyed a circulation of 30,000.[37]

With Methodists and Oberlin perfectionists leading the way, the holiness crusade approached a climax shortly before the Civil War. Ministers of most denominations joined in the campaign for perfection. In 1858 William E. Boardman, a Presbyterian minister, published *The Higher Christian Life*, an attempt to interpret sanctification to those outside the Methodist tradition. At once this volume became a best-seller and gained influence in England as well as in America. In 1859 A. B. Earle, the nation's leading Baptist evangelist, professed to be sanctified and published his experience in another best-seller, *The Rest of Faith*. Everywhere men were seeking perfection. "The ethical ideals to which Emerson and Henry David Thoreau aspired on a highly sophisticated level, plain men of the time sought at a Methodist mourners' bench or class meeting." It was a kind of "evangelical transcendentalism" which thrived in the idealism of a young and growing America. By 1856 holiness had become so popular that Jesse T. Peck's book, *The Central Idea of Christianity*, seemed to express the feeling of a large segment of Protestantism in America.[38]

This crusade for holiness, however, was not without disruptive and schismatic tendencies. Along with the drive for perfect sanctification, there arose a parallel drive to stamp out the evil of slavery. Sanctified Christians came to believe that slavery was a blot on society and the church and that it should be abolished. Anti-slavery thought was the direct cause of the formation of the Wesleyan Methodist Church in New York and New England in 1843-44. Leaders of the new sect charged that by compromising with the evil of slavery the Methodist Episcopal Church had renounced its duty to become "evangelically anti-slavery." In 1844 the great division finally came within the Methodist Church itself, with

---

37 Smith, *Revivalism and Social Reform*, pp. 115-117; Delbert R. Rose, *A Theology of Christian Experience* (Minneapolis, 1965), pp. 32-39.

38 Bucke, *The History of American Methodism*, II, 610-612; Smith, *Revivalism and Social Reform*, pp. 114-134. See Warfield, *Perfectionism*, II, 463-558, for an excellent treatment of the "Higher Life Movement" led by William E. Boardman after 1859.

THE DOUBLE CURE 31

the Southern division espousing and defending slavery and the Northern division becoming more openly anti-slavery in practice.[39]

The climactic revival in America with a holiness emphasis came in 1858. This *annus mirabilis* was also the last religious awakening preceding the Civil War. Unfortunately, the Southern states were largely untouched by this revival. Beginning in New York City and spreading over most of the Northeast, the 1858 awakening proved to be primarily urban and Northern. In this remarkable movement business workers turned out *en masse* to sing hymns, while stevedores knelt on the docks to pray. Telegraph companies allowed messages to be sent to "sinners" free of cost at certain times of the day. Soon a "thousand mile prayer meeting" was inaugurated that struck one city after another. Even Henry Ward Beecher, that crusty old opponent of "got up" revivals, joined the crusade after his church filled to capacity night after night with no special urging. The revival of 1858 was as deep and intense as Whitefield's revival of 1740, with one exception — the slave-holding South never felt its impact.[40]

Long before 1858, the Southern churches had largely abandoned the quest for holiness, in theory and in practice. From about 1830 until the outbreak of war, Southern theological energies were directed toward supporting and defending the institution of slavery. A study of the literature of the Methodist Episcopal Church, South, before the war shows that perfectionism was barely discernible. In a volume representing the best thought of the church in 1858, only one out of eighteen "representative" sermons was Wesleyan

[39] Smith, *Revivalism and Social Reform*, pp. 184, 185; Peters, *Christian Perfection*, pp. 125-128; Cross, *The Burned-Over District*, pp. 263-267.

[40] Robertson, *Old-Time Religion*, pp. 68-69; Smith, *Revivalism and Social Reform*, pp. 63-79. The perfectionist aspect of the revival can be seen in J. A. Wood, *Perfect Love, Or Plain Things for Those Who Need Them* (Chicago, 1880), pp. 315-330. Much of a pentecostalist atmosphere surrounded services in the Methodist Church in Binghampton, N. Y., in 1858 where the pastor "fell out for three hours" and then prayed all night. During one service "some shouted, some laughed, some wept, and a large number lay prostrate from three to five hours, beyond the power of shouting or weeping."

in regard to sanctification. Holiness had become a dead letter in the Southern church.[41]

As the nation drifted inexorably into war, the thrust of American thought became almost entirely political and secular. Men forgot about theological differences and denominational distinctions as the verbal dispute over slavery became a military contest. When the guns of Fort Sumter opened fire in April 1861, they signalled the end of the early holiness movement in the United States and proved that the perfection that so many had sought, through the double cure of conversion and sanctification, had failed to avert the imperfection of war.

[41] See *The Methodist Pulpit, South* (Washington, 1858), *passim;* also Gaddis, "Christian Perfectionism," pp. 424, 425. For pro-slavery sermonizing see Eric McKitrick, *Slavery Defended: The Views of the Old South* (Inglewood Cliffs, New Jersey, 1963), pp. 86-98.

Chapter Two

ECHOES FROM THE FOREST TEMPLE - THE NATIONAL HOLINESS ASSOCIATION 1867-1894

We affectionately invite all . . . to come together and spend a week in God's great temple of nature.
—Alfred Cookman

The American Civil War was the greatest phase of the nineteenth-century drive toward the reform and perfection of American society. With the evil of slavery abolished from American life, reformers could now turn their attention to eliminating other evils. Fiery-eyed reformers would henceforth involve themselves with such causes as prohibition, women's rights, and political reform. Few causes lacked supporters, and zealous reformers were not lacking causes.

The reforming zeal that was to produce the populist revolt and the progressive movement also permeated the churches of the nation. No denomination was exempt from the ferment of the times. All churches experienced the challenge to established religion thrown down by Darwinism, socialism, higher criticism, and the social gospel. The flow of American population to urban areas threatened the very foundations of a way of life that remained dominated by a rural mentality. The rise of big industrial empires with all the attendant evils of monopolies, unequal distribution of wealth, and political corruption, posed a special dilemma to Protestantism. More and more the ethics and morality of big business began to dominate the thinking of the churches. President W. J. Tucker of Dartmouth College wrote somewhat ruefully of the decades that followed the Civil War: "The generation which was beginning to take shape and character when I came of age was to have the peculiar fortune, whether to its disadvantage or to its distinction, of finding its way into what we now call the 'modern world.' "[1] For better or for worse, the churches, along with the rest of America's institutions, had to make the same painful transition.

The years that followed the Civil War were characterized by a moral depression in America. Returning soldiers with "battlefield ethics" entered not only the houses of business, but also the halls of government and the sanctuaries of the churches. Many of the younger recruits to the ministry entered their vocations with less training than their elders and lacked the same respect for the traditions and doctrines of the church. No denomination felt the winds of change more than the Methodist Church. Such ancient usages of that church as the "mourner's bench" for penitent sinners, class meetings for the "perfection of the saints," and camp meetings for the benefit of both had been abandoned during the war. With the return of peace, little effort was made to revive these honored forms.[2]

The first region of the United States to experience a religious revival after the war was the South. In the dark days following the war, the impoverished states of the defeated Confederacy turned to religion for solace. During 1865-1867 "a sound of revival was heard from one border to the other." The journals of Methodism teemed with news of great evangelistic efforts. The bishops of the Methodist Episcopal Church, South, meeting in General Conference in 1866, called for a return to Wesleyan principles as an answer to the postwar moral crisis.[3]

1 Degler, *Out of Our Past*, pp. 338-378.

2 W. W. Sweet, *Methodism in American History*, pp. 332-333; Bucke, *et al.*, *The History of American Methodism*, II, 324-326.

3 *Journal of the General Conference of the Methodist Episcopal Church, South, 1866*, pp. 15-21. Also see the statement on holiness in

In spite of this short-lived Southern revival, Protestant Christianity suffered a gradual decline in membership and in interest during the last decades of the century. In 1860, 23 percent of the American population were church members, but it was not until 1890 that the proportion again reached that figure.[4] Within the ranks of Methodism, both North and South, arose a conviction that a return to the holiness revival that had swept much of the country in 1858 would be a welcome relief. In 1870, the bishops of the Southern church again called for a re-emphasis on sanctification: "Nothing is so much needed at the present time throughout all these lands, as a general and powerful revival of scriptural holiness."[5]

Many churchmen lamented the loss of old Methodist institutions, such as the class meeting, the camp meeting, and the emphasis on plainness of dress. As young "progressive" ministers joined the ranks, older preachers looked sadly on at such innovations as robed choirs, organs, and seminary-trained ministers. Some warned that if the camp meeting ceased, then the "heroic fire of Methodism" would die out. Many conservative Methodists believed that the general religious inertia of the times could be cured only by a return to the camp-meeting revivalism that preceded the Civil War.[6]

While Southern leaders grappled with the massive problems of reconstruction and called for a revival of holiness, moves were being made in the North which eventually resulted in the revival of the camp meeting and a new crusade for holiness. In August 1866, J. A. Wood, who had written the best-seller *Perfect Love* in 1860, remarked to a friend, Mrs. Harriet E. Drake of Wilkes-Barre, Pennsylvania, that the doctrine of sanctification was suffering an eclipse within Methodism. Even opposition to "the doctrine and distinctive experience of entire sanctification" was often encountered in

the 1866 *Discipline* of the M. E. Church, South, pp. 3, 74-75; Gaddis, "Christian Perfectionism in America," p. 442.

[4] Robertson, *Old-Time Religion*, p. 70.

[5] Gross Alexander, *History of the Methodist Episcopal Church, South* (New York, 1894), p. 94.

[6] Bucke, *et al.*, *The History of American Methodism*, II, 326; George A. Smith, *The History of Georgia Methodism from 1786 to 1866* (Atlanta, 1913), pp. 396-398.

some Methodist camp meetings. In an offhand remark, Wood
said he believed "that some camp meetings for the special
work of holiness ought to be held." Mrs. Drake, an ardent
devotee of the experience of sanctification, immediately
volunteered to pay one-half of the cost of a holiness camp
meeting if one could be arranged. Wood became obsessed
with the idea and later shared it with the Reverend William B.
Osborn of the New Jersey Methodist Conference. Also
enthused by the idea, Osborn traveled to New York City in
April 1867 to lay the matter before the Reverend John S.
Inskip, pastor of the Green Street Methodist Episcopal
Church. With great feeling, Osborn told Inskip, "I feel God
would have us hold a holiness camp meeting." Osborn's
enthusiasm was so contagious that Inskip immediately
approved the idea. With the winning of Inskip the holiness
movement gained its leading figure and its eventual nationally
acknowledged leader.[7]

Inskip and Osborn immediately set the wheels moving for
the first camp meeting. A call, signed by thirteen Methodist
ministers of New York, was issued for a larger meeting to be
held in Philadelphia on June 13, 1867. This call, published in
several church papers, was for those interested in "holding a
camp meeting, the special object of which should be the
promotion of the work of entire sanctification." Meeting in
Philadelphia on the appointed date, the men present voted to
hold a camp meeting at Vineland, New Jersey, July 17
through 26, 1867, appointing committees to prepare accommodations and publicity for the event. Naming themselves
"The National Camp Meeting Association for the Promotion
of Christian Holiness," the group issued a call written by a
well-known Methodist pastor, the Reverend Alfred Cookman,
addressed to all, "irrespective of denominational ties."
Especially welcome were those "who feel themselves com-
paratively isolated in their profession of holiness." It was
hoped that all would "realize together a Pentecostal baptism
of the Holy Ghost" and return "with a view to increased
usefulness in the churches of which we are members." The
call ended with a plea for unity and revival:

7 J. A. Wood, *Auto-Biography of Rev. J. A. Wood* (Chicago, 1904),
p. 73. For an excellent treatment of the National Holiness Association
see Delbert R. Rose, *A Theology of Christian Experience*, pp. 23-78.

> Come, brothers and sisters of the various denominations, and let us, in this forest-meeting, as in other meetings for the promotion of holiness, furnish an illustration of evangelical union, and make common supplication for the descent of the Spirit upon ourselves, the church, the nation, and the world.[8]

With the opening of the Vineland, New Jersey, camp meeting on July 17, 1867, the modern holiness crusade began. This may properly be considered the beginning of the modern holiness movement in the United States. Those who attended felt unanimously that this meeting was destined to "exert an influence over all Christendom" as well as "to initiate a new era in Methodism." Little did these men realize that this meeting would eventually result in the formation of over a hundred denominations around the world and indirectly bring to birth a "Third Force" in Christendom, the pentecostal movement.[9]

The first "National Camp Meeting for the Promotion of Holiness" was an unqualified success. Although clearly interdenominational, the meeting was dominated by Methodists. Even the famous Methodist Bishop Matthew Simpson and his family attended. Near the end of the meeting a committee of twenty-one was elected to continue the organization and to call for a similar meeting the following year. Inskip was elected the first president of the group, and George Hughes the first secretary. The name adopted for the new group was the "National Camp Meeting Association for the Promotion of Holiness." A call was made for another camp meeting to be held the following year.[10]

In the years following 1867 "National Camp Meetings" were held in Manheim, Pennsylvania, Round Lake, New York, and in many other locations. From 1867 to 1883 a total of fifty-two "national camps" were held, mostly on

[8] Rose, *A Theology of Christian Experience*, p. 52. Also see A. M. McLean and Joel W. Eaton, eds., *Penuel, Or Face to Face with God* (New York, 1869), pp. 6-15, for Inskip's version of the beginning of the Association; and George Hughes, *Days of Power in the Forest Temple. . .* (Boston, 1874), pp. 39-60.

[9] Rose, *A Theology of Christian Experience*, pp. 52-53.

[10] *Ibid.*, pp. 52-61. In later years the name of the group was shortened to "The National Holiness Association," a name which is still used (1970).

Methodist campgrounds and in connection with Methodist annual conferences. Perhaps the most notable "National Camp Meeting" was the one held in Round Lake, New York, in 1874 where seven bishops from the Northern and Southern Methodist Churches attended, along with 20,000 other worshippers. The high point was reached when President U. S. Grant arrived for one day of services. The closing meeting was a sacramental service presided over by Bishop Matthew Simpson, who exhorted the ministers with great passion: "Brethren, there never was a day when we needed more power than now. We are called to meet, in this land, the tide of heathenism rolling in upon our shores. Infidelity is making its fiercest onset. We need and must have apostolic power." On the final Sunday over four hundred persons testified at a "love feast" to having been sanctified in the meeting.[11]

For several years it seemed as if the Methodist Church would once again become the chief holiness sect of America. Of eight new bishops elected in the Northern General Conference of 1872, four were sympathetic to the holiness movement and none was opposed. In 1869, Randolph S. Foster, one of the newly elected bishops, had published a new edition of his most popular book, *Christian Purity, Or the Heritage of Faith* in which he took the view that sanctification could and should be an instantaneous work of grace. In 1878, the bishops of the Southern church went so far as to criticize their preachers for "the infrequency of its (Christian perfection) proclamation from the pulpit and the irregularity of its experimental power in the church." They called for a new emphasis in the denomination, exhorting, "Let us more than ever reassert this grand doctrine."[12]

Throughout the 1870's and 1880's the movement was aided by a flood of literature that issued from independent holiness and official Methodist presses alike. The National Holiness Association began publication in 1870 of two new periodicals in addition to *Guide to Holiness*, now edited by

11 McLean and Eaton, *Penuel*, p. 468; cf. pp. 254-268; Gaddis, "Christian Perfectionism in America," p. 443; Bucke, *et al.*, *History of American Methodism*, II, 612-613.

12 *Journal of the General Conference, 1878*, p. 33.

Inskip: *The Christian Standard and Home Journal,* published at Philadelphia, and *The Advocate of Holiness,* printed in Boston. The books and tracts of Phoebe Palmer enjoyed a particularly wide distribution, *The Way of Holiness* appearing in fifty-two editions by 1867. In addition to these independent publications, the denominational *Christian Advocate, Methodist Quarterly Review, Zion's Herald,* and *Northern Christian Advocate* were filled with holiness articles and appeals.[13]

By 1870 the holiness crusade had assumed nationwide proportions and soon found some of its most ardent supporters in the South. Throughout the period from 1870 to 1885 the idea spread rapidly throughout Southern Methodism. During this time, Inskip, President of the National Holiness Association and a full-time revivalist, conducted "holiness revivals" in the South. Preaching in Savannah and Augusta, he found such interest that he organized a "Georgia Holiness Association" in connection with the Georgia Conferences of the Methodist Episcopal Church, South. The leading ministers of the North Georgia Conference joined the organization. Georgia leaders were the Reverends A. J. Jarrell, pastor of the First Methodist Church of Athens, Asbury Dodge, W. P. Lovejoy, Lovick Pierce, and R. P. Martin.[14]

During the height of the movement in Georgia Methodism, 200 of the 240 ministers of the North Georgia Conference professed to have received the experience of sanctification as a "second blessing." Most of these joined the Holiness Association of the North Georgia Conference. A similar association was formed for the South Georgia Conference.[15]

The "Holiness Association" movement became the nationwide arm of the National Holiness Association, with state and local associations being formed in many states of the union. Some were regional, such as the "New England Holiness Association" and the "Iowa Holiness Association," while

[13] Bucke, *et al., History of American Methodism,* II, 613-615; Smith, *Revivalism and Social Reform,* pp. 114-128.

[14] Smith, *History of Georgia Methodism,* p. 410.

[15] Joseph H. King and Blanche L. King, *Yet Speaketh: Memoirs of the Late Bishop Joseph H. King* (Franklin Springs, Georgia, 1949), p. 85.

others reached down to city and county levels. In the South, there were associations for every Methodist district conference as well as for the annual conferences. So fundamental was this movement in Southern Methodism that one preacher from the Old Dominion declared that his church was "reconstructing Virginia upon the basis of holiness." Some Southerners felt that reconstruction based on holiness would be much more effective than the political reconstruction of the South which was then in process.[16]

As in other regions of the nation, the holiness movement in the South began as an urban force among the better educated circles. Leading advocates of the movement were often also leading figures in the Methodist Church. The patriarch of Georgia Methodism, Lovick Pierce, who had been a Methodist preacher since the early days of the nineteenth century, pronounced the holiness movement to be nothing more than "old line, pioneer" Methodism.[17] In the early years of the movement, annual meetings were held in the leading churches of the conference. So great was interest that Asbury Dodge and some of his friends began publication of a weekly newspaper devoted to holiness and established a holiness camp meeting in a refurbished campground at Indian Springs near Jackson, Georgia.[18]

The holiness crusade found unusual acceptance in the Methodist Church in this period for several reasons. Many conservatives felt that this movement might be a bulwark against the urbane and highly educated "progressive" ministers who were gaining in numbers and influence. In some places these "progressives" had introduced organs into the churches with robed choirs. Even more disturbing was the tendency among them of dispensing with class meetings and altar services where seekers knelt to pursue holiness of heart.

---

16 Bucke, *et al.*, *History of American Methodism*, II, 613. Associations similar to those in Georgia were formed in all the Southern states during the 1870's, with the greatest strength being in Mississippi, Georgia, Texas, and Kentucky.

17 Lovick Pierce, *A Miscellaneous Essay on Entire Sanctification, How It Was Lost to the Church and How It May and Must Be Regained* (n.p., 1897), p. 1.

18 Smith, *History of Georgia Methodism*, p. 401; Rose, *A Theology of Christian Experience*, pp. 70-71.

They also began to admit new members without the aid of previous indoctrination. Many older ministers were also shocked at the fashionable modes of dress that these ministers allowed their members to wear. Perhaps the new emphasis on holiness would stem the tide of these disturbing developments.[19]

Others supported the movement because of the theological views held by many of the new "progressive" ministers, many of whom had been educated in Germany. Their favorable views toward the current work of the German "higher critics" disturbed the older ministers. Should certain passages of Scripture prove to have been falsely included in the sacred canon, might not all the biblically based arguments for Christian perfection fall? Also deeply disturbing to many were the discussions concerning the theories of Charles Darwin. The more recently educated ministers seemed to know too much about "evolution" for the comfort of the older ministers. Perhaps the holiness movement would prove to be a bulwark against these "heretical teachings."[20]

Many Methodists also saw the holiness revival as a unifying force which, by crossing denominational barriers, could help unify Methodism. The holiness camp meetings were opportunities for Methodists of the North and South to unite on a common platform and to begin healing the breach caused by the Civil War and reconstruction. Perhaps Wesley's "perfect love" could end bitter divisions in the church and also help in the reuniting of the nation.

Others felt that the National Holiness Movement might save the camp meeting, which seemed on the verge of dying out in Methodism. Many of the old campgrounds were still in use, but the long rows of tents had begun to be replaced by well-built cottages; and rather than the old-time revival services that had been the normal ritual under the "shed," the services were now interspersed with lectures on semi-religious and even secular subjects. "Old-time" religious

[19] Smith, *ibid.*, pp. 396-401; Pierce, *A Miscellaneous Essay*, pp. 16-57; Sweet, *Methodism in American History*, pp. 332-339.

[20] For an example of current theological thought, see Andrew C. Zenos, *The Elements of Higher Criticism* (New York, 1895), pp. 1-13ff. See also Joseph E. Campbell, *The Pentecostal Holiness Church, 1898-1948* (Franklin Springs, Georgia, 1951), pp. 102-110.

fervor with its shouts and hallelujahs was being replaced by gossip and visiting, as the camps were transformed into "respectable middle-class summer resorts with only a tinge of religion."[21]

The National Holiness Movement was as successful in reviving the camp meeting as it was in reviving the doctrine of sanctification. By 1887 the National Association reported that it had held "sixty-seven national camp meetings and eleven Tabernacle meetings . . . distributed through sixteen states of the Union, extending to both shores of the Continent and to the far off East." At least twenty-eight camps, officially designated "National Camp Meetings," were in operation by the 1880's.[22]

There was no lack of preachers to fill the pulpits of these hundreds of holiness churches and camp meetings. By 1887 the National Holiness Association listed 206 "holiness evangelists" who gave full time to preaching the doctrine. By 1891 the list had grown to 304. Also contributing to the movement were scores of "weekday meetings for the promotion of holiness" patterned after the famous "Tuesday Meeting" of Phoebe Palmer. By 1891 there were no less than 354 of these meetings listed by the National Association, most of them gathering in private homes.[23]

The holiness movement was not confined to the United States alone. The many preaching tours of the Palmers from 1853 to 1859 had brought the message to the Methodists of Canada. When they traveled to England in 1859, the revival of holiness which resulted helped to revitalize the very homebase of Methodism. In 1875, Inskip returned to Canada and held successful revivals there. But the "grand tour" of the holiness advocates came in 1880 when Inskip, Wood, and William McDonald made an "around-the-world tour" which reached England, Italy, and India with the doctrine of perfect love. The campaign in India attached a strong holiness cast to

21 Sweet, *Methodism in American History*, p. 333.

22 Peters, *Christian Perfection and American Methodism*, p. 138; Bucke, *et al.*, *American Methodism*, II, 613.

23 Peters, *Christian Perfection and American Methodism*, p. 138.

the Methodist Mission which was to figure in the pentecostal revival of the early twentieth century.[24]

The later British campaigns of the Palmers, Inskip, and William E. Boardman awakened an interest in the doctrine of holiness in England which rivaled that in America. Among those joining in the British holiness crusade were William Booth, founder of the Salvation Army, and Canon Harford-Battersby, Vicar of Keswick. In time a series of summer conventions at Keswick for the promotion of the "higher life" became the British equivalent of the American National Holiness Association.[25]

During the 1880's the holiness awakening reached its peak of acceptance and popularity in America. Inskip, the acknowledged leader of the movement, had held huge revivalistic campaigns throughout the nation during the decade before his death in 1884. Supported not only by Methodists, but also by Presbyterians, Baptists, and Congregationalists, this fervent preacher carried his message from California to Georgia. A high point of the movement came when Inskip and a supporting team of preachers held a preaching campaign in Salt Lake City, the center of Mormonism. Night after night Brigham Young and his elders attended in an attempt to intimidate the speakers. Undaunted, the intrepid evangelists obliged their visitors with sermon after sermon on holiness and climaxed the campaign by denouncing Young and the Mormons in a sermon called the "Last Judgment."[26]

The success of the holiness movement was nowhere more pronounced in the South than in Georgia. An early advocate of the movement in that state was the Reverend Warren Candler, pastor of the fashionable St. John's Methodist Church in Augusta. In 1883 he stirred the entire city with a sermon on holiness. The *Augusta News* reported that Christians of all denominations were discussing his question: "Is it possible for one to live without sin?"[27] In 1884 Candler, who later became the first president of Emory

[24] Rose, *A Theology of Christian Experience*, p. 44; Timothy L. Smith, *Called Unto Holiness* (Kansas City, 1962), pp. 22-23.

[25] Smith, *Called Unto Holiness*, pp. 23-25.

[26] Bucke, *et al.*, *American Methodism*, II, 613.

[27] Alfred M. Pierce, *Giant Against the Sky* (New York, 1958), p. 47.

University in Atlanta, hosted the annual convention of the North Georgia Holiness Association at St. John's Church. Although he never embraced fully the "second blessing" theory, Candler approved of fiery sermons and lusty denunciations of sin, especially the sins practiced by uptown congregations like his own. Candler himself was unmatched in his "holiness sermons" on the evils of drinking, dancing, theater-going, card playing, swearing, and "even wine on the family tables."[28]

Candler used the holiness movement in the North Georgia Conference to gain the Bishopric of the Southern Methodist Church. Sensing the strength of the movement, he allied himself with it in the 1880's and was elected Bishop largely because of the support he mustered among its advocates. In later years Candler stood with his church in opposition to the movement, but at heart he remained a "holiness preacher."[29]

The holiness movement within Methodism continued with increasing force until the mid-eighties. High recognition of the doctrine was given by the delegates to the Methodist Centennial Conference in 1884. There it was stated that Christian perfection had become so popular among other denominations, "in fact, if not in form," that no longer could Methodists claim it "as their peculiar heritage." Indeed, the newly imported Salvation Army of General William Booth claimed holiness as its distinguishing doctrine and social work as its public manifestation of the sanctifying grace. The Society of Friends made it clear during this decade that they also were a "holiness church," the doctrines of George Fox being identical with those of John Wesley. The Evangelical United Brethren Church, always closely related to Methodism, inserted a strong holiness section in their *Discipline* during this period. The Cumberland Presbyterian Church also joined in the cause by inserting a paragraph on sanctification

28 *Ibid.*, pp. 158, 159. See Candler's booklet entitled, *On with the Revolution: By One of the Revolutionaries* (n.p., 1887), pp. 1-12; and *Christus Auctor, A Manual of Christian Evidence* (Nashville, 1900), which refutes "higher criticism" and defends traditional Methodist social views.

29 Harold W. Mann, *Atticus Greene Haygood* (Athens, 1965), pp. 154-167.

which, if not entirely Wesleyan, gave recognition to the importance of the doctrine.[30]

In spite of the great popularity of the doctrine of holiness after 1867, controversy over it began to be felt in the Methodist Church during the 1880's. There were many factors that led to controversy and to the rise of opposition to the holiness movement in general, not the least of which was the independent character of the National Holiness Association. From the beginning, this group had been led and supported largely by Methodists, but yet remained an inter-denominational body. This type of independency was re-pugnant to the traditionally well-organized and tightly knit polity of the Methodist Church. By 1888 it was reported that there were four publishing houses devoted exclusively to publishing holiness literature. Four years later there were forty-one holiness periodicals being published throughout the country. Most of these enterprises were wholly independent of any church control and were associated with the National Holiness Association.[31]

As early as 1878, searching criticism of the movement had been voiced by Methodist leaders. In that year D. D. Whedon had written in the *Methodist Quarterly Review* that:

> The holiness association, the holiness periodical, the holiness prayer meeting, the holiness preacher, are all modern novelties. They are not Wesleyan. We believe that a living Wesley would never admit them into the Methodist system.[32]

The Southern Methodist Church early became a defender of the movement through Leonidas Rosser, editor of the *Southern Methodist Review.* Reminding Methodists that they must avoid "law without liberty," he warned his brethren that "Methodism, itself a great holiness association, was organized in the Church of England." He challenged further, "Let all opposers of these associations . . . show their errors,

[30] Bucke, *et al., American Methodism,* II, 616, 618; Redford, *Rise of the Church of the Nazarene,* p. 38; *Discipline of the United Brethren Church, 1951* (Harrisburg, 1951), pp. 51-56; Smith, *Called Unto Holiness,* pp. 25, 26.

[31] Peters, *Christian Perfection and American Methodism,* pp. 138, 139.

[32] *Ibid.,* p. 139.

excesses, and evils, or withdraw their opposition; for in opposing them they oppose Methodism." Such charges and countercharges as these reflected the rift that the holiness movement was erecting among Methodists, and it portended deep trouble for the years ahead.[33]

The most disturbing development to loyal churchmen was the appearance of a "come-outism" movement during the 1880's among the more radical holiness spokesmen. In 1880 Daniel S. Warner had organized the "Church of God," with headquarters in Anderson, Indiana, on an anti-denominational platform. Hardin Wallace, from Illinois, began somewhat earlier the holiness "Band" movement in rural East Texas. Also S. B. Shaw of Michigan, one of the most respected leaders of the movement, in the early 1880's organized a short-lived sect known as the Primitive Holiness Mission. Adding fuel to the fire was the publication in 1887 of the "textbook of come-outism," *The Divine Church*, by John P. Brooks. Brooks, from Bloomington, Illinois, had been a loyal Methodist and had edited *The Banner of Holiness* for some years. In 1885 he left the Methodist Church denouncing the "easy, indulgent, accommodating, mammonized" kind of Wesleyanism which tolerated church parties, festivals, and dramatic presentations and "erected gorgeous and costly temples to gratify its pride." Threatened with defiant "come-outism," every Methodist Bishop and minister was forced to stand with or against the holiness movement during the last two decades of the nineteenth century.[34]

The primary battleground in the controversy eventually became the South and Middle West where the holiness movement was making its greatest inroads. By 1885 the most radical section of the holiness ranks was being filled by rural Methodists in these two regions. Traveling evangelists, mostly from Kentucky, Iowa, and Texas, began to tour these areas preaching a much more radical brand of holiness than had been heard in the uptown churches during the earlier phases

33 *Ibid.,* p. 140; Sweet, *Methodism in American History*, p. 342; Gaddis, "Christian Perfectionism in America," pp. 436-451.

34 Bucke, *et al.*, *American Methodism*, II, 619; Smith, *Called Unto Holiness*, pp. 28-33. "Come-outism" meant leaving the Methodist Church in favor of the independent holiness churches.

of the movement. Great emphasis was laid on dress and "worldly amusements" by these preachers, who in addition were not averse to denouncing the "coldness" and "formality" of the Methodist Church itself. These preachers succeeded in capturing the holiness associations in some states, thereby further alienating Methodist loyalists. When the Texas Holiness Association became dominated by "comeouters" under Hardin Wallace, loyal Methodist churchmen organized in 1883 the "Northwest Texas Holiness Association" to counteract the "radicalism" of the older group.[35]

The holiness movement in Texas illustrated another development that was highly disturbing to loyal churchmen and to the older leadership of the National Holiness Association. This was the rise of new doctrines that had never before been emphasized in Methodism. Among the "fanaticisms" and "heresies" taught in Texas were "sinless perfection," freedom from death, "marital purity," a third work following sanctification called "the fire," abstinence from pork or coffee, and that all "doctors, drugs, and devils" are done with when one is sanctified. To older leaders such as Isaiah Reed, founder of the Iowa Holiness Association, these views were "innovations" and never presented as a part of the holiness movement for nearly half a century.[36]

The movement to end the controversy by reading the holiness faction out of Methodism began in the Southern church. The prime mover in this development was Atticus Greene Haygood, a Georgia Methodist minister who later became a leading bishop in his church. In July 1885 he was invited to preach at the Oxford District Conference on the subject of sanctification. Haygood chose the topic "Growth in Grace" and in his sermon denied the need for a "second blessing" of instantaneous holiness, calling instead for a gradual attainment of the sanctified state. To him, holiness teaching was a "do-it-yourself" doctrine of salvation. For the

[35] Smith, *Called Unto Holiness*, pp. 30-33.

[36] References to these teachings may be seen in the *Beulah Christian* (Providence, R.I.), November 1896, p. 2; January 1897, p. 2; March 1898, p. 4; and *Sent of God* (Tabor, Iowa), April 15, 1897, p. 7; June 3, 1897, p. 8; June 15, 1899, p. 2. Also see S. B. Shaw, *Echoes of the General Holiness Assembly* (Chicago, 1901), pp. 325-326; Rose, *A Theology of Christian Experience*, pp. 73-78.

next decade Haygood led the wing of Methodism which opposed the holiness faction and which eventually discredited the movement in the Southern church.[37]

Another factor which led to the downfall of the holiness faction in the Southern Methodist Church was the opposition to the doctrine of sanctification expressed in the seminaries of the church. Before the 1880's the seminaries had been sympathetic to the movement, acting as a theological shelter to its advocates. But the picture began to change in 1884 when Wilbur F. Tillett, a theologian at Vanderbilt University, openly challenged the concept of sanctification as taught by the holiness partisans. Calling all varieties of holiness teaching "semi-pelagian," Tillett felt that the effect of holiness teaching "was to convince Methodists that they could attain salvation through willing it."[38]

After the opening volleys of Tillett and Haygood, Methodist preachers, writers, and teachers throughout the nation joined the fray. In 1888 J. M. Boland published his highly controversial *The Problem of Methodism*, which questioned the "second blessing" and even Wesley's advocacy of it. The editor of the *Southern Methodist Quarterly Review* warmly applauded the volume and called for an end to all doctrine that "recognized a second change." Following this book came others that only added fuel to the fire. George H. Hayes' *The Problem Solved* and James Mudges' *Growth in Holiness Toward Perfection, or Progressive Sanctification* offered further indictments of holiness teachings.[39]

As more and more of the intellectual and ecclesiastical leaders of Methodism questioned the basic premises of the holiness movement, more defenders of the doctrine arose to

37 Mann, *Atticus Greene Haygood*, pp. 154-161. Holiness people have felt that Haygood did much to end the movement in Southern Methodism. It is often pointed out by believers that Haygood's subsequent alcoholism and humiliation at presiding over an annual conference while inebriated were retributions for his opposition to the holiness movement.

38 *Ibid.*, pp. 161-162.

39 Bucke, *et al., American Methodism*, II; Smith, *Called Unto Holiness*, pp. 42-47. Also see J. M. Boland, "A Psychological View of Sin and Holiness," *Quarterly Review of the M. E. Church, South*, XII (1892), 339-354, for an intellectual approach to the anti-holiness argument.

speak in its behalf. In 1896, Daniel Steele, who had written a holiness classic, *Love Enthroned*, in 1877, pitched into the fray with a book entitled, *A Defense of Christian Perfection*. The Southern church found a staunch defender of the holiness movement in the Reverend Lovick Pierce, whose career as a Methodist minister went back to 1842. In 1897 he published a volume whose title amply fixed his position in the controversy, *A Miscellaneous Essay on Entire Sanctification: How It Was Lost to the Church and How It May and Must Be Regained*. In this work, Pierce lamented that "Methodism was never so nearly divorced from holiness as it is now." He further asserted that "holiness meetings are absolutely ridiculed by some of our people," causing the church to be "turned over to Satan and the world." Later a bruising attack on the intellectuals who had criticized cherished holiness beliefs was delivered by George W. Wilson in his *Methodist Theology vs. Methodist Theologians*, which appeared in 1904. In this volume Wilson declared that "New England Methodism, where much of this new theology is born, is slowly dying." The reason for it, he felt, was "spiritual compromise in urban congregations" where dancing, card playing, and the theater had detracted members from attending revivals.[40]

An example of the bitterness created by the controversy was the famous Pickett-Smith debate of August 1896 in Terrell, Texas. In fourteen turgid debates, the combatants argued five points of doctrine, Pickett defending and Smith denouncing holiness views. Held under holiness auspices and before a holiness audience, Pickett's arguments seem to have prevailed, but not before much strife and bitterness had been engendered.[41]

As the controversy deepened, defenders of holiness became less loyal to the church, and defenders of the church became less loyal to the doctrine of holiness. By the mid-nineties Methodist officials in the Southern church were

[40] Bucke, *et al.*, *American Methodism*, II, 623-624; Pierce, *A Miscellaneous Essay*, pp. 4-69; Daniel Steele, *A Defense of Christian Perfection* (New York, 1895); George W. Wilson, *Methodist Theology vs. Methodist Theologians* (Cincinnati, 1904).

[41] L. L. Pickett, *The Pickett-Smith Debate on Entire Sanctification* (Louisville, 1897), *passim*.

assigning "holiness preachers" to "hard-scrabble" circuits to lessen their influence. If a holiness pastor had been fairly successful in indoctrinating a congregation, his successor would be furnished with an "anti-holiness squad" and instructed to correct his predecessor's folly. In 1885 the North Georgia Conference assigned most of the "holiness" preachers to the Gainesville District, thereby hoping to localize the contagion, but the holiness advocates nearly took over the district. A writer to the Georgia *Wesleyan Advocate* complained that year:

> They have changed the name of our meetings, substituting Holiness for Methodist. They preach a different doctrine. . . , they sing different songs; they patronize and circulate a different literature; they have adopted radically different words of worship. . . .[42]

The great turning point in the struggle came in 1894 at the General Conference of the Methodist Episcopal Church, South. With the Gainesville experience clearly in mind and with Haygood now occupying a Bishop's chair, it was inevitable that the conference would take some positive action to stem the tide of controversy which threatened to engulf the church. The statement which resulted bore a curious resemblance to the statement previously printed in the *Wesleyan Advocate* and was unquestionably a disavowal of the holiness movement and a declaration of open warfare against its proponents:

> But there has sprung up among us a party with holiness as a watchword; they have holiness associations, holiness meetings, holiness preachers, holiness evangelists, and holiness property. Religious experience is represented as if it consists of only two steps, the first step out of condemnation into peace and the next step into Christian perfection. The effect is to disparage the new birth, and all stages of spiritual growth from the blade to the full corn in the ear. . . . We do not question the sincerity and zeal of these brethren; we desire the church to profit by their earnest preaching and godly example; but we deplore their teaching and methods in so far as they claim a monopoly of the experience,

42 Mann, *Haygood*, pp. 164-165.

practice, and advocacy of holiness, and separate themselves from the body of ministers and disciples.[43]

With this statement a "war of extermination" began which eventually resulted in the creation of scores of new "holiness" denominations and churches throughout the United States. To holiness partisans, the statement of the Southern church fell like a bombshell. It simply meant that there was no longer any hope of re-creating the Methodist Church in a holiness image. The loyalists in the holiness movement were now faced with an agonizing decision, whether to stay with the old church or whether to join the "come-outers" in the new "Bands," churches, and denominations that soon were being formed everywhere.[44]

Many of the most committed holiness advocates determined to stay with the Methodist Church in spite of its new policy. In Georgia such holiness stalwarts as Jarrell, Pierce, and Dodge lived and died in their church. But many others felt that it was impossible to remain in the church. An example of the turmoil some experienced is indicated in the title of a volume describing the problems of B. F. Haynes, one-time editor of the *Tennessee Methodist* and President of Asbury College in Kentucky. In *Tempest-Tossed on Methodist Seas*, Haynes described his life as "simply one of protest" in which his "voice and pen have been kept busy in dissent."[45] As far away as California, other Methodists felt that the time had come to break with their church. In Los Angeles Phineas Bresee and Dr. J. P. Widney organized in 1895 the first congregation of the "Church of the Nazarene," which was destined in time to become the nation's largest holiness church. In Georgia, a young pastor near Royston, J. H. King, felt that he could no longer continue in the Methodist connection in the light of the negative attitude toward holiness that the church seemed to be taking. In 1898 he made the decision to leave after being "almost forced to

[43] *Journal, General Conference, M. E. Church, South, 1894*, pp. 25, 26. See also Peters, *Christian Perfection and American Methodism*, p. 148; and Sweet, *Methodism in American History*, p. 343.

[44] Bucke, *et al.*, *History of American Methodism*, II, 624-625.

[45] B. F. Haynes, *Tempest-Tossed on Methodist Seas* (Kansas City, 1914), pp. 98ff.; see also Smith, *Called Unto Holiness*, pp. 44-45.

separate from the church I loved better than life." The stories of Hayes, Bresee, Widney, and King were repeated by the hundreds throughout the United States.[46]

It is a matter of interest that the holiness movement fragmented into over a score of denominations in the period from 1895 to 1905, instead of forming one large, unified group. The machinery was already in operation by which all of these groups could easily have been transformed into a national holiness denomination. The National Holiness Association with its great camp meetings and large convocations, although loosely organized, might have served as the vehicle for such a movement. A simple resolution for a constitutional convention could have produced a new united denomination of possibly one million members, if such a program had been desired. Three "General Holiness Assemblies" were held during the period of controversy over the holiness question, any one of which could have resolved itself into a new denomination. At the Assemblies which met in Jacksonville, Illinois, in 1880, and in Chicago in 1886 and 1901, many delegates asked for such a step, but leaders steadfastly counseled against "come-outism" and directed the delegates to remain loyal to their denominations. However, this insistence on loyalty caused the movement to fragment, as groups in different annual conferences left the churches piecemeal in disputes over local conditions.[47]

Placing the holiness break from Methodism in its historical setting produces other interesting possibilities. It is a matter of record that the most radical elements in the holiness movement were in the rural South and Midwest and that most of the holiness denominations began in those regions from 1895 to 1900. It is also a matter of record that the agrarian revolt which culminated in populism and the candidacy of William Jennings Bryan in 1896 also occurred in the same regions at the same time. Both the holiness and the

46 King and King, *Yet Speaketh*, pp. 77-87; E. A. Girvin, *P. F. Bresee, A Prince In Israel* (Kansas City, Mo., 1916), pp. 23-151; Smith, *Called Unto Holiness*, pp. 91-121.

47 See Rose, *A Theology of Christian Experience*, pp. 69-77; and Shaw, *Echoes of the General Holiness Assembly*, pp. 274-277. For interesting speculations on what might have happened, see Gaddis, "Christian Perfectionism in America," pp. 455-459.

populist movements were protests against the Eastern "establishment." In the same period that Tom Watson and Bryan were fulminating against the "banking interests" of Wall Street and the "monopoly powers" of big business, holiness dissenters were preaching livid sermons against the "autocracy" and "ecclesiastical power" of the Methodist "hierarchy." Whether the populist and holiness revolts were triggered by the exigencies of the panic of 1893 is something for other writers to explore. Nevertheless, it appears that the rise of the holiness denominations after 1894 was a religious revolt which paralleled the political and economic revolt of populism.[48]

Of the score of holiness denominations that began after 1894, most of them began in the Midwest and the South. The most radical of these groups was the "Fire-Baptized Holiness Church," which began in Iowa in 1895 and was organized into a denomination in South Carolina in 1898. The eight states where this church began were roughly the same areas where the Northwestern and Southern Farmers' alliances were also strong: Iowa, Kansas, Texas, Oklahoma, Florida, Georgia, North Carolina, South Carolina, and Virginia.[49]

As the nineteenth century drew to a close, these holiness groups were well on their way toward development as full-fledged denominations. Never before in the history of the nation had so many churches been founded in so short a time. A measure of the intensity of the conflict over sanctification is the fact that twenty-three holiness denominations began in the relatively short period of seven years between 1893 and 1900. One reason for the magnitude of the problem was the fact that during the last decade of the century, the Methodist Church formed the largest body of

[48] See Smith, *Called Unto Holiness*, pp. 27-53; Bucke, *History of American Methodism*, II, 608-627; Peters, *Christian Perfection and American Methodism*, pp. 133-193; Gaddis, "Christian Perfectionism in America," pp. 462-515; Joseph E. Campbell, *The Pentecostal Holiness Church, 1898-1948* (Franklin Springs, Georgia, 1951), pp. 192-201.

[49] King and King, *Yet Speaketh*, pp. 85-87. Interviews with surviving ministers of the 1894-1900 era confirm the loyalty of most holiness people to populism and to William Jennings Bryan (Interview with Reverend L. R. Graham, November 10, 1966). The following chapters of this work will further document this hypothesis.

Protestants in the nation. Any schism within such a large communion was necessarily of great importance. Of the four million Methodists in the United States during the nineties, probably one-third to one-half were committed to the idea of sanctification as a second work of grace. That those who left Methodist churches to form the holiness denominations numbered no more than 100,000 indicates that loyalty to the church's organization was greater than loyalty to the church's doctrines.[50]

The men who issued the call for the first gathering of the National Holiness Association in 1867 little knew that they were inadvertently laying the groundwork for the formation of dozens of new denominations. Yet this week spent "in God's great temple of nature" was destined to echo throughout the religious world. The direct result of the holiness crusade of 1867-1894 was the formation of the family of denominations known as the holiness movement and the still larger group which became known as the pentecostal movement.

[50] Gaddis, "Christian Perfectionism in America," p. 570. George P. Fisher, in his *History of the Christian Church* (New York: Charles Scribner's Sons, 1898), p. 581, estimates that in 1887 the Methodists in America numbered 4,532,658, while the Catholics counted approximately 4,000,000, and the Baptists 3,727,020.

Chapter Three

THE FIRE-BAPTIZED WAY

Christ is our commander, we know no defeat,
We've sounded the trumpet that ne'er calls retreat,
Then onward, right onward at His blest command,
Clear the way, we are coming, the fire-baptized band.
                                    —Thurman A. Carey

The last quarter of the nineteenth century was a period of fundamental change in most phases of American life. In the social and intellectual life of the nation, no institution, however sacred, escaped the searching scrutiny of the critics. In particular, the religious life of America was subjected to heavy criticism by many writers. The climate of thought which prevailed before 1900 was especially unfavorable toward traditional Protestantism, with its emphasis on individualism and seeming neglect of the pressing problems of society. Many American writers from 1870 to 1900 engaged in a concerted attack on what they considered an "outmoded theology."[1]

Among the writers who most deeply questioned traditional American religious concepts were Edward Eggleston, Harold Frederick, and John W. De Forest. Eggleston, in particular, was critical of his own Methodist Church. In his 1873 novel, *The Circuit Rider*, Eggleston questioned primitive Methodism, calling it "no longer adequate." Although admitting that

[1] Billy Hawkins Gilley, "Social Trends as Reflected in American Fiction, 1870-1901" (Unpublished Ph.D. dissertation, University of Georgia, 1966), p. 124.

it had served a civilizing purpose on the frontier, he felt that "by 1870 primitive Methodism had outlived its usefulness." Reminding contemporary Methodists that their "stern forbears" had often thrown "weak saints" and "obstinate sinners" alike into contortions of "the jerks," he felt that such practices were now "hypocritical and ostentatious." Although originally the reaction of a "sincere people," these demonstrations were, in his view, "actually alienating the masses."[2]

Other writers saw an end to Protestantism as it had been known before the Civil War. In Harold Frederick's *The Damnation of Theron Ware*, Arlo Bates' *The Philistines*, and John W. De Forest's *The Wetherel Affair*, calls were made for an accommodation with the evolutionary theories of Darwin along with a more "rational thought" which would lead to "social salvation."[3] Other observers saw that the Protestant churches had become centers of middle-class thought and values, while the workingmen were going elsewhere. Samuel Loomis said in 1887 that "the Catholic church is emphatically the workingmen's church. She rears her edifices in the midst of the densest populations, provides them with many seats and has the seats well filled." With Protestantism becoming more divided theologically, socially, and intellectually, and with Catholicism rising both in numbers and self-assurance, it was certain that the religious life of the nation would be greatly altered in the twentieth century.[4]

Another theological movement arose during the last years of the century that deeply disturbed conservative religious leaders, and in particular those in the holiness ranks. This movement, known as "the Social Gospel," was the brainchild of Washington Gladden, a Congregational minister from Massachusetts, and Walter Rauschenbusch, a Baptist minister

2 Edward Eggleston, *The Circuit Rider: A Tale of the Heroic Age* (New York, 1909), pp. 158-159.

3 Arlo Bates, *The Philistines* (Boston, 1888), p. 324.

4 Carl Degler, *Out of Our Past*, p. 349; Harold Frederick, *The Damnation of Theron Ware* (Cambridge, 1960 [1896]), pp. 72-137; John W. De Forest, *The Wetherel Affair* (New York, 1873), pp. 52-53. Also see Gilley, "Social Trends," pp. 124-150; and Henry F. May, *Protestant Churches in Industrial America* (New York, 1949), pp. 92-93.

and teacher at Rochester Theological Seminary. Rejecting capitalism and "capitalistic Christianity," they requested a new system which they called "Christian Socialism." Believing that such "social sins" as poverty, irresponsible use of wealth, social ostracism, and unhealthful and indecent living conditions were as bad as individual sins, they called for a "social conversion" of American life. Gladden's *Workingmen and Their Employers* (1876), *Applied Christianity* (1887), and *Tools and Men* (1893) laid the intellectual foundations for the movement. Rauschenbusch, on the other hand, brought the message to the church in his *Christianity and the Social Crisis* (1907), *Christianizing the Social Order* (1912), and *The Theology of the Social Gospel* (1917). This movement deeply affected all the major churches of America, but none as deeply as the Methodist Church, which by 1908 had adopted the "Social Creed of the Churches" along with other members of the newly created Federal Council of Churches.[5]

The fact that the holiness and pentecostal movements arose during the same period that such intellectual currents as Darwinism, higher criticism, the social gospel, and the ecumenism of the Federal Council of Churches were gaining ascendancy in much of Protestantism, demands an analysis of relationships. It could well be that the holiness ministers who severed their connections with the various denominations felt that they were protesting against these developments within their churches. Writers within the holiness and pentecostal movement generally cite these currents of thought as the "false doctrines" against which the movements protested. In this sense, the holiness and pentecostal churches represented a conservative counterweight among the lower classes to the liberal thinking of the upper and middle classes. In leaving the older churches, the holiness people were protesting against these "modernistic" developments and were attempt-

---

[5] See Sweet, *The Story of Religion in America*, pp. 356-357, 389-390, and *Methodism in American History*, pp. 355-368; Curti, *The Growth of American Thought*, pp. 610-614; and Rauschenbusch, *Christianity and the Social Crisis* (New York, 1964 [1907]), pp. viii-xx of the Introduction. For an interpretive view of the movement see Carl Degler's *Out of Our Past*, pp. 338-351.

ing to keep alive the "old-time religion" which seemed in danger of dying out in American Protestantism.[6]

The social gospel movement actually owed a great deal to the perfectionist thought that also produced the holiness movement. Gladden in his *Tools and Men* (1893) wrote: "The end of Christianity is two-fold — a perfect man in a perfect society. These purposes are never separated; they cannot be separated. No man can be redeemed and saved alone. . . ." The impulse toward social reform had originally sprung from the pre-Civil War holiness crusade, and the greater part of Christian social service following the war had been carried out by the perfectionistic Salvation Army and its offspring, The Volunteers of America. In a sense the social gospel movement was a logical outcome of the holiness crusade because both groups shared the assumption that man could be perfected. The two movements parted company, however, on the question of the perfectibility of society, the holiness advocates holding that society would be perfected only with the second coming of Christ and the institution of the millennium.[7]

Interestingly enough, the very groups that the social gospel advocates wished to help, that is, the poor, the destitute, and the underprivileged, were the very ones who joined the holiness and pentecostal churches and most bitterly denounced the Gladdens and the Rauschenbusches. In fact, the holiness people taught a negative "social gospel" of their own. Rather than trying to reform society, they rejected it. In the holiness system of values the greatest "social sins" were not poverty, inequality, or unequal distribution of the wealth, but rather the evil effects of the theater, ball games, dancing, lipstick, cigarettes, and liquor. Perhaps the most serious objection to the social gospel from all religious conservatives was the unsettling suspicion that the leaders of

6 For examples of protest thought within the holiness and pentecostal movements see: Redford, *Rise of the Church of the Nazarene*, pp. 1-40; Campbell, *The Pentecostal Holiness Church*, pp. 27-145; Carl Brumback, *Suddenly from Heaven, A History of the Assemblies of God* (Springfield, Missouri, 1961), pp. 25-31.

7 See Smith, *Revivalism and Social Reform*, pp. 225-237; Sweet, *Methodism in American History*, p. 357; Timothy Smith, *Called Unto Holiness* (Kansas City, Mo., 1962), pp. 200-204.

this movement would neglect individual salvation altogether and substitute "social works" for "saving grace."[8]

It was against the background of these theological, intellectual, and social changes that the holiness churches completed their schism from traditional Methodism. It is apparent that theological differences over the subject of entire sanctification as a "second blessing" were not the only factor in the breaks that came after 1894. Indeed, the Methodist churches never entirely discarded the doctrine of the "double cure." As late as 1919 an apologist for Southern Methodism, Hilary T. Hudson, included a section on "holiness or sanctification" in his book *The Methodist Armor* which might have been acceptable to most holiness people, but by that time the holiness churches were already well established.[9]

Most of the holiness groups began in the decade after 1894, although a few began earlier and some as late as 1917. The quadrennium following the 1894 General Conference of the Southern Methodist Church saw the greatest number of new churches organized. Of the score or more of major holiness groups with beginnings during this period, only four later became pentecostal, and all of these were in the South. The first of the postwar holiness churches was the "Church of God" with headquarters in Anderson, Indiana. Led by Daniel S. Warner, this group began in 1880 as a secession from the Winebrenner Church of God, a Methodist-like German body. In 1887 the Christian and Missionary Alliance was established in New York by A. B. Simpson, who emphasized foreign missions and divine healing as well as sanctification. These two movements were not fully products of the National Holiness Movement, having had their begin-

[8] Liston Pope, *Millhands and Preachers* (New Haven, 1942), pp. 117-140, 162-186.

[9] Hilary T. Hudson, *The Methodist Armor or a Popular Exposition of the Doctrines, Peculiar Usages and Ecclesiastical Machinery of the Methodist Episcopal Church, South* (Nashville, 1919), pp. 108-111. On page 109 sanctification is presented as "a work commencing *in* and carried on *after* conversion. It is a *second* blessing, in harmony *with*, yet separate *from*, and subsequent *to*, the work of conversion." For an account of the continuation of the holiness movement within Methodism through the 1940's see Rose, *A Theology of Christian Experience*, pp. 76-270.

nings in the period before the doctrine of sanctification became controversial.[10]

The two largest holiness denominations that resulted from the National Holiness Movement, the Church of the Nazarene and the Pilgrim Holiness Church, were both the results of a complicated series of mergers of widely separated holiness groups. The Church of the Nazarene emerged in 1914 as a merger of the following groups: the "People's Evangelical Church," which began in New England in 1887; the "Pentecostal Churches of America," beginning in Brooklyn, New York, in 1894; the "New Testament Church of Christ," founded at Milan, Tennessee, in 1894; the "Church of the Nazarene," started in Los Angeles, California, in 1895; the "Pentecostal Mission," which began in Nashville, Tennessee, in 1898; and the "Independent Holiness Church," organized in 1900 in Texas. In 1914, most of these bodies were merged into one national denomination at Pilot Point, Texas, with the name "The Pentecostal Church of the Nazarene."[11]

The Pilgrim Holiness Church began in 1897 in Cincinnati, Ohio, under the leadership of the Reverend Martin W. Knapp, a Methodist minister. Originally called the "International Apostolic Holiness Union," this church took its name in 1922 after mergers with the "Holiness Christian Church" of Pennsylvania, the "Pentecostal Rescue Mission" of New York, and the "Pilgrim Church" of California. Later accessions made the church somewhat larger after 1922.[12]

In addition to the Church of the Nazarene and the Pilgrim Holiness Church, there were dozens of smaller groups that fragmented from Methodism and other denominations during

10 For accounts of the backgrounds of these groups see Elmer T. Clark's *Small Sects in America* (New York, 1949), pp. 76-81; and F. E. Mayer's *Religious Bodies of America* (St. Louis, 1954), pp. 313, 339.

11 The most scholarly history of the Church of the Nazarene is Timothy Smith, *Called Unto Holiness.* Other histories are J. B. Chapman, *A History of the Church of the Nazarene* (Kansas City, 1926), and Redford, *The Rise of the Church of the Nazarene* (1951). In 1919 the "Pentecostal Church of the Nazarene" dropped the word "pentecostal" to distinguish itself from the tongue-speaking "pentecostal movement," which began in 1906. Since that time it has been known simply as the "Church of the Nazarene."

12 Clark, *Small Sects in America,* p. 76; Gaddis, "Christian Perfectionism in America," pp. 509-514.

the 1890's and after, but because of their small size and lack of significant growth they played minor roles in the holiness and later pentecostal movements. With interesting variations of doctrine, government, and worship, these groups continued their existence under such names as "The Missionary Bands of the World," "The Church of Daniel's Band," the "Burning Bush," the "Hepzibah Faith Missionary Association," and "The Pillar of Fire."[13]

Many other holiness denominations arose during this period that became a part of the later pentecostal movement. In much the same way that populist politics underwent its most convulsive phase in the South and Middle West, the holiness movement had its most turbulent experience in the same areas.

One of the most radical of the holiness denominations that issued from the National Holiness Association movement was the "Fire-Baptized Holiness Church," which had its beginnings in Iowa in 1895. It was perhaps inevitable that a new church should come from Iowa, since that state was a major holiness stronghold of the nation. Organized in 1879 by Isaiah Reed, the "Iowa Holiness Association" became the first such organization west of the Mississippi River. By the 1890's it had spread into the neighboring states of Missouri and Nebraska. By the late 1890's the Iowa Association had grown to encompass a larger enrollment of ministers and laymen than had the rest of the National Association. It was in Iowa that many of the more radical doctrines that later influenced the rise of pentecostalism had their beginnings.[14]

The founder of the Fire-Baptized Holiness Church was Benjamin Hardin Irwin of Lincoln, Nebraska, a member of the Iowa Holiness Association. Born and reared in Mercer County, Missouri, Irwin was educated for the law profession. After some years of mediocre practice, he was converted in a Baptist church and later forsook law to enter the Baptist

[13] Information about these groups may be found in Clark, *Small Sects in America*; F. E. Mayer, *The Religious Bodies of America* (St. Louis, 1956); and Benson I. Landis, *Yearbook of American Churches* (New York, 1966).

[14] Rose, *A Theology of Christian Experience*, pp. 74, 75; Campbell, *The Pentecostal Holiness Church*, pp. 192-195.

ministry. It was as an ordained minister that Irwin came into contact with holiness teachings by ministers of the Iowa Association, which at that time embraced Lincoln, Nebraska, his home. Seeking and receiving the experience of sanctification, Irwin became a devout advocate of the doctrine. Being a studious young man, he began to study the Scriptures and the writings of John Wesley and his colleague, John Fletcher.

Out of the vast amount of Methodist and holiness theological literature, Irwin was most influenced by the writings of Fletcher, who seemed to teach an experience following sanctification called a "baptism of burning love." More often the terminology "baptism with the Holy Ghost and fire" was used. Fletcher also taught that one could receive several "baptisms," if such were needed. In his *Checks to Antinomianism*, Fletcher called for the sanctified to "enter the full dispensation of the Spirit" until they lived "in the pentecostal glory of the church . . . baptized with the Holy Ghost. . . ." In other passages he spoke of those who were "baptized with fire" and thereby "endued with power from on high." These and other statements led Irwin to conclude that there was a third experience beyond sanctification called "the baptism with the Holy Ghost and fire" or simply "the fire."[15]

Having already been sanctified, Irwin began to seek the "baptism of fire" for himself. Eventually he received such an experience, which came to him with great ecstasy and demonstrations of joy. Afterward he began to preach this "third experience" among the holiness people of the Middle West. Soon his services began to draw large crowds, a special attraction being the renewed exhibition of the emotional phenomena which had characterized the Cane-Ridge revivals earlier in the century. Those receiving "the fire" would often shout, scream, speak in other tongues, fall into trances, and even get the "jerks." For several years beginning in the early 1890's Irwin's teaching became the talk of the holiness movement. His doctrine also gained currency in the many

[15] John Fletcher, *The Works of John Fletcher* (New York, 1851), II, 356, 632-669; IV, 230-232; J. H. King, "History of the Fire-Baptized Holiness Church," *The Pentecostal Holiness Advocate*, March 24, 1921, p. 4; Campbell, *The Pentecostal Holiness Church*, pp. 194-195.

holiness periodicals to which he contributed. The people of the South first met his doctrine in the monthly *Way of Faith*, a holiness paper published in Columbia, South Carolina. A regular contributor to this paper, Irwin often advertised his booklet *Baptism of Fire* for two cents a copy.[16]

Although many thousands attended Irwin's meetings and professed to receive the "baptism of fire," the greater part of the holiness movement rejected his message. The holiness people had always taught that the "second blessing" of sanctification was also the "baptism with the Holy Spirit" and that both were aspects of the same experience. The older "loyalist" wing of the holiness movement, made up of such stalwarts as Isaiah Reed and S. B. Shaw, denounced the doctrine as "the third blessing heresy" and forbade its being preached in their churches. Despite this opposition, the "Fire-Baptized" movement continued to grow, especially in the rural areas of the Middle West and South.[17]

The Fire-Baptized apostle Irwin continued to preach with such fervor and success until the entire holiness movement became familiar with his doctrine. In time the opposition of Reed and the well-organized Iowa Holiness Association caused him to form his own separate group. Finally, in 1895 the "Iowa Fire-Baptized Holiness Association" was formed at Olmitz, Iowa, to propagate the doctrine in holiness ranks. With this Iowa Association as a base, Irwin traveled over the nation preaching his fiery gospel and organizing state associations wherever he went.[18]

Irwin also organized in 1895 Fire-Baptized Holiness Associations in Kansas, Oklahoma, and Texas. Everywhere people fell "under the power" and came out claiming the experience of "the fire." The South received the message in a series of revivals that Irwin held from 1896 through 1898.

16 See *The Way of Faith*, April 15, 1896, p. 4. This paper was the outstanding holiness periodical in the South, and later played a leading part in reporting the pentecostal outbreak in California.

17 For denunciations see Shaw, *Echoes of the General Holiness Assembly*, p. 106; the *Beulah Christian* (Providence, R. I.), "Fanaticism," November 1896, p. 2; "New Theories," January 1897, p. 2; "Sanctification and Fire," March 1898, p. 4; *Sent of God* (Tabor, Iowa), "Fanaticism," June 15, 1899, p. 2.

18 Campbell, *The Pentecostal Holiness Church*, p. 197.

The first Southern city to hear him was Piedmont, South Carolina, where in December 1896 services were held in the Wesleyan Methodist Church. It was reported that he "struck the South in cyclone fashion." Even stalwart holiness advocates felt that his services were "on the wild order," but this was no deterrent. He continued his canvass of the South, organizing Fire-Baptized Associations wherever he went. During 1897 he preached in Royston, Georgia; Williston, Florida; and Abbottsburg, North Carolina. As a result of these efforts, the Florida, Georgia, South Carolina, North Carolina, and Virginia Fire-Baptized Holiness Associations were formed. In addition to these associations, others were formed in the Canadian provinces of Ontario and Manitoba in the same year. Unsuccessful efforts were made to organize associations in Pennsylvania, Tennessee, and Ohio.[19]

By mid-1898 definite state and provincial organizations had been formed in Iowa, Kansas, Texas, Oklahoma, South Carolina, North Carolina, Georgia, Florida, Virginia, Ontario, and Manitoba. In each association Irwin had appointed an "overseer" to conduct the affairs of the group, while he took for himself the title "General Overseer." With such a rapidly growing organization behind him, Irwin then decided to organize a central governing authority. Consequently, from July 28 to August 28, 1898, a national convention was held in Anderson, South Carolina, where a *Discipline* was adopted along with other general rules for the infant denomination. Irwin was named General Overseer for life and various other offices were created and filled. The fact that Irwin could license and ordain ministers and assign them to churches illustrates the ecclesiastical nature of the union. It was in every respect a new denomination.[20]

The following year Irwin was able to raise enough money to purchase a printing plant with which to issue a periodical for the new group. The new press was set up adjacent to his residence in Lincoln, Nebraska, and in October 1899 the first

19 King, "History of the Fire-Baptized Holiness Church," March 31, 1921, pp. 10-11.

20 *Ibid.*, p. 11; see also King and King, *Yet Speaketh*, pp. 77-87; Campbell, *The Pentecostal Holiness Church*, pp. 198-201; and *Constitution and General Rules of the Fire-Baptized Holiness Church* (Royston, Georgia, 1905), pp. 2-4.

issue of *Live Coals of Fire* appeared. With Irwin as editor, and a Canadian, A. E. Robinson, as printing assistant, the paper was distributed throughout the United States. It was the first publication in the nation that taught that the baptism of the Holy Ghost and fire was subsequent to sanctification. As such, it was quite influential in producing the climate of thought and doctrinal interpretation that produced the pentecostal movement a few years later. Although the Fire-Baptized movement did not teach that speaking with other tongues was the initial evidence of receiving the baptism with the Holy Spirit, this phenomenon was quite common among those who received "the fire."[21]

The Fire-Baptized Church might have consolidated a large element of the holiness movement if Irwin had exercised more foresight in his leadership of the new church. Its mushroom-like growth indicated a wide acceptance of his views among holiness people, even those within the Methodist Church. *Live Coals of Fire* carried reports of extraordinary meetings and successes that were colored with references of the blood and thunder variety. One writer reported in an early issue that "the fire is still spreading. People may oppose us, preachers may preach against the experience, and devils may howl, but we have come to stay to preach blood and fire till Jesus comes."[22]

Attending the 1898 Anderson organizational meeting was J. H. King, a Methodist pastor from Royston, Georgia, who cast his lot with the new church. Also joining the movement at this time was a Negro minister, W. E. Fuller, who was elected to the general board of the denomination. Fuller became overseer of the Negro churches that were formed,

[21] An interested observer of Irwin's meetings was Charles Parham, the patriarch of the pentecostal movement, who was repelled by the noise and emotion of the meetings, but who was impressed by his "third blessing" doctrine. See *The Apostolic Faith*, April 25, 1925, pp. 9-14, for Parham's views of Irwin's meetings. Prominent Fire-Baptized people who spoke in tongues before 1906 were Miss Agnes Ozman in Kansas, and Mrs. Sarah A. Smith of Camp Creek, North Carolina. See John Nichols, *Pentecostalism* (New York, 1966), p. 104; Clyde S. Bailey, *Pioneer Marvels of Faith* (Morristown, Tennessee, n.d.), p. 20; and Campbell, *The Pentecostal Holiness Church*, pp. 208-209.

[22] Thurman A. Carey, quoted in *Live Coals of Fire*, April 4, 1906, p. 2.

most of them resulting from his own efforts. The church continued to be interracial until 1908, when the Negro churches, reflecting the growing trend toward segregation, separated with the blessings of the whites to form their own group under Fuller's leadership.[23]

Several developments between 1898 and 1900 prevented the Fire-Baptized movement from developing into the national church that it promised to become. One was the inclusion of additional doctrines that frightened even "radical" holiness people away. Taking Fletcher's premise that many "effusions" or "baptisms" might be necessary to perfect the experience of Christian believers, Irwin began to teach that there were additional "baptisms of fire." These he named the baptisms of "dynamite," "lyddite," and "oxidite." By early 1900 the Fire-Baptized faithful were being taught not only a "third blessing" but also a fourth, a fifth, and even a sixth. This "chemical jargon" never took root within the movement and was later rejected by King and other leaders when Irwin left the church. But for a time the movement was pervaded by the "pathetic pursuit of this religious rainbow's end."[24] The influence of this explosive terminology continued to be felt, however, long after the doctrine was rejected by the body as a whole. In 1904 Fuller wrote to the *Live Coals of Fire* reporting that he was "still on this blood, fire and dynamite line. . . ." He further praised God for "the blood that cleans up, the Holy Ghost that fills up, the fire that burns up, and the dynamite that blows up." Such vivid preaching characterizes the Negro branch of the church to this day.[25]

In addition to the "dynamite heresy," Irwin taught many other doctrines that were later rejected by the movement. Like all other holiness churches, the Fire-Baptized Church opposed extravagance of dress and the wearing of "needless

23 *Discipline of the Fire-Baptized Holiness Church of the Americas, 1962* (Atlanta, Georgia), p. 9.

24 Charles R. Conn, *Like a Mighty Army, Moves the Church of God* (Cleveland, Tennessee, 1955), p. 43; Campbell, *The Pentecostal Holiness Church*, p. 204. The vast majority of holiness people rejected these "experiences" as Irwin taught them because they were not found to be taught in the Scriptures.

25 *Live Coals of Fire*, January 11, 1904, p. 2.

ornamentation" by women members. This emphasis was as old as John Wesley and was generally accepted by the National Holiness Movement. Indeed the puritanical temper of the late Victorian age was nowhere observed more stringently than in holiness circles. Irwin, however, carried this belief to its logical conclusion and placed male members under the same restrictions as women. It thus became a sin for a man to wear a necktie, Irwin and his preachers declaring that they would "rather have a rattlesnake around their necks than a tie." Also, Irwin taught that it was a sin to eat hog meat, catfish, oysters, or anything forbidden by the dietary laws of the Old Testament.[26]

A blow that almost destroyed the young church came in late 1899 when it was discovered that Irwin, the founder of the church, was living a life which resembled that of an apostate rather than an apostle. By the spring of 1900 he confessed to "open and gross sin" which brought "great reproach" to the church. Loyal members of the movement were shocked and saddened at this development. When his disgrace was known, Irwin resigned as Overseer of the church and his place was taken by King, the thirty-one-year-old Georgian, who, with a heavy heart, traveled to Olmitz, Iowa, in June 1900 to conduct the second "General Council" of the denomination. King was formally elected to succeed Irwin as "General Overseer" and as editor of *Live Coals of Fire* on June 5, 1900, and later moved to Iowa to conduct the affairs of the badly shaken denomination. Irwin's defection caused much havoc within the church he had founded. Since several of the state associations ceased to function, the youthful King faced the task of holding the infant church together in the discouraging years after 1900.[27]

[26] G. F. Taylor, "Our Church History," *The Pentecostal Holiness Advocate*, February 3, 1921, p. 9.

[27] King, "History of the Fire-Baptized Holiness Church," April 7, 1921, p. 10; Campbell, *The Pentecostal Holiness Church*, pp. 200-201; King and King, *Yet Speaketh*, pp. 102-106. Also see King's earlier work which is his first published autobiography, *From Passover to Pentecost* (Memphis, 1917), pp. 163-167. The Fire-Baptized Holiness Church later merged with the Pentecostal Holiness Church in 1911 and took the name of the latter group. Organized as a national church in 1898, it is

The Fire-Baptized Holiness Church served as an important link in the chain that later produced the modern pentecostal movement. By teaching that the baptism of the Holy Ghost was an experience separate from and subsequent to sanctification, it laid the basic doctrinal premise of the later movement. It is probable that Charles F. Parham, the man who initiated the pentecostal revival in Topeka, Kansas, in 1901, received from Irwin, with whom he was associated in several meetings before 1901, the basic idea of a separate baptism of the Holy Ghost following sanctification. In the social, doctrinal, and intellectual sense, the Fire-Baptized Holiness Church was a direct precursor of the modern pentecostal movement.[28]

Throughout the 1890's and early 1900's several other holiness groups were formed in the nation with the doctrine of entire sanctification as their major tenet. All of them owed their doctrine to Methodism, although not all of them were Methodists. Almost everywhere new churches were organized as "holiness" preachers traversed the countryside, preaching in schoolhouses, tents, abandoned churches, and under "brush arbors." Many of these new churches, often numbering no more than fifteen to thirty members, were to become mother congregations of groups that eventually developed into major denominations. Indeed, it would seem that most preachers who "came out" of their denominations during this time inevitably made holiness doctrines the hallmark of their creeds.[29]

The holiness movement of the late 1890's was not entirely rural or Methodist, as many have assumed, but included significant urban groups also. Some of these groups were inaugurated by Presbyterian ministers who adopted the theology of the holiness movement. Two Southern ones were

the oldest denomination which later became a part of the pentecostal movement.

28 For other evaluations of Irwin's Fire-Baptized movement and its relation to the pentecostal movement see Kendrick, *The Promise Fulfilled*, p. 33; Brumback, *Suddenly from Heaven*, p. 9; and Campbell, *The Pentecostal Holiness Church*, p. 195.

29 The group of churches known as the "churches of God" will be treated in the next chapter because of their importance to the entire picture of Southern pentecostalism.

the Brewerton Presbyterian Church of Greenville, South Carolina, and the Pentecostal Mission of Nashville, Tennessee. The former was organized as a result of the preaching of the Reverend N. J. Holmes, pastor of the Second Presbyterian Church of Greenville, South Carolina. Before entering the Presbyterian ministry, Holmes had been a prominent lawyer in South Carolina, having been educated for the profession at the University of Edinburgh in Scotland. After preaching for some years in various Presbyterian Churches, he heard of Dwight L. Moody's emphasis on sanctification and became interested in this doctrine. After a long talk with Moody on a trip to Massachusetts, Holmes sought for and obtained the experience of sanctification in 1896. Because of his new emphasis on entire sanctification, he was tried by his Presbytery and withdrew from the Presbyterian Church. He later joined the Brewerton Presbyterian Church, which had been founded in 1899 by other holiness-minded Presbyterians. This group had amended the "longer" and "shorter" Presbyterian catechisms to include the doctrine of sanctification as a "second blessing."[30]

Having always felt an urge to teach theology to young people planning to enter the ministry, Holmes inaugurated a Bible institute near Greenville in November of 1898. As early as 1893 he had conducted short Bible courses at a cottage on Paris Mountain near Greenville. The first name of the young school was the "Altamont Bible and Missionary Institute," and it was Wesleyan in doctrine. After many changes in name and location, the school was permanently located in Greenville, South Carolina, and was eventually renamed "The Holmes Theological Seminary." From its earliest days, Holmes' school maintained ties with the Fire-Baptized Holiness Church and the later Pentecostal Holiness Church. Although Holmes questioned Irwin's idea of a "baptism of fire," he later joined the pentecostal movement, bringing his school with him. With a continuous history dating back to

[30] N. J. Holmes, *Life Sketches and Sermons* (Franklin Springs, Georgia, 1920), pp. 7-97. Also see Iva Thomas, *The History of Holmes Theological Seminary* (Greenville, S. C., n.d.), pp. 2-9; *The Voice of Holmes*, May 1948, pp. 2-3; Campbell, *The Pentecostal Holiness Church*, pp. 263, 423-432.

1898, Holmes eventually could claim to be the oldest pentecostal school in the world.[31]

Another Presbyterian minister who joined the ranks of the holiness movement was the Reverend J. O. McClurkan of Nashville, Tennessee. Of the Cumberland Presbyterian persuasion, McClurkan started the "Pentecostal Mission" in 1898 in Nashville after hearing revivalist Sam Jones praise the holiness people in a city-wide campaign in 1897, asserting that he had "never seen a holiness man that wasn't a prohibitionist from his hat to his heels."[32]

Also contributing to McClurkan's interest in the doctrine was the appearance in 1897 of Presbyterian evangelist J. Wilbur Chapman's book, *The Surrendered Life*. The "Pentecostal Mission" became the center for several holiness-minded ministers, including John T. Benson, later prominent as a publisher, and B. F. Haynes, former editor of the *Tennessee Methodist*. Due to McClurkan's Calvinistic background, the theology of the "Pentecostal Mission" was closer to the Oberlin theology of Charles G. Finney than the National Holiness Movement. For many years this group endeavored to unite all the holiness factions in the Southeast and at one time allied itself with A. B. Simpson's Christian and Missionary Alliance. Holmes attended the conventions of this group as an observer until 1907 when his defection to the pentecostal movement closed the doors of fellowship with most other holiness people.[33]

McClurkan's "Pentecostal Mission" was in many ways more radical than the National Holiness Movement. From its beginning it taught the doctrine of divine healing "as in the atonement," the "premillennial second coming of Christ," and a view of sanctification which emphasized the indwelling of the Holy Spirit rather than the cleansing aspect of the doctrine. Rejecting the pentecostal doctrine of speaking with tongues as evidence of receiving the Holy Spirit, the Pentecostal Mission eventually merged with the Church of

31 Holmes, *Life Sketches and Sermons*, pp. 93-149. According to notes found in his Bible, Holmes received the "baptism of fire" on one occasion but later repudiated it.

32 Smith, *Called Unto Holiness*, p. 181.

33 Holmes, *Life Sketches and Sermons*, p. 152.

the Nazarene in 1915 and became the major strength of that denomination in the Southeast. This group is the only major holiness group in the South that did not later enter the pentecostal movement.[34]

Another holiness church that was destined to play a major role in the pentecostal movement was the Pentecostal Holiness Church, which began in North Carolina. The founder of this group was a Methodist minister from Sampson County, North Carolina, the Reverend A. B. Crumpler, who in the 1880's had moved to Missouri where he came into contact with holiness teachings. In 1890, at a District Conference of the Methodist Church, he was sanctified under the preaching of Beverly Carradine, a leading preacher in the National Holiness Movement. Returning to North Carolina after 1890, Crumpler began to preach sanctification in the Methodist Churches of his native state. By 1897 an outbreak of interest in the doctrine caused by Crumpler's preaching led him to organize the "North Carolina Holiness Association." Becoming quite active in holiness circles, he also contributed articles and reports of his meetings to J. M. Pike's *Way of Faith* magazine in Columbia, South Carolina, and to George Watson's *Living Words*, published in Pittsburgh, Pennsylvania. At the height of the 1896 holiness revival, Crumpler preached to thousands in churches, tents, and arbors all over the state. In only one week of services he reported 80 souls "converted" and 125 "wholly sanctified," with the movement "sweeping this country."[35]

Since the Southern Methodist Church had declared war on the holiness movement at the 1894 General Conference, Crumpler ran into trouble with his superiors in the church. In October 1899 the North Carolina Annual Conference tried him for insubordination for refusing to stop preaching the doctrine of sanctification after being enjoined from doing so by his ecclesiastical superior. Crumpler thereupon witl.drew from the church "for the sake of peace and harmony,"

[34] Smith, *Called Unto Holiness*, pp. 180-204; Redford, *Rise of the Church of the Nazarene*, pp. 40-60.

[35] *The Way of Faith*, April 15, 1896, p. 5; *Living Words*, April 1903, p. 16; June 1903, p. 16.

feeling that he had been tried for "preaching the glorious doctrine of Methodism."[36]

Following his separation from the Methodist Church, Crumpler continued to preach throughout the eastern part of North Carolina, bringing great controversies to the Methodist churches of that area. Adding to the conflict was a paper that he began to publish in 1900 called *The Holiness Advocate*. Since the large number of people that had been sanctified in his meetings felt unwelcome in their Methodist Churches, he also formed a new church for them. Meeting in the spring of 1900 in Fayetteville, North Carolina, Crumpler and a few other former Methodist ministers formed a new denomination which they named "The Pentecostal Holiness Church." The reasons for creating this new church were stated by Crumpler: "That those who had been saved and sanctified, many of whom belonged to no church, and many of whom had been turned out of their churches for professing holiness, might have a congenial church home." Before leaving Fayetteville, Crumpler framed a *Discipline* for the new denomination and made plans to organize new churches as soon as possible. Before the end of 1900 churches had been organized in Antioch, Goldsboro, and Magnolia, with prospects for several more in other communities.[37]

Crumpler's Pentecostal Holiness Church was quite similar to all the other holiness groups that had been founded during the last quarter of the century. Its statement of faith contained all the usual Wesleyan language regarding "entire sanctification as a second definite work of grace." Other holiness doctrines were also spelled out which marked this group as a part of the "radical" wing of the holiness movement. Divine healing and premillennialism also received a prominent place, as did strictures against "worldliness," "oyster stews," "needless ornamentation," and "tobacco."[38]

36 G. F. Taylor, "Our Church History," January 20, 1921, p. 9; Campbell, *The Pentecostal Holiness Church*, pp. 217-220.

37 Taylor, "Our Church History," February 17, 1921, pp. 8-10; Campbell, *The Pentecostal Holiness Church*, pp. 221-232; *Discipline of the Pentecostal Holiness Church, 1961* (Franklin Springs, Georgia, 1961), pp. 5-6; *The Holiness Advocate*, July 15, 1904, pp. 4-5.

38 See the *Discipline of the Pentecostal Holiness Church, 1902*, pp. 9-18.

In 1901 the group changed its name to "The Holiness Church," dropping the name "Pentecostal." This step was taken because many members were using the term "pentecostal church" to identify themselves, rather than the more "reproachful" term "Holiness Church." This name continued to be used until 1909 after the church had changed its articles of faith in 1908 to make it officially a part of the pentecostal movement. Then the adjective "pentecostal" was restored to the name.[39]

Also developing in North Carolina was one of the few Baptist groups in the nation to accept the Wesleyan doctrine of holiness. The Free-Will Baptist Church, which had beginnings in New England in the eighteenth century, reached the state in 1855. In that year the Stony Run Free-Will Baptist Church was organized and with it the Cape Fear Conference of the denomination. Originally an Arminian reaction to the stern Calvinism of New England Protestantism, the Free-Will Baptists from the beginning accepted the basic premises of Methodism.[40]

It was not until the height of the holiness crusade of the 1880's that this group adopted a strictly Wesleyan perfectionist creed. The 1883 *Discipline* stated that sanctification "commences at regeneration" and continues with one "constantly growing in grace." This language showed definite evidence of being influenced by Finney's Oberlin views of holiness. The statement in the *Discipline* of 1889, however, was changed to be much more Wesleyan in tone, showing the influence of the National Holiness Movement on the denomination. In this issue sanctification was presented as "an instantaneous work of God's grace in a believer's heart whereby the heart is cleansed from all sin and made pure by the blood of Christ." With this statement the Free-Will Baptists of North Carolina followed the trend of perfectionist thinking that was permeating other denominations in addition to the Methodist. This group also followed the trend

[39] Campbell, *The Pentecostal Holiness Church*, pp. 234, 251. The *Discipline* (1961) states that the word "pentecostal" was dropped because they did not speak with other tongues as on the day of Pentecost (Acts 2:4), but this seems to be a later interpolation; see p. 6.

[40] *Discipline of the Pentecostal Free-Will Baptist Church* (n.p., n.d.), pp. 8-9.

among Southern holiness churches after 1906 of adopting the pentecostal view of the baptism of the Holy Spirit. In 1912 a division occurred within the Cape Fear Conference resulting in the formation of the "Pentecostal Free-Will Baptist Church," which henceforth became completely dissociated from the main body of the denomination.[41]

Another North Carolina holiness denomination that began in this period was the "United Holy Church" with origins near Wilmington in the town of Method, North Carolina. In 1886 a revival was held in a Negro Baptist church in Method in which the doctrine of sanctification was preached. The officials of the church recognized the fact that the doctrine was contrary to Baptist theology and practice. The holiness faction was asked to leave the church after the revival closed. The small group of dissidents organized a church which became the nucleus of a small holiness denomination. Other groups in other sections of North Carolina joined the small church at various times between 1886 and 1902, when a formal organization was effected.[42]

The leader in the organizational meeting was an Elder in Irwin's Fire-Baptized Holiness Church, one W. H. Fulford. The first president of the new denomination was Elder C. M. Mason of Wilmington, North Carolina. Because of its doctrinal position, the new denomination adopted the name "The United Holy Church of America." In 1903 Elder Fulford was elected President, and served in this capacity until 1916 when Elder H. L. Fisher was chosen to lead the group. Although founded by a minister of the Fire-Baptized Holiness Church, the United Holy Church developed as an independent denomination and spread over the South as a completely Negro group. Dependent on the white churches for theological direction, this denomination followed other Southern holiness groups into the pentecostal movement after the turn of the century.[43]

Throughout the South there were hundreds of local independent holiness congregations formed during this period

41 *Ibid.*, p. 10.
42 H. L. Fisher, *History of the United Holy Church of America* (n.p., n.d.), pp. 1-7.
43 *Ibid.*, p. 8.

that never expanded beyond their local areas. Many others were formed in community-shaking revivals and then quietly died due to subsequent indifference or to acute persecution. Most of the Southern holiness churches, as has been pointed out, belonged to the more "radical" wing of the holiness movement, emphasizing such new doctrines as divine healing, the premillennial second coming of Christ, a "third blessing" of "the fire," and puritanical modes of dress.

Although some of the holiness churches of the South, such as McClurkan's Tennessee-based "Pentecostal Mission," joined the more conservative groups, such as the Church of the Nazarene and the Wesleyan Methodist Church, most of them followed the Midwestern and Southern trends toward the radicalism that represented the temper of the times. A long-run result of this trend was that the greater part of the Southern holiness movement was predisposed to accept the even more radical doctrines of the pentecostal movement when it began in 1906.

The conservative holiness denominations, which included the Church of the Nazarene, the Pilgrim Holiness Church, the Wesleyan Methodist Church, the Christian and Missionary Alliance, and the Free Methodist Church, ultimately accounted for only a small proportion of the holiness population of the Southern states. An example of the trend of the times was the fact that Irwin's first meetings in South Carolina and Georgia resulted in the Wesleyan Methodist Churches, which invited him, disbanding and becoming Fire-Baptized Holiness Churches. Indeed many of the older churches of the pentecostal-holiness movement of today began their existence as Wesleyan Methodist Churches.[44]

One of the most far-reaching manifestations of holiness religion in the nation occurred among the people who adopted variations of the name "Church of God." Because of their importance they will be considered in detail in the next chapter, but it should be remembered that they developed in the same context as did the Fire-Baptized Holiness Church,

---

[44] An interesting example is the Beulah Church near Elberton, Georgia, which was organized in 1896 as a Wesleyan Methodist Church, but which later reorganized as a Pentecostal Holiness Church in 1911. See *The Minutes of the Beulah Pentecostal Holiness Church, 1896-1956* (Franklin Springs, Georgia), pp. 1-16.

the Pentecostal Holiness Church, and the others discussed in this chapter. These groups, along with all the others, were a result of the holiness crusade of 1867-1900 and were destined to become pentecostal after 1906.

In the end it was the more radical "Fire-Baptized Way" that prevailed among the holiness people of the South and Midwest, rather than the more conservative Nazarene Church concept of sanctification. The "third blessing heresy" of Irwin's church was destined to become the orthodox position of the Southern holiness-pentecostal groups, with the single addition of speaking with other tongues as the evidence of one's having received the baptism of the Holy Ghost. By the time this doctrine swept over the holiness movement in 1906, the Southern segment of the movement was psychologically and doctrinally prepared to accept it as an integral part of their beliefs.

Chapter Four

THE CHURCHES OF GOD

Like a mighty army, moves the Church of God;
Brothers, we are treading where the saints have trod.
We are not divided, all one body we,
One in hope and doctrine, one in charity.
—Sabine Baring-Gould

As the holiness movement fragmented from the older denominations throughout the United States, new sects sprang into being in every section of the nation. As has been noted, many of these groups used the term "holiness" in their names, while others preferred the word "pentecostal." However, no other name became as popular as "The Church of God." Between 1880 and 1923 no less than two hundred groups adopted some version of that name to designate their churches. Out of this number, perhaps a score could be classed as major groups.[1]

The first holiness body to call itself "The Church of God" was D. S. Warner's church, which began in 1880 in Anderson,

---

[1] Frank S. Mead, *Handbook of Denominations in the United States* (New York, 1965), p. 74; Clark, *Small Sects in America*, pp. 102-105; Mayer, *Religious Bodies of America*, pp. 331-338. There are so many independent bodies in the nation with this name that a full investigation and classification of them all would be impossible. They range from "The (Original) Church of God" to the "Runaway Church of God," and endorse a wide variety of doctrines and practices. Most of the earlier groups chose the name without knowledge of the existence of the other groups. In most cases it was chosen because it was a "Bible name," being mentioned several times in the New Testament.

Indiana. The body represented a split from the older "Winebrenner Church of God," which had churches in the Northeast and Midwest. Three years later one A. M. Kiergan organized the "Church of God (Holiness)" in protest against official Methodist pressure against the holiness associations of the South and Midwest.[2] These and several other more insignificant groups formed sects using the name "Church of God" before the period of sect formation began in earnest shortly after 1894. Those formed before 1894 generally belonged to the holiness persuasion and were not to identify themselves with the pentecostal movement after 1906. Those beginning after 1894 generally became pentecostal later.

The greatest sect-forming years in the South fell in the quadrennium of 1894-98, following the anti-holiness policy statement of the General Conference of the Southern Methodist Church. In widely scattered places outbreaks of holiness preaching produced new churches that called themselves "Church of God." The only connecting link between them was the doctrine of entire sanctification, which occasionally caused great excitement in communities where it was first preached. The cause of the excitement, which sometimes took the form of opposition, was the charge, whether founded or not, that holiness people taught that one could live totally without sin.

In 1895 the doctrine of sanctification was introduced to McCreary County, Kentucky, with the preaching of J. H. Parks, a United Baptist pastor. This new doctrine, as Parks preached it, claimed the attention of three other Baptist pastors in the area: Steve Bryant, Tom Moses, and William Douglas. All of these ministers were affiliated with the local South Union Baptist Association of the United Baptist Church. From 1895 to 1903 they preached the most un-Calvinistic doctrine of holiness, winning many converts. The rise of this "heresy" among their preachers and churches gave great concern to the leaders of the Baptist Association. Finally, in 1903 a trial was held by the association in a full session and Parks and his followers were excluded from the Baptist denomination. The ministers' credentials were also

2 Mayer, *Religious Bodies*, pp. 331-332; Harold Paul, "The Religious Frontier in Oklahoma" (Unpublished Doctoral dissertation, University of Oklahoma, 1965), pp. 19-20.

revoked completing the separation. The charge against them was that they taught that "men could be lost after regeneration," a most serious heresy to these predestinarian Baptists. After the trial five Baptist churches left the denomination in sympathy with the holiness leaders.[3]

By 1906 these five churches met in a "General Assembly" at the "Jellico Creek Church" in Whitley County, Kentucky, and organized a new denomination which they named "The Church of God." Several years later this small group of holiness people, isolated in the Kentucky mountains, were told that other denominations also were using the same name. Accordingly, in 1911 they added the words "Mountain Assembly" to distinguish their group from the others.[4]

The year 1895 also saw the beginning of another holiness group which eventually emerged as the largest Negro pente-costal denomination in the nation, the "Church of God in Christ." The founders of this group were Elders C. H. Mason and C. P. Jones, ministers of missionary Baptist churches in Mississippi. Mason, the dominant personality of the two founders, had been licensed as a Baptist minister in 1893. Later that year he had entered Arkansas Baptist College to further prepare himself for the ministry, but left after three months because he felt "there was no salvation in schools or colleges."[5]

Two years later Mason and Jones traveled to Lexington, Mississippi, where they came in contact with the holiness doctrine of entire sanctification. The two men accepted the doctrine and began vigorously to preach it in the Baptist churches of that area. Soon they were ejected from their Baptist Association for preaching and claiming to have received the experience. These churchless preachers then held a "holiness" revival in February 1897 in a cotton gin house in Lexington, Mississippi, which became the organizational meeting for a new denomination. The name chosen for the new group was "The Church of God in Christ," a designation that Mason had previously settled on while walking the street

[3] Luther Gibson, *History of the Church of God, Mountain Assembly* (n.p., 1954), pp. 4-5.

[4] *Ibid.*, p. 8.

[5] C. A. Ashworth, *Yearbook of the Church of God in Christ* (Memphis, 1961), p. 9; Kendrick, *The Promise Fulfilled*, p. 197.

in Little Rock, Arkansas. In late 1897 the new church was incorporated in Memphis, Tennessee, as a chartered denomination.[6]

This church was the first Southern holiness denomination to become legally chartered, a source of great advantage to the group. Because of this factor, ordained ministers of Mason's church could claim clergy rates on the railroads and legally perform marriages. Consequently, many white ministers of independent holiness congregations received ordination from Mason, making his organization interracial. This situation became even more pronounced after the pentecostal revival of 1906 when scores of white ministers joined Mason's church.[7]

Like many of the holiness and pentecostal bodies, the Church of God in Christ owed its existence to a strong and dominating founder. Mason stamped his personality on his church far more emphatically than any other holiness leader. Called by his followers a "Greater than the Apostle Paul," Mason outlived all the other founders of major holiness sects and during his lifetime saw his group become the largest Negro pentecostal sect in the world and the second largest of all the pentecostal denominations in the United States.[8]

The year following the separation of the Church of God in Christ saw the beginnings of another group in the mountains of Tennessee and North Carolina which was destined to make the term "Church of God" a household word in the South. In 1896 the doctrine of entire sanctification reached the hill folk of Western North Carolina when three men from East Tennessee came over the mountains and

6 See *The Evangelist Speaks*, November and December 1966, p. 1. This is the national paper of the denomination. Also see U.S. Bureau of the Census, *Religious Bodies: 1926*, II, 380-381. The only biography of Mason is Mary Mason, *The History and Life Work of Bishop C. H. Mason, Chief Apostle, and His Co-Laborers* (Memphis, 1934); see pp. 1-12 of this work.

7 *The International Outlook* (Los Angeles, 1963), January-March 1963, p. 4.

8 Mason died in 1963 at the age of 97 and was buried in his massive (10,000 seats) "Mason's Temple" in Memphis, Tennessee, the first such burial allowed in the history of the city. The street where his temple is located was renamed "Mason Street" in his honor. See the 1966 *Official Convocation Program* (Memphis, 1966), p. 61.

held a revival in the Schearer Schoolhouse in Cherokee County, North Carolina. These three, William Martin, Joe M. Tipton, and Milton McNabb, were self-proclaimed "evangelists" belonging to local Methodist and Baptist Churches in the Cokercreek Community near the North Carolina border. Revival fires were burning throughout the Carolinas in 1896, as Irwin and Carradine preached in South Carolina and Crumpler spread the holiness flame in Eastern North Carolina. Tipton and Martin had been in contact with the Fire-Baptized movement, which had made an abortive attempt at organizing a state association in Tennessee. Centering their efforts in East Tennessee, near the Cokercreek home of Mrs. Sarah A. Smith, an association was never formally effected, but the Fire-Baptized doctrine spread throughout the countryside. The revival that began in the Schearer Schoolhouse in 1896 formed the nucleus of what later became the "Church of God" of Cleveland, Tennessee.[9]

An unusual feature of this revival was the fact that several of those who received sanctification spoke in other tongues when they "prayed through." This manifestation, which seemed strange to the mountain folk, caused great excitement in the community. The Baptist and Methodist pastors in the locality soon were denouncing this new "heresy." As the tongues-speaking spread, even children experienced the phenomenon. Because of these demonstrations heavy persecutions broke out against the people engaged in the meeting. Before the revival ended, several houses were burned as mobs led by "leading Methodist and Baptist members" ransacked and pillaged the homes of the worshippers. Leading the group was a justice of the peace and the local sheriff. After the meeting house to which the group had moved was burned, the band of worshippers moved to the home of one W. F. Bryant, who assumed leadership of the group.[10]

For the next six years the band of people that had

[9] L. Howard Juillerat, *Book of Minutes, General Assemblies, Churches of God* (Cleveland, Tennessee, 1922), pp. 7-14; Charles W. Conn, *Like a Mighty Army, Moves the Church of God* (Cleveland, Tennessee, 1955), pp. 16-18; S. Claude Bailey, *Pioneer Marvels of Faith* (Morristown, Tennessee, n.d.), p. 20.

[10] Juillerat, *Book of Minutes*, pp. 11-12.

gathered in the revival of 1896 worshipped as an unorganized band of holiness believers. From time to time they were visited by an itinerant Baptist preacher from Tennessee, R. G. Spurling, Jr., who had been expelled from his church near Turtletown, Tennessee, in 1892 for teaching the doctrine of sanctification to his congregation at the Liberty Baptist Church. Spurling preached the need of a new reformation in Christianity comparable to the Protestant Reformation of the sixteenth century. Spurling's ideas had come from his father, R. G. Spurling, Sr., who had gone so far as to organize a band of like-minded followers into a "Christian Union" in 1886 in Monroe County, Tennessee. The Junior Spurling had joined the group which, however, later disbanded for lack of interest, the members returning to their former churches. Spurling, however, kept alive his desire for a reformation, and when the holiness revival began in Cherokee County, he became one of the favorite speakers that Bryant invited to address the group.[11]

The doctrines that Bryant and Spurling preached to the congregation which met in the Camp Creek community were quite similar to those taught in the holiness movement at large. The more radical doctrines of divine healing, the baptism of fire, and the second advent of Christ gained acceptance with the group. Entire sanctification, with a complete rejection of society, was the central doctrine. But all was not well with this small, unorganized band of worshippers. Irwin's idea of the baptisms of "dynamite," "lyddite," and "oxidite" swept the community, exciting its more emotional members and repelling its most thoughtful. In addition, such Fire-Baptized prohibitions as no neckties, no meats, no candies, and no medicines were imposed on the group. Others engaged in prolonged fasts until they became gaunt and weak. By the turn of the century such "fanaticisms" as these led Pastor Bryant to conclude that a form of government was necessary if the group was to survive.[12]

In order to curb these evils, Bryant later decided to form

11 Conn, *Like a Mighty Army*, pp. 7-16; Juillerat, *Book of Minutes*, p. 13; Homer Tomlinson, ed., *The Diary of A. J. Tomlinson* (New York, 1949), I, 52-53.

12 E. L. Simmons, *History of the Church of God* (Cleveland, Tennessee, 1938), pp. 11-12; Conn, *Like a Mighty Army*, pp. 39-40.

an organization which would confer the authority to discipline erring members. Accordingly, on May 15, 1902, the first local church was organized, which was to become the nucleus of the Church of God. The name chosen for the new body was "The Holiness Church at Camp Creek." Bryant was ordained into the ministry and the itinerant Spurling was chosen as pastor. Thus almost unwittingly the denomination which was to become one of the world's largest pentecostal churches was born.[13]

The appearance in 1903 of another itinerant preacher, A. J. Tomlinson, who was destined to dominate the infant church and through his organizational talents spread its churches throughout the nation, was to make that year a memorable one in the history of the Camp Creek church. Tomlinson was a mystical Quaker from Indiana who traveled over the Southeast selling Bibles and tracts for the American Bible Society. He had been an interested observer during the 1896 holiness revival at Camp Creek and had later settled in Culbertson, North Carolina, near the Georgia border. A restless wanderer, he had sold Bibles as a colporteur for the American Bible Society from Maine to Georgia. A deeply religious man, he had already received the experience of sanctification before reaching North Carolina. After settling in Culbertson, he began an orphanage on a farm he had bought and began publication of a religious monthly paper he called *Samson's Foxes.*[14]

[13] Juillerat, *Book of Minutes,* p. 13; *The Church of God Evangel,* April 7, 1945, pp. 3-15; Conn, *Like a Mighty Army,* pp. 44-45. The Camp Creek church seems to have been the first continuous congregation of the several branches of the Church of God with headquarters in Cleveland, Tennessee. Some controversy exists as to whether the modern pentecostal movement originated with this group, which had antecedents going back to 1886. For various viewpoints see Conn, *Like a Mighty Army,* pp. xix-xxii; Carl Brumback, *Suddenly from Heaven* (Springfield, Missouri, 1961), p. 57; Vinson Synan, *Emmanuel College—The First Fifty Years* (Washington, D.C., 1968), p. 4; Nils Bloch-Hoell, *The Pentecostal Movement* (Oslo, Norway, 1964), p. 18.

[14] A. J. Tomlinson, "A Journal of Happenings" (Manuscript version of Tomlinson's *Diary* at the Church of God headquarters in Cleveland), pp. 1-10; Lillie Duggar, *A. J. Tomlinson* (Cleveland, Tennessee, 1964), pp. 17-33. Several versions of Tomlinson's *Diary* exist, including the three-volume one published by Homer Tomlinson from 1949 to 1955

Not satisfied with his membership in the Society of Friends, Tomlinson attended religious services wherever he traveled. Although not an ordained minister, he was often called on to preach. In 1901, on a trip to Shiloh, Maine, he had been baptized by a Mr. Sandifer in the Androscogin River. The name of the church he joined was called "The Church of the Living God for the Evangelization of the World, Gathering of Israel, New Order of Things at the Close of the Gentile Age." This group must have meant little to the Hoosier colporteur, since he never spoke of it again in any of his writings.[15]

The members of the Camp Creek church had known Tomlinson for seven years when in 1903 they asked him to join the group. Often he had been invited to preach for them, and in time he came to be regarded as more highly educated than Bryant or Spurling. The decision to join was a difficult one for Tomlinson to make. Before the day on which he was to join, he went to the top of a nearby hill, called Burger Mountain, to pray over his decision. Here, on what his followers now call "prayer mountain," Tomlinson "prevailed in prayer" and received a vision of "the Church of God of the last days." According to his revelation:

> Jesus had started the Church of God when He was here on earth, and a record was kept of its progress and activities for several years after the death of its founder. The period of history known as the Dark Ages had come after the Church of God had departed from the faith and the church was lost to view.[16]

Now Tomlinson had discovered the "True Church of God" at Camp Creek, and accordingly joined the small group the next day, June 13, 1903, with the understanding "that it is the Church of God of the Bible." With the accession of this traveling Bible salesman from Indiana, the struggling little group of mountaineers gained a gifted preacher and organizer

(New York, Church of God World Headquarters). References used here are from the manuscript entitled "Journal of Happenings."

15 A. J. Tomlinson, *Answering the Call of God* (Cleveland, Tennessee, 1942), pp. 1-15; Tomlinson, "Journal of Happenings," p. 12.

16 *The Evening Light and Church of God Evangel*, March 1, 1910, p. 1; Duggar, *A. J. Tomlinson*, p. 34.

who, more than any other individual, was responsible for the phenomenal growth of the church into a national church today.[17]

The local reputation of Tomlinson as a deep Bible student and well-traveled agent for the American Bible Society caused the Camp Creek congregation to elect him immediately as the pastor of their church. Spurling and Bryant then departed from Camp Creek to evangelize other mountain communities. Within three years the Camp Creek preachers had established congregations in three other communities, two in Tennessee and one in Georgia. In 1904, Tomlinson was chosen as pastor of three of the four congregations—Union Grove and Luskville in Tennessee, and Camp Creek in North Carolina. The other church, at Jones, Georgia, met in a private home and was soon abandoned.[18]

The Hoosier minister traversed the countryside preaching in his three churches and at many other points. As he preached, the ideas that were to shape the Church of God movement and eventually to divide it, came into sharper focus. To Tomlinson the group with which he was associated was the only true and valid Christian communion "this side of the Dark Ages." In the early church "the full blaze of light beamed forth from the Pentecostal chamber and shined forth with radiant glory in the early morning of the Gospel day." Then intervened the long period of apostasy known as the "dark ages" when the church of God was dormant and back-slidden. Now that the true church had been rediscovered in the mountains of North Carolina, "the evening light, the true light is now shining, and the sheep are hearing His voice and are coming from every place where they have been scattered during the cloudy and dark day." In order to prepare the world for the second coming of Christ and the end of the age, the church of God was destined to reap "the precious fruit of the earth" before it was too late. Eventually the faithful Christians of all denominations in every nation of the world would return to the true church of God and the

[17] Tomlinson, *Answering the Call of God*, p. 17; "Journal of Happenings," p. 17; Duggar, *A. J. Tomlinson*, p. 35.

[18] Tomlinson, "Journal of Happenings," *passim*, entries from 1903-1906; Juillerat, *Book of Minutes*, pp. 13, 14.

Lord would set up his kingdom, beginning at Burger Mountain and ending in Jerusalem.[19]

This apocalyptic view of the mission of the church was at once a source of strength and weakness for the movement. To those who accepted the message, there was only one true church, all others being part of the "dark ages" of apostasy. This idea bred an exclusivism which bound the members to the church with a tenacious loyalty. It also created a strong urge to bring others into the true "Church of God" fold, thereby producing a spirit of competition for the members of other holiness churches.

The preaching of Tomlinson, Spurling, and Bryant also produced the emotional reactions that had been so familiar in frontier American revivalism. In meetings in Tennessee, Georgia, and North Carolina, Tomlinson reported that the Spirit worked in many ways, with many saints "shouting, weeping, clapping their hands, jerking, and hand shaking." Once at the Union Grove church he reported that people "fell on the floor, and some writhed like serpents," while others "seemed to be off in a trance for four or five hours." In all of this the preacher felt that the "church seemed to be greatly edified." In most services some claimed to be converted and others sanctified. These demonstrations attracted large crowds to the services wherever Tomlinson preached. Crowds of five hundred to seven hundred were reported in many of the early services that he conducted.[20]

With surprisingly little opposition from the community, the four churches made great progress under Tomlinson's leadership. By the end of 1905, it was felt that a general meeting of the four churches should be held to better organize the work of the groups. Accordingly a "General Assembly" was planned to convene at the Camp Creek church in January of 1906 to organize a new denomination.

19 A. J. Tomlinson, *The Evening Light and Church of God Evangel*, March 1, 1910, p. 1; Homer Tomlinson, *The Shout of a King* (New York, 1968), pp. 14-20. This exclusivist view continued with little modification until 1937 when it began to moderate and eventually disappear in official church documents. See the *Church of God Evangel*, January 17, 1914, pp. 1-3; July 3, 1915, pp. 1-4; April 1, 1916, p. 1; May 13, 1916, p. 1; June 30, 1934, p. 5; August 14, 1937, pp. 3-14.

20 Tomlinson, "A Journal of Happenings," pp. 21-23.

Rather than meet in the church house, the Assembly decided to meet in the home of a member of the church, one J. C. Murphy, because of its convenience and size. In this house delegates from the four churches met on January 26 and 27 and conducted the short and simple business of the group. As pastor of the home church, Tomlinson acted as "ruling elder" and secretary and gave direction to the Assembly. It debated such subjects as "feet washing," tobacco, family worship, and the Sunday school. It was decided that feet washing was an ordinance on the same level as the sacrament of communion. Like most other holiness groups, a strong statement condemning the use of tobacco was adopted. Other resolutions supporting family worship and the establishment of Sunday schools were also approved. As the work of the Assembly concluded, the twenty-one participants engaged in observing a sacramental and foot-washing service.[21]

The delegates to this Assembly discountenanced the idea that they were establishing a new denomination. The first resolution adopted declared that "we do not consider ourselves a legislative or executive body but judicial only." At the end of the meeting, Secretary Tomlinson wrote on the margin of the minutes:

> We hope and trust that no person or body of people will ever use these minutes, or any part of them, as articles of faith upon which to establish a sect or denomination. The subjects were discussed merely to obtain light and understanding. Our articles of faith are inspired and given us by the holy apostles and written in the New Testament which is our only rule of faith and practice.[22]

Despite the denial of any sect-forming motives, the work of the Assembly inevitably led to the development of a separate denomination. Although Tomlinson had traveled widely and was well aware of the existence of other holiness denominations, he made no effort to affiliate his group with any of them. This body of worshippers thus was and continued to remain a *sui generis* religious group.

[21] Juillerat, *Book of Minutes*, pp. 15-19; Duggar, *A. J. Tomlinson*, p. 39; Conn, *Like a Mighty Army*, pp. 61-69.

[22] Simmons, *History of the Church of God*, p. 16; Conn, *Like a Mighty Army*, p. 303.

The Second General Assembly of the new movement convened at the Union Grove church in Bradley County, Tennessee, in 1907. It made some far-reaching decisions. As of that time this nascent organization did not have a name, the local congregations calling themselves simply "holiness churches." The problem of anonymity was solved when the delegates voted "harmoniously" to designate the new denomination "Church of God," citing New Testament usages of the term as their authority. This action seems to have been taken without any reference to other churches which already used the name.[23]

Another problem that faced the Second General Assembly was which form of church government to adopt. Some favored the congregational system for the selection of pastors, while others called for appointment by a higher church authority, as in the episcopal system. The decision was a compromise which in reality paved the way for a strong episcopal government: "sometimes the church calls, sometimes sent by those having the responsibility and authority." In time the Church of God developed the most centralized government of all the holiness or pentecostal denominations in America.[24]

With the closing of the Second General Assembly, the Church of God had become a fully developed, if yet small, denomination. It was also fully a part of the National Holiness Movement, although rather isolated from the other groups across the nation. The vitality of the new church was seen in the great growth that followed the 1902 organization of the Camp Creek church. At that time the body had only 20 members in one church. By 1910 there were 1,005 members in 31 churches scattered throughout the Southeast. In that year the church also began publication of its first official organ, which it named *The Evening Light and Church of God Evangel.* By 1911 the number of churches had grown to 58 and the phenomenal growth that would make it, with its numerous subsequent branches, one of the largest pentecostal church bodies in the United States had begun.[25]

23 Juillerat, *Book of Minutes*, p. 22. The Scriptures cited were I Corinthians 1:2 and II Corinthians 1:1.
24 *Ibid.*, p. 23.
25 Juillerat, *Book of Minutes*, pp. 37-41. In 1911 the name of the

The choice of Tomlinson as the first "General Overseer" of the denomination was a fateful one. With his Indiana accent and background as a Bible salesman, he seemed the obvious choice to lead the infant church. Ironically the most Southern of the pentecostal denominations counted as their organizer and greatest propagator a Northerner, who originally had viewed the poverty-stricken South as little more than a mission field. Associated with Tomlinson in the early days of the Church of God movement was his eldest son Homer, who was to gain fame as both presidential candidate of the "Theocratic Party" and self-proclaimed "King of the World." Indeed, before the twentieth century had reached the halfway mark the Tomlinson family could claim the distinction of organizing three denominations, each calling itself the "Church of God."[26]

In later years the Tomlinsons were to claim that the entire holiness and pentecostal movements stemmed directly or indirectly from the work of A. J. Tomlinson. This, of course, represented a distortion of the facts, since the Church of God movement developed in relative isolation from the National Holiness Movement. The theological and organizational foundations of the holiness movements were laid much earlier in the National Holiness Association under Inskip and his successors, and the basic premises for pentecostalism were laid by Irwin's Fire-Baptized movement well before Tomlinson joined the holiness church at Camp Creek.[27]

In addition to these bodies, many other groups adopted

paper was changed to *The Church of God Evangel,* making it the oldest continuous publication in the pentecostal world.

[26] A. J. Tomlinson organized "The Church of God" (Cleveland, Tennessee) in 1906, and later "The Church of God of Prophecy" in 1923 to which his younger son, Milton, became heir after the father's death in 1943. Disgruntled, Homer then began the "Church of God" (World Headquarters) with offices in Queens, New York.

[27] See Homer Tomlinson, ed., *Diary of A. J. Tomlinson,* I, 5-13; and *The Shout of a King* (New York, 1968), pp. 1-20. Unfortunately, Homer Tomlinson's many unfounded claims found their way into such otherwise reputable works as Elmer T. Clark's *Small Sects in America* (New York, 1949), pp. 100-107. More recent and reliable scholarship accords Tomlinson a very important place in the early pentecostal movement, but finds the doctrinal origins of the movement elsewhere. See Klaud Kendrick, *The Promise Fulfilled* (Springfield, Missouri, 1961), pp. 32-68.

the name "Church of God." Among them were: The
(Original) Church of God, The Bible Church of God, The
Remnant Church of God, The Justified Church of God, The
Holstein Church of God, the Glorified Church of God, the
Church of God, Inc., and The Church of God (Apostolic).
Practically all of them were holiness groups of the more
radical type and identified themselves with the pentecostal
movement after 1906.[28]

By 1906 most of the major holiness bodies in the nation
had been formed and were in the process of building
denominations. Little thought was given to mergers, as most
groups were relatively isolated from each other. When the
Church of God in Kentucky heard of the Tennessee group, an
attempt was made at a merger which eventually failed when
the Kentucky group refused to submit to Tomlinson's authority.[29]

The body of holiness doctrine had become well established
in these new movements by the first decade of the century.
In general all of the groups were basically Arminian in their
theology and Wesleyan in their view of sanctification. In
addition to these premises, which might be considered
"orthodox" for the National Holiness Movement, the Southern groups had added several more radical views which set
them apart. The "Baptism of Fire" was perhaps the most
radical departure from the accepted views of the holiness
movement. Yet time had added many more rules and
doctrines that were to make the Southern holiness bodies
unique. At one General Assembly of the Church of God it
was decided that Coca Cola, chewing gum, rings, bracelets,
and earbobs were sinful and therefore prohibited to members
of the church.[30] Furthermore, the Pentecostal Holiness
Church held that it was sinful for a member to wear a necktie
or attend a county fair. Most of the groups also denounced
lodges, political parties, and labor unions as "instruments of
Satan." Buying life insurance was frowned upon as an
indication of lack of faith in God. Divine healing was taught
in such a way that it was almost placed on a level with the

---

28 See Mayer, *The Religious Bodies of America*, pp. 336-337.

29 Gibson, *Church of God, Mountain Assembly*, p. 10.

30 Juillerat, *Book of Minutes*, pp. 125-127.

new birth. The prevailing view was that physical healing for the body was provided "in the atonement" along with salvation for the soul. Medicines were widely believed to be "poisons" dispensed by doctors to the faithless. Hence persons who took medicines or visited doctors were considered weak or even completely lost.[31]

The movement was not without its apostates and critics. Because of the emotional aspects of most holiness services the epithet "holy rollers" was applied to most of the people who joined them. This term, similar in its origin to "Quaker," "Shaker," and "Methodist," was never accepted by any branch of the holiness movement.[32] More serious was the criticism leveled by ministers and theologians of other denominations. Perhaps the most damaging broadside was the volume of criticism by H. A. Ironside entitled *Holiness, The False and the True*, which appeared in 1912. The holiness churches were described by Ironside as hotbeds of "pharisaism," "tattling," "selfishness," and even frequent immorality. Speaking as a former member of the Salvation Army, Ironside's book was taken by many critics to discredit the entire movement, becoming a veritable textbook of anti-holiness theology.[33]

Other critics pointed to the antics of Alexander Dowie, the balding Australian who brought his divine healing services to Zion, Illinois, in the 1890's. By 1906 he had organized the "Christian Catholic Church" and had preached to crowds of 15,000 in Madison Square Garden in New York. He gained his greatest fame, however, at the Chicago World's Fair in 1893 where his "healing services" vied with Buffalo Bill's show for popular acclaim. At the turn of the century, Dowie became demented, claiming to be "Elijah the Prophet," and eventually was cast out of the church that he had founded. Wherever he traveled and whatever he said made headline

[31] *Ibid.*, pp. 25, 125, 176-177. Campbell, *The Pentecostal Holiness Church*, pp. 203-205.

[32] Most holiness churches repudiated the term "holy roller" in official statements, although they were the obvious objects of the epithets. A typical repudiation called the term "slanderous," "reproachful," and "malignant." See Juillerat, *Book of Minutes*, p. 200.

[33] H. A. Ironside, *Holiness, The False and the True* (Neptune, New Jersey, 1912), pp. 1-38.

news, most of it ludicrous and damaging to the holiness movement. Unfortunately "Dowieism" became associated with "holy rollerism," perhaps because both emphasized divine healing. The result was much ill-informed criticism of the holiness movement, though little of the American aspect of this movement had any connection with Dowie.[34]

Despite the criticism and occasional violence directed against the holiness movement, it continued to make progress throughout the nation. By the turn of the century there were at least a dozen major holiness bodies that were well organized. Most conspicuous among the Southern groups were the Church of God, the Pentecostal Holiness Church, the Fire-Baptized Holiness Church, and the Church of God in Christ. These four bodies were to display a remarkable similarity in doctrine and government, and they were to play leading roles in the pentecostal movement which began in 1906.

All these denominations were directed by men with powerful and dynamic personalities. The Church of God continued to grow from its mountain headquarters in Cleveland, Tennessee, under the leadership of the colorful Tomlinson, while the Church of God in Christ, with offices at the other end of the state in Memphis, was led by the soft-spoken, but firm, C. H. Mason. The Fire-Baptized Holiness Church spread out from its headquarters in Royston, Georgia, under the leadership of the scholarly and ascetic J. H. King, while the reins of the Pentecostal Holiness Church were held by A. B. Crumpler in Goldsboro, North Carolina. All of these men led denominations that were practically identical in doctrine and which operated in the same general territory.

These leaders were all busily engaged in the ecclesiastical affairs of their churches, when news arrived in the spring of 1906 that a meeting, heralded as rivaling the events that transpired on the day of Pentecost in Jerusalem, was then in progress in Los Angeles, California, at the Azusa Street Mission. The future course of the holiness movement in

34 Gordon Lindsay, *The Life of John Alexander Dowie* (Dallas, 1951), pp. 149-160.

America would be profoundly affected by the reactions of the leaders of the various bodies to the startling news from California. The Southern churches were to be particularly affected since they were the only major holiness groups in the nation to join the pentecostal movement.

Chapter Five

THE AMERICAN JERUSALEM— AZUSA STREET

Weird Babel of Tongues
New Sect of Fanatics is breaking Loose
Wild Scene Last Night on Azusa Street
Gurgle of Wordless Talk by a Sister.
—Los Angeles Times,
April 18, 1906

The doctrinal revolution which occurred in the holiness movement in 1906 came to the attention of the religious world through reports of a sensational revival meeting in Los Angeles. The City of the Angels was first told of the new movement in a report to the *Los Angeles Times* on April 18, 1906. Under a headline proclaiming "Weird Babel of Tongues," the writer reported that, "breathing strange utterances and mouthing a creed which it would seem no sane mortal could understand, the newest sect has started in Los Angeles." The paper further reported that:

Meetings are held in a tumble-down shack on Azusa Street, near San Pedro Street, and the devotees of the weird doctrine practice the most fanatical rites, preach the wildest theories and work themselves into a state of mad excitement in their peculiar zeal. Colored people and a sprinkling of whites compose the congregation, and night is made hideous in the neighborhood by the howlings of the worshippers, who spend hours swaying forth and back in a nerve-racking attitude of prayer and supplication. They claim to have the "gift of tongues" and to be able to comprehend the babel.[1]

This new doctrine was extreme even for Los Angeles, which already was the home of "numberless creeds." The "startling" claims of the new group were considered to be "fanatical" and "irreverent" by the reporter to the *Times*. With amazing accuracy, it was said that "a new sect . . . is breaking loose."[2] Little did *Times'* readers realize that this was the first report of one of the most far-reaching religious meetings of the twentieth century.

Los Angeles in April of 1906 boasted a population of 228,298, an increase of 30,684 over the past year. Every month 2,789 people were coming to live in this city, each one bringing his own ideas of politics, society, and religion.[3] While newspapers were filled with articles reflecting the pride of a dynamic and growing city, stories revealing the racism and religious intolerance of the times were usually given front-page coverage. The antics of Dowie and his struggles in Zion City, Illinois, were followed daily in the press. The *Times* scored him on April 22, 1906, for being a religious "fakir" and a "colossal humbug." Indeed the baldheaded divine healer was offered a thousand dollars a week to perform on vaudeville by shrewd show business promoters.[4]

The reputation of Los Angeles as a congenial home for new religious ideas was already well founded before 1906. The largest holiness denomination in America had already begun its history in the city when Phineas Bresee founded the "Church of the Nazarene" there in 1895. For a decade Bresee had conducted "mass holiness meetings" in his "Peniel Tabernacle" on Main Street to the shouts and hallelujahs of his working class congregation. By 1906 the Nazarenes had

1 *Los Angeles Times,* April 18, 1906, p. 1.

2 *Ibid.*

3 *Ibid.,* April 14, p. 1.

4 *Ibid.,* April 11, 1906, p. 1; April 22, 1906, p. 3. Other articles appeared daily in April-June 1906 concerning Dowie's struggle with rebellious members for control of Zion City.

spread to about a dozen congregations in the Los Angeles area, some of them among the Negroes.[5]

Another religious innovator in Los Angeles was Joseph Smale, the former pastor of the First Baptist Church, who had opened a mission called the "First New Testament Church" at Burbank Hall. Smale advertised his group in the *Times* as "a fellowship for evangelical preaching and teaching and pentecostal life and service." Holiness people who became dissatisfied with the attitude of the Methodist Church toward sanctification had by 1906 begun to attend services at Smale's and Bresee's churches. These two preachers represented the holiness "radical fringe" of the religious life of the city. For several years their churches had grown until by 1906 each could boast of over a thousand attendants at their Sunday services.[6]

Smale had begun his religious odyssey, which resulted in his entering the holiness ranks, after a visit to Wales in 1904 where he participated in the famous Welsh revival under Evan Roberts. Returning to Los Angeles, he had conducted a fifteen-week revival meeting in the First Baptist Church of that city. When the deacons of this church tired of the revival, Smale resigned to start his New Testament Church. The news of the Welsh revival was spread mainly by means of S. B. Shaw's book, which appeared in 1905, entitled *The Great Revival in Wales*. Also widely read was G. Campbell Morgan's pamphlet, "Revival in Wales." The story of how the twenty-six-year-old Roberts had led the sensational revival, which had seen over 30,000 conversions and 20,000 new church members, swept over the holiness movement with a compelling force.[7]

A young man attending Pastor Smale's services was Frank Bartleman, a holiness minister who also frequented services at Bresee's Peniel Mission. Bartleman had for some time been a regular contributor to J. M. Pike's *Way of Faith* in Columbia,

[5] Smith, *Called Unto Holiness*, pp. 112-121; *Los Angeles Times*, April 14, 1906, II, 71.

[6] *Ibid.*, May 12, 1906, II, 7.

[7] See S. B. Shaw, *The Great Revival in Wales* (Toronto, 1905), which includes accounts of the revival by Morgan, and other ministers, in addition to numerous excerpts from the *London Times* and several denominational periodicals.

South Carolina, and to Martin W. Knapp's *God's Revivalist* in Cincinnati, Ohio. Already well known in holiness circles, he fell under the spell of the Welsh revival and began to work toward a similar revival in Los Angeles. Deeply impressed by Smale's account of the Welsh phenomenon, Bartleman wrote to Roberts in Wales asking him to pray for a "new pentecost" in Los Angeles. In all, he wrote three letters, Roberts answering each of them. By March 1906, Bartleman became so agitated for such a revival that he wrote a tract entitled "The Last Call" in which he predicted one last "world-wide revival" before judgment came. Closing the tract, he prophesied, "Some tremendous event is about to transpire."[8]

A startling feature of nineteenth-century British revivalism which so impressed Bartleman was the appearance of "glossolalia," or speaking with other tongues. This phenomenon had first been seen in Edward Irving's services at the Presbyterian Church on Regent's Square, London, in 1831. Although he never spoke in tongues himself, Irving saw many of his parishioners, including a member of Parliament named Henry Drummond, display this evidence of "receiving the Holy Ghost." At the height of public interest in the proceedings at Regent's Square, Thomas Carlyle and his wife attended services to see what was happening. As more people began to manifest the tongues phenomenon in his services, Irving attempted to calm the worshippers and to maintain order, but his efforts largely failed. After being accused of "losing mental balance," Irving was tried by the London Presbytery in 1832 and deposed from his pulpit. Afterwards he formed his own denomination which he named "The Catholic Apostolic Church."[9]

Another instance of glossolalia in London occurred in

8 Frank Bartleman, *How "Pentecost" Came to Los Angeles* (Los Angeles, 1925), pp. 5-43. This book, which includes excerpts from Bartleman's diary and articles from his contributions to various holiness periodicals, constitutes the most reliable record of the Los Angeles revival. It was through Bartleman's reports that much of the holiness movement first heard of the Los Angeles meeting. Some writers, notably British, look on the pentecostal movement as being an outgrowth of the Welsh revival.

9 Jean Christie Root, *Edward Irving, Man, Preacher, Prophet* (Boston, 1912), pp. 70-112.

1875 when Dwight L. Moody preached at a Y.M.C.A. meeting at the Victoria Hall. After speaking to a small group of men in an afternoon service, Moody left the group "on fire" with the young men "speaking with tongues" and "prophesying." In a sense Moody could be classified as a pre-pentecostal preacher, although tongues could not be said to have characterized his revival services. This instance, however, indicated that glossolalia sometimes accompanied his preaching.[10]

Tongues were also prevalent in the Welsh revival of 1904, although those who participated had probably not heard of the experiences of Irving or Moody. The *Yorkshire Post* reported that at the height of the revival under Roberts, young men and women who knew nothing of Old Welsh would in their ecstasy speak in that tongue.[11] It is quite probable that Bartleman and Smale were aware of this aspect of the Welsh revival when they began efforts to duplicate it in Los Angeles.

America had also experienced an outbreak of the tongues phenomenon during the same period of time that the Welsh revival was in progress. The person responsible for introducing this practice as a formally stated doctrine was the Reverend Charles Fox Parham of Kansas. It was Parham who first singled out "glossolalia" as the only evidence of one's having received the baptism with the Holy Ghost, and who taught that it should be a part of "normal" Christian worship rather than a curious by-product of religious enthusiasm. It was his teaching that laid the doctrinal and experimental foundations of the modern pentecostal movement. It was Parham's ideas preached by his followers that produced the Azusa Street revival of 1906 and with it the worldwide pentecostal movement.[12]

[10] Walter J. Hollenweger, "Handbuch Der Pfingstbewegung" (Unpublished Doctoral dissertation, University of Zurich, 1965), II, 360. See also John C. Pollock, *Moody* (New York, 1963), pp. 90-91.

[11] *The Yorkshire Post,* December 27, 1904, quoted in Lincoln Moore Vivier, "Glossolalia" (Unpublished Doctoral dissertation, University of Witwatersrand, Johannesburg, 1960), p. 117; also *West Africa,* IX, 219 (February 25, 1905), 163.

[12] Most pentecostal writers acknowledge Parham's place as the formulator of the pentecostal doctrine, but none call him the "father"

Parham had begun his ministerial career in Linwood, Kansas, as a supply pastor in the Methodist Episcopal Church. It was from Methodism that he received the teaching of entire sanctification as a second work of grace, an experience which he had received and preached in the Methodist Church. During the last decade of the century, Parham had come in contact with the more radical elements of the holiness movement and after much study had adopted the doctrine of faith healing as a part of "the atonement." He had also been in services with Irwin's Fire-Baptized people and had rejected the extreme emotion, but not the idea of a "third experience" of a "baptism with the Holy Ghost and fire." After 1895, when "come-outism" became rampant in Methodism, Parham dissociated himself from the Methodist Episcopal Church and adopted an anti-denominational view to which he adhered for the rest of his life.[13]

In 1898 Parham felt that he should begin a "divine healing home" in Topeka where he could gather those who were sick and infirm and pray for their healing. Accordingly, the "Bethel Healing Home" was begun in that year and also a bi-monthly paper entitled *Apostolic Faith.* Two years later he instituted a school near Topeka which he named the "Bethel Bible School." This school began in October 1900 in a large, rambling house that the local people had christened "Stone's Folly" because of the builders' inability to finish it in the grandiose style he had desired. It was here that forty holiness students gathered for the only year that the school was to exist.[14]

Parham's theology by 1900 had come from many sources. Just prior to the opening of the Topeka school, he had traveled to Chicago to hear Alexander Dowie. From there he

of the movement. Because of later questions about his personal ethics his place in pentecostal history has been de-emphasized. Many refer to the pentecostal movement as "a movement without a man." See Brumback, *Suddenly from Heaven,* pp. 48-63; Bloch-Hoell, *The Pentecostal Movement,* pp. 18-21.

13 Sarah E. (Mrs. Charles F.) Parham, *The Life of Charles F. Parham, Founder of the Apostolic Faith Movement* (Joplin, Missouri, 1930), pp. 6-24. Parham had been active in the prohibition movement in Kansas and after leaving the Methodist Church blamed his "persecutions" on what he termed "the drinking class." (See p. 25.)

14 *Ibid.,* pp. 39-50.

had gone to Nyack, New York, to hear A. B. Simpson of the Christian and Missionary Alliance, and to Shiloh, Maine, to investigate Sandifer's "Holy Ghost and Us" church. Returning to Topeka, he felt that there was still something beyond the experience of sanctification that would be needed "to meet the challenge of the new century."[15]

By December 1900, Parham had led his students through a study of the major tenets of the holiness movement, including sanctification and divine healing. When they arrived at the second chapter of Acts they studied the events which transpired on the day of Pentecost in Jerusalem, including speaking with other tongues. At that juncture, Parham had to leave the school for three days for a speaking engagement. Before leaving, he asked the students to study their Bibles in an effort to find the scriptural evidence for the reception of the baptism with the Holy Spirit. Upon returning he asked the students to state the conclusion of their study, and to his "astonishment" they all answered unanimously that the evidence was "speaking with other tongues." This they deduced from the four recorded occasions in the Book of Acts when tongues accompanied the baptism with the Holy Spirit.[16]

Apparently convinced that his conclusion was a proper interpretation of the Scriptures, Parham and his students conducted a watchnight service on December 31, 1900, which was to continue into the new year. In this service, a student named Agnes N. Ozman requested Parham to lay hands on her head and pray for her to be baptized with the Holy Ghost with the evidence of speaking in tongues. It was after midnight and the first day of the twentieth century when Miss Ozman began "speaking in the Chinese language" while a "halo seemed to surround her head and face." Following this experience, Ozman was unable to speak in English for three days, and when she tried to communicate by writing, she invariably wrote in Chinese characters. This event is commonly regarded as the beginning of the modern

[15] *Ibid.*, p. 48; Brumback, *Suddenly from Heaven*, p. 21. Tomlinson was baptized into Sandifer's church in 1901, before joining the holiness church in Camp Creek, North Carolina. (See above.)

[16] Parham, *Charles F. Parham*, pp. 51-53. The scriptural references are Acts 2:4; 10:46; and 19:6; and I Corinthians 14:1-33.

pentecostal movement in America. After Ozman experienced "tongues" the rest of the students sought and received the same experience. Somewhat later Parham himself received the experience and began to preach it in all his services.[17]

In a short time the news of what was happening at "Stone's Folly" reached the press of Topeka and Kansas City. Soon reporters, government interpreters, and language experts converged on the school to investigate the new phenomenon. A few days later the *Topeka Capitol* reported in headlines, "A Queer Faith, Strange Acts . . . Believers Speak in Strange Languages." *The Kansas City World* said that "these people have a faith almost incomprehensible at this day." The wire services picked up the story when Parham and his group of students visited Galena, Kansas, late in January. Concerning this meeting, the *Cincinnati Enquirer* reported that it was doubtful if anything in recent years had awakened the interest, excited the comment, or "mystified the people" as the events in Galena.[18]

A remarkable claim made during these meetings was that the students, Americans all, spoke in twenty-one known languages, including French, German, Swedish, Bohemian, Chinese, Japanese, Hungarian, Bulgarian, Russian, Italian, Spanish, and Norwegian. In a conversation with a *Kansas City Times* correspondent, Parham claimed that his students had never studied these languages and that natives of the countries involved had heard them spoken and had verified their authenticity. Taking these events at face value, Parham immediately began to teach that missionaries would no longer be compelled to study foreign languages to preach in the mission fields. From henceforth, he taught, one need only receive the baptism with the Holy Ghost and he

---

17 Parham, *Charles F. Parham*, pp. 52-53; Agnes N. La Berge (Ozman), *What God Hath Wrought—Life and Work of Mrs. Agnes N. O. La Berge, Nee Miss Agnes N. Ozman* (Chicago, 1921), pp. 28-39. The next night Ozman went to Topeka and, after speaking in tongues, was told by a Bohemian that he understood her perfectly.

18 Parham, *Charles F. Parham*, pp. 70-96. These articles are reprinted in Parham's *Apostolic Faith*, November 1927, pp. 2-5. Charles F. Parham, *A Voice Crying in the Wilderness* (Joplin, Missouri, 1944), pp. 29-38.

could go to the farthest corners of the world and preach to the natives in languages unknown to the speaker.[19]

After the meetings in Missouri in 1901, Parham closed his school at Topeka and began a whirlwind tour of revivals which lasted for four years. During this period the pentecostal doctrine was spread through Kansas, as well as Kansas City, Lawrence, Galena, Melrose, Kwelville, and Baxter Springs, Missouri. By the fall of 1905, he moved his headquarters to Houston, Texas, at the request of friends there, and in a short while had opened another Bible school for the propagation of his views. Housed in a large, three-storied house, this institution was called simply "The Bible Training School," and had an enrollment of about twenty-five students during the few months of its operation. It was at this school that W. J. Seymour, the apostle of Azusa Street, received his theological training.[20]

Seymour, a Negro born in Louisiana, had moved to Texas early in life and had become a Baptist minister in the Houston area. Coming in contact with the holiness movement, he had accepted the idea of sanctification as a "second blessing" and had begun to preach in a local holiness church. A short, stocky man, minus one eye, Seymour in 1905 was a poverty-stricken Southern Negro with little or no knowledge of religious history. Hearing of Parham's new school, he determined to improve his religious training if possible.[21]

The racial mores of the South dictated that Seymour, a Negro, could not attend Parham's school. However, his great desire to attend classes and his apparent thirst for knowledge led Parham to allow him to attend the Bible classes during the day. For several months Seymour heard the new pentecostal theology from his teacher, Parham. He was taught that the holiness movement had been wrong in asserting that sanctification was also the baptism with the Holy Spirit. It was rather a "third experience" separate in

---

[19] Parham, *Voice Crying in the Wilderness*, pp. 31-32. Very few pentecostal leaders accepted this premise, although Parham held to it until his death.

[20] Parham, *Charles F. Parham*, pp. 131-146.

[21] R. L. Fidler, "Historical Review of the Pentecostal Outpouring in Los Angeles at the Azusa Street Mission in 1906," *The International Outlook*, January-March 1963, p. 3.

time and nature from the "second blessing." Sanctification cleansed and purified the believer, while the baptism with the Holy Spirit brought great power for service. The only biblical evidence that one had received the "baptism" was the act of speaking with other tongues as the 120 disciples had done on the day of Pentecost. Any other "baptism," whether it was called sanctification or the "baptism of fire," was not the true baptism of the New Testament. One should not be satisfied, therefore, until he had spoken with tongues as "proof" that he had received the Holy Ghost.[22]

All of this Seymour accepted unquestioningly and uncritically. Yet while he studied under Parham in Houston, he never experienced speaking with tongues, while many others became quite adept at the practice. The *Houston Chronicle* sent reporters to the school in August to report on the events taking place there. It was reported that Houstonians were witnessing "miracles" as students "speak in all tongues known to man." Some claimed that twenty Chinese dialects were spoken, while others were able to "command the classics of a Homer or talk the jargon of the lowest savage of the African jungle."[23]

While these events continued in Parham's school, great numbers of Houston people visited the services and many received the pentecostal experience as Parham taught it. Among those who came was a Negro lady by the name of Neely Terry, a native of Los Angeles. Becoming a friend of Seymour, she received the experience of speaking with tongues in services at the school. Later returning to her home in Los Angeles, Miss Neely found that her family and some close friends had been excommunicated from the Negro Second Baptist Church for professing holiness doctrine. Subsequently they had organized a small Negro holiness mission which they associated with Bresee's Church of the Nazarene. The mission had then elected a Mrs. Hutchinson to act as pastor of the group. When Miss Neely arrived in Los

22 Charles Parham, "A Critical Analysis of the Tongues Question," *The Apostolic Faith*, June 1925, pp. 2-6. Other sources of Parham's teachings are in Parham, *Charles F. Parham*, and Charles Parham, *A Voice Crying in the Wilderness, passim.*

23 The *Houston Chronicle*, August 13, 1905, quoted in Parham, *Charles F. Parham*, p. 121.

Angeles in March 1906, she recommended that the little congregation invite Seymour to come and assume the duties of pastor. After accepting the invitation, Seymour arrived early in April on a mission which was to exceed any of his fondest expectations.[24]

As he traveled to Los Angeles, Seymour stopped at well-known holiness missions on the way. One of his stops was in Denver, Colorado, at the headquarters of Alma White's "Pillar of Fire" movement, a small holiness group which specialized in the "holy dance" as the evidence of sanctification. Stopping at White's Bible school, Seymour introduced himself as a "man of God" and asked for lodging and meals. Seymour's reception was anything but warm in the Pillar of Fire center. Seymour impressed Mrs. White as a "very untidy person . . . wearing no collar." Writing many years later, she recalled, "I had met all kinds of religious fakirs and tramps, but I felt he excelled them all." Such was the reception of the Apostle of Pentecost at the Pillar of Fire headquarters.[25]

Seymour, the central personality of the Azusa Street revival, was a typical Southern Negro holiness preacher. At first a Baptist minister, he had adopted holiness views and in 1906 was pastor of a small holiness church near the city when Parham arrived to open his Bible school. He had built a reputation in his area as a very humble man, but one extremely interested in holiness religion. Described by many observers as "dirty and collarless," he hardly seemed to be the person to lead the historic revival that would usher in the pentecostal movement. Probably the only theological training he ever received was in Parham's Houston school.[26]

[24] Fidler, "Historical Review," p. 3; Brumback, *Suddenly from Heaven*, pp. 34-36; Kendrick, *The Promise Fulfilled*, p. 64.

[25] Alma White, *Demons and Tongues* (Zeraphath, New Jersey, 1949), pp. 68-69. Mrs. White became a bitter critic of the pentecostal movement in later years, and her description of Seymour was probably colored by her theological propensities as well as racial prejudice.

[26] Michael Harper, *As at the Beginning, The Twentieth Century Pentecostal Revival* (London, 1965), p. 28; Frank Ewart, *The Phenomenon of Pentecost, A History of the Latter Rain* (St. Louis, 1947), pp. 36-37. A description of Seymour was given in the *Los Angeles Times* on September 9, 1956, on the occasion of the fiftieth anniversary of the Azusa Street revival. See Brumback, *Suddenly from Heaven*, pp. 37-38.

When Seymour preached his first sermon at the Nazarene Church on Santa Fe Street, he took as his text Acts 2:4 and declared that speaking in tongues was the initial evidence of receiving the Holy Spirit, although he, as yet, had not received the experience. Mrs. Hutchinson, feeling that this teaching was contrary to accepted holiness views, padlocked the church door the next night to keep Seymour out, although most of her members enthusiastically accepted his message. The hapless evangelist, with no place to stay in the city, thereupon was invited to stay in the home of one Richard Asbury, who at that point refused to accept his teaching. Nevertheless, the evangelist began to preach in the living room of the home, which was located at 312 Bonnie Brae Street.[27]

For several days prayer services continued in the Asbury home until the night of April 9, 1906, when Seymour and seven others fell to the floor in a religious ecstasy, speaking with other tongues. When this occurred, a daughter of the Asbury's fled through the kitchen door terrified by what she saw. The news of the unusual events on Bonnie Brae Street spread quickly through the neighborhood as the newly baptized enthusiasts went to the front porch to conduct their strange services. Soon the curious began to gather as one of the worshippers, Jennie Moore, the future wife of Seymour, began to play the piano and sing in what was thought to be Hebrew. In the services that followed, demonstrations of tongues were so pronounced that huge crowds gathered in the streets to see what was happening. Soon whites began to mingle in the crowd as Seymour addressed them from a makeshift pulpit on the front porch. As crowds pressed into the house and onto the porch, the pressure became so great that at one point a floor caved in, but no one was hurt.[28]

With such interest in evidence, Seymour decided to find larger quarters where revival services could be conducted in a more conventional manner. After a search of the city, an old abandoned Methodist Church building at 312 Azusa Street was secured to continue the meetings. This building was

27 Fidler, "Historical Review," pp. 3-4.
28 *Ibid.*, p. 4; "When the Spirit Fell," *Pentecostal Evangel*, April 6, 1946, p. 7.

located in a business section of Los Angeles and had most recently been used as a combined tenement house and livery stable. This old two-story building was by 1906 a shambles. The windows and doors were broken out and debris littered the floor, but in many ways it was ideal for such a meeting. Far from residential areas, it could be used for the all-night meetings that characterized the early pentecostals. It also had the rough-hewn camp meeting-like atmosphere to which the holiness people had grown accustomed in their annual pilgrimages to the "forest temple." Another advantage of the "Azusa Stable" was that the poorest of the lower classes could come to it and not be intimidated by the stained-glass trappings of the traditional church. In these unpretentious surroundings, Seymour began to preach to the crowds that followed him from Bonnie Brae Street.[29]

No sooner had Seymour begun preaching in the Azusa location than a monumental revival began. Scores of people began to "fall under the power" and arise speaking in other tongues. News of the Azusa meeting reached the *Los Angeles Times* by mid-April and a reporter described what he called the "wild scenes" of this new "sect of fanatics." Describing Seymour as "an old colored exhorter" who acted as "major-domo of the company," the reporter felt that his "stony optic" eye served to hypnotize unbelievers. Old "colored mammys" were seen to "gurgle wordless talk" in a "frenzy of religious zeal."[30] This first news release of the Azusa Street revival ended with a prophecy that had been given in a vision to a man in the service. In his vision, he saw the people of Los Angeles "flocking in a mighty stream to perdition." He then prophesied "awful destruction to this city unless its citizens are brought to a belief in the tenets of the new faith."[31]

"Awful destruction" did come the very next day, but to San Francisco instead of Los Angeles. On April 19, the *Times* headlines screamed, "Heart is Torn from Great City," its

[29] Fidler, "Historical Review," pp. 4-5; Brumback, *Suddenly from Heaven*, pp. 36-37; Stanley H. Frodsham, *With Signs Following, The Story of the Pentecostal Revival in the Twentieth Century* (Springfield, Missouri, 1946), pp. 32-33.

[30] *Los Angeles Times*, April 18, 1906, p. 1.

[31] *Ibid.*

pages telling of the devastation of the sister city to Los Angeles. The worshippers at Azusa Street felt the tremors that shook the entire coast of California and in their religious zeal felt that there was a divine connection between the two. The natural earthquake in San Francisco was followed by a "spiritual earthquake" on Azusa Street which rose to a near hysteria level after the April 18th earthquake.[32]

As the Azusa revival continued, hundreds and later thousands of both the curious and the serious began to flock to the mission. Every day trains unloaded numbers of visitors who came from all over the continent. News accounts of the meeting spread over the nation in both the secular and the religious press. The most interested observers were the members of the holiness movements around the country. Scores of reports in such papers as *The Way of Faith* in South Carolina, carried minute accounts of the events in Los Angeles. Also publicizing the revival was a four-page free paper entitled *The Apostolic Faith*, which was published from Azusa Street by Seymour and his assistants.[33]

A visitor to Azusa Street during the three years that the revival continued would have met scenes that beggared description. Men and women would shout, weep, dance, fall into trances, speak and sing in tongues, and interpret the messages into English. In true Quaker fashion, anyone who felt "moved by the Spirit" would preach or sing. There was no robed choir, no hymnals, no order of services, but there was an abundance of religious enthusiasm. In the middle of it all was "Elder" Seymour, who rarely preached and much of the time kept his head covered in an empty shoe box behind the pulpit. At times he would be seen walking through the crowds with five- and ten-dollar bills sticking out of his hip

[32] *Los Angeles Times*, April 19, 1906, pp. 1-10. Early pentecostals made much of the coincidence of the earthquake and the Azusa meeting, one writer asserting that "in all God's great moves, nature sympathizes with Him." See Frank Ewart, *The Phenomenon of Pentecost*, p. 18; Bartleman, *How Pentecost Came to Los Angeles*, pp. 47-53.

[33] *The Apostolic Faith* (Azusa Street, September 1906), p. 1; Bartleman, *How Pentecost Came to Los Angeles*, pp. 61-63; Ewart, *The Phenomenon of Pentecost*, p. 43; also see issues of *The Way of Faith* for 1906-1908 where continuous reports of the meetings were published by eyewitnesses.

pockets which people had crammed there unnoticed by him. At other times he would "preach" by hurling defiance at anyone who did not accept his views or by encouraging seekers at the woodplank altars to "let the tongues come forth." To others he would exclaim: "Be emphatic! Ask for salvation, sanctification, the baptism with the Holy Ghost, or divine healing."[34]

Seymour and the workers in the mission lived on the upper floor where there was also a long room they called "the Pentecostal upper room," a place where seekers were sent to receive their own "pentecostal experience." Visitors to the meeting claimed they could feel a "supernatural atmosphere" within several blocks of the mission. Part of this atmosphere was created by a recurrence of the physical manifestations which had been common at Cane-Ridge in 1800. Sounds of shouting and rejoicing echoed over the lumber yards, stables, and tombstone shops that surrounded the mission. As the meetings continued week after week, more and more people began to attend, until by the summer of 1906 people of every race and nationality in the Los Angeles area were mingling in the crowds that pressed into the mission from the street. There was no racial prejudice in the services. Negroes, whites, Chinese and even Jews attended side by side to hear Seymour preach. Eventually what began as a local revival in a Negro church became of interest to people all over the nation, regardless of race. In a short while the majority of the attendants were white, but always there was complete integration of the races in the services, one man exclaiming, "The color line was washed away in the blood."[35]

Throughout 1906 the revival increased in fervor and interest. In August, Bartleman wrote to *The Way of Faith* that "Pentecost has come to Los Angeles, the American Jerusalem."[36] Reports from the *Apostolic Faith* published at the

[34] Ewart, *The Phenomenon of Pentecost*, pp. 40-49; *Los Angeles Times*, April 18, 1906, p. 1; Bartleman, *How Pentecost Came to Los Angeles*, p. 58.

[35] Bartleman, *How Pentecost Came to Los Angeles*, p. 54. Also see Frodsham, *With Signs Following*, pp. 33-34; and Ewart, *The Phenomenon of Pentecost*, p. 42.

[36] *The Way of Faith*, August 1, 1906, quoted in Bartleman, *How Pentecost Came to Los Angeles*, p. 63.

mission indicated that hundreds were speaking with tongues in addition to the numbers saved, sanctified, and healed. "The waves of Pentecostal salvation are still rolling in Azusa Street Mission," the paper reported. It was also claimed that a woman named Anna Hall had gone to a Russian church in Los Angeles and preached to its communicants in their own language, although it was unknown to her. It was reported that the hearers were "so glad to hear the truth that they wept and even kissed her hands." By December 1906 the paper reported that "the Lord God is in Los Angeles in different missions and churches in mighty power, in spite of opposition." Indeed, by the end of the year many other missions had been opened in the Los Angeles area and others were beginning to operate in cities all over the United States as visitors to Azusa Street carried the "fire" to their own homes.[37]

As the meetings continued at Azusa Street many attended who were critical of the proceedings. Some felt that the emotionalism and enthusiasm that characterized the services were too extreme, even for holiness people, many of whom were not known for especially decorous services. Many of the more radical holiness churches and missions closed their services and came *en masse* to Azusa Street when the services there became well known. Soon such physical demonstrations as the "jerks" and "treeing the devil" were in evidence in the mission. Before long spiritualists and mediums from the numerous occult societies of Los Angeles began to attend and to contribute their seances and trances to the services. Disturbed by these developments, Seymour wrote Parham for advice on how to handle "the spirits," and begged him to come to Los Angeles and take over supervision of the revival. Others reported to Parham that "all the stunts common in old camp meetings among colored folks" were being performed in the services. Even more disturbing to him was the report that "white people [were] imitating [the] unintelligent, crude negroisms of the Southland, and laying it on the Holy Ghost." Parham, therefore, advised Seymour to continue the services while he went to Zion City to preach to the

37 *The Apostolic Faith*, September 1906, pp. 1-4; October 1906, pp. 1-4; December 1906, pp. 1-4; December 1907, pp. 1-4.

followers of "Elijah" Dowie who were in a state of confusion due to the efforts of some members to unseat the now obviously deranged "prophet."[38]

Although Seymour attempted to de-emphasize tongues and the uncontrolled fervor of the Azusa Street crowds, his efforts were futile. Nettie Harwood, a disciple of Alma White, visited the mission late in 1906 and reported that people were singing songs "in a far away tune that sounded very unnatural and repulsive." This critic also claimed that there was much kissing between sexes and even races. She was incensed at seeing a colored woman with her arms around a white man's neck "praying for him." To many of the holiness people who rejected Seymour's baptism he was an "instrument of Satan." To Mrs. White and her Pillar of Fire followers the "winds of perdition" were blowing in Los Angeles.[39]

If some came to criticize, many more came out of curiosity and went away convinced that a genuinely historical revival was occurring. One foreign-born reporter from a Los Angeles newspaper came on assignment to report on the "circus-like" meeting in the Azusa Street "stable." While there, an ignorant woman rose to her feet, looked straight at him and spoke in his native tongue, telling him secrets that only he could have known. He left convinced of the authenticity of the "tongues" experience. The first white man to receive the experience at Azusa was one A. G. Garr, pastor of a holiness mission in Los Angeles. After his "baptism," Garr and his wife went to India where they expected to preach to the natives in their own languages. However, when this was attempted, it ended in failure. After their fiasco in India the Garrs traveled to Hong Kong where they set up a mission and learned Chinese in the more conventional manner. This was the outstanding attempt at carrying out Parham's teaching concerning the missionary use of tongues, and it ended in failure.[40]

[38] Parham, *Charles F. Parham*, pp. 160-163.

[39] White, *Demons and Tongues*, pp. 71-73; Ewart, *The Phenomenon of Pentecost*, p. 45.

[40] Ewart, *The Phenomenon of Pentecost*, pp. 47, 106; *The Apostolic Faith* (Azusa Street), October 1906, p. 2; Homer A. Tomlinson, in *Twentieth Anniversary of the Garr Auditorium* (Charlotte, North Carolina, 1950), p. 3. Garr was known as the "first

It was in October 1906 that Parham, whom Seymour claimed as his "father in the Gospel of the Kingdom," arrived in Los Angeles for his much-heralded "general union revival." When he came to Azusa Street, he was shocked by the "holy roller" aspects of the services and made efforts to correct the "extremes and fanaticism," which he felt had gone "beyond the bounds of common sense and reason." After preaching two or three times, the "Apostle of the Apostolic Faith" was told by some of Seymour's followers that he "was not wanted in that place." He then was invited to leave because of his denunciations of the "hypnotists" and "spiritualists" who seemed to have taken over the services. He left "disgusted" because many "came through chattering, jabbering and sputtering, speaking in no language at all." After being barred from the Azusa Mission, which now ironically carried the name "Apostolic Faith Gospel Mission," after Parham's own organization, the rejected prophet opened services in a local W.C.T.U. building on the corner of Broadway and Temple Streets. This meeting, however, was short-lived and failed to alter the course of the Azusa Street revival, which continued unabated, night and day, for three more years. After the barring of Parham from Azusa Street, Seymour and his teacher suffered a total break which was never healed, Parham later denouncing the Azusa leader as being "possessed with a spirit of leadership." For the rest of his life, Parham continued his denunciation of the Azusa Street meeting as a case of "spiritual power prostituted" to the "awful fits and spasms" of the "holy rollers and hypnotists."[41]

During the three years that the Azusa Street revival continued, reports were written by visitors from all parts of the nation who attended the services. These reports were read avidly by most of the holiness people of the United States. Word also eventually spread to Europe that an unusual outpouring of Pentecost had come to California. Hundreds of preachers from around the continent traveled to Los Angeles

foreign missionary of the pentecostal movement." In 1930, Garr settled in Charlotte, North Carolina, founding the famous "Garr Auditorium," one of the outstanding urban pentecostal churches in the South.

41 Parham, *Charles F. Parham*, pp. 164-202; Parham, "Sermon by Charles F. Parham," *The Apostolic Faith* (Baxter Springs), April 1925, pp. 9-14. One probable reason why Seymour rejected his authority was

to see for themselves what was taking place. Most of them were convinced of the genuineness of the teachings and practices that they saw, receiving their own "pentecost" with the evidence of speaking with other tongues before returning to their churches. Many who came were destined to found entire denominations of pentecostal believers. In later years anyone who was an "Azusa recipient" was looked on with awe and covered with an aura of respect and "glory" by his co-religionists. A list of the "pilgrims to Los Angeles" eventually became a veritable honor roll of early pentecostal leadership.[42]

Among those who later became prominent in the pentecostal movement was Florence Crawford, who brought the message to the Northwest in her "Apostolic Faith" movement with headquarters in Portland, Oregon. Mrs. Crawford was an early worker with Seymour at Azusa Street, adopting the name "The Apostolic Faith" from Parham's and Seymour's groups. Her movement, which developed into a small denomination, never was officially connected with Parham's group of the same name with headquarters in Baxter Springs, Kansas. Another, the Reverend William H. Durham of Chicago, traveled to Los Angeles and then returned to his "North Avenue Mission" to found the pentecostal movement in the Midwest. From Durham's church, leaders of the later Pentecostal Assemblies of Canada received the pentecostal message. New York City saw its first pentecostal church organized in December 1906 when a Negro preacher, "Elder" Sturdevant, arrived from Los Angeles and opened a mission in a room at 351 West Fortieth Street. The New York City press reacted to the West Side group in similar fashion to that of Los Angeles when Azusa Street started a few months earlier. Calling the votaries in the hall "a group of Negroes of the poor and uneducated class," the papers declared that

the reports that Parham was a practicing homosexual, a charge often made and repeatedly denied by Parham. See Bloch-Hoell, *The Pentecostal Movement,* p. 19; H. J. Stolee, *Speaking in Tongues* (Minneapolis, 1963), p. 63; *Zion's Herald,* July 26, 1907, p. 1; *The Burning Bush,* September 19, 1907, pp. 5-7, which quotes court proceedings reported in the *San Antonio Express,* 1907.

[42] Brumback, *Suddenly from Heaven,* pp. 64-87; Bartleman, *How Pentecost Came to Los Angeles,* pp. 54-60.

"the heights of frenzy they reach seem in many instances to go beyond the limits of normal physical endurance."[43]

Others who spread the message from Azusa Street were: Mrs. Rachel Sizelove in Missouri, Samuel Saell in Arizona, Glenn A. Cook in Indiana, D. W. Kerr in Ohio, Marie Burgess in New York, R. E. McAlister in Ottawa, Canada, C. H. Mason in Tennessee, and G. B. Cashwell in North Carolina. [44] One of the most important persons influenced by the Azusa Street revival was the Norwegian Methodist pastor T. B. Barratt, who was on a tour of the United States in 1906-1907. While in New York, he heard of the Los Angeles meeting and began a correspondence with Seymour about the new pentecostal doctrine. In November 1906, he received the pentecostal experience in New York and shortly thereafter returned to Oslo. Beginning an Azusa-type meeting in Oslo in December 1906, Barratt soon had Norwegian Methodists and Baptists speaking in other tongues, as well as performing the "holy laugh" and the "holy dance." Spectacular news coverage caused great public interest in the Norwegian capital, which insured great crowds of spectators at the meetings which followed. From 1906 till his death in 1940, Barratt served as a veritable prophet of Pentecost in Northern Europe. He is credited with beginning the pentecostal movements in Sweden, Norway, Denmark, Germany, France, and England.[45]

The Azusa Street revival is commonly regarded as the beginning of the modern pentecostal movement. Although many persons had spoken in tongues in the United States in the years preceding 1906, this meeting brought this belief to the attention of the world and served as the catalyst for the formation of scores of pentecostal denominations. Directly or indirectly, practically all of the pentecostal groups in existence can trace their lineage to the Azusa Mission. Even

43 The *New York American*, December 3, 1906, quoted in Bloch-Hoell, *The Pentecostal Movement*, pp. 39-51; R. R. Crawford, *et al., A Historical Account of the Apostolic Faith* (Portland, 1965), pp. 44-64.

44 Mason and Cashwell will be treated in detail in the next chapter because of their importance to the movement in the South.

45 T. B. Barratt, *When the Fire Fell* (Oslo, 1927), pp. 99-126; Bloch-Hoell, *The Pentecostal Movement*, pp. 65-86, 178-179.

in India an outbreak of tongues was reported in 1908 that had all the characteristics of the Azusa meeting. Under the direction of one Pandita Ramabai, the inmates of a girls' orphanage spoke and prayed in English, Greek, Hebrew, and Sanskrit in the years 1905-1908. Indeed, the years following the 1894 break with Methodism reached a climax in Los Angeles in 1906, and from there the holiness-pentecostal movement spread to the farthest reaches of the world.[46]

Historians have experienced difficulty in explaining the conditions which produced the pentecostal movement and in placing it in its proper ecclesiastical perspective. Some have suggested that pentecostalism arises "during or immediately after great national or cosmic catastrophes," or during periods of "widespread religious apathy." In the case of the California pentecostal revival centering on Azusa Street, none of these factors seemed to be present. No great wars or catastrophes brought it on, although the San Francisco Earthquake occurred after the meeting began. The great holiness controversy which had convulsed the religious world since 1867 indicated that these were not years of religious apathy.[47]

The pentecostal movement arose as a split in the holiness movement and can be viewed as the logical outcome of the holiness crusade which had vexed American Protestantism for forty years, and in particular the Methodist Church. The repeated calls of the holiness leadership after 1894 for a "new pentecost" inevitably produced the frame of mind and the intellectual foundations for just such a "pentecost" to occur. In historical perspective the pentecostal movement was the child of the holiness movement, which in turn was a child of Methodism. Practically all the early pentecostal leaders were firm advocates of sanctification as a "second work of grace" and simply added the "pentecostal baptism"

[46] *The Chicago Daily News,* January 14, 1908, carried reports of the glossolalic outburst in India; quoted in Vivier, "Glossolalia," p. 118. See also Turner, *Pentecost and Tongues,* pp. 134-136; Donald Gee, *All with One Accord* (Springfield, Missouri, 1961), p. 29.

[47] F. E. Mayer, *The Religious Bodies of America,* p. 315. It also may be added that World War I, the depression, and World War II failed to produce any new movements equaling those of the 1894-1906 period.

with the evidence of speaking in tongues as a "third blessing" superimposed on the other two. Both Parham and Seymour maintained fully the Wesleyan view of sanctification throughout their lives.[48]

The Azusa Street Mission continued to function as an independent Negro city church for several years after the original revival had ended in 1909, the white people leaving it in exclusive charge of the Blacks. Seymour later left the mission and traveled extensively throughout the United States as an evangelist. The building eventually was torn down in 1928, some years after Seymour's death. A prominent pentecostal denomination refused an offer to buy it because, as was explained, "we are not interested in relics." Parham returned to his home in Baxter Springs, Kansas, where his annual Apostolic Faith Convocations attracted thousands of followers until his death in 1929. Yet the movement they unleashed in Topeka and Los Angeles was destined to begin a new and important chapter in the history of Christianity.[49]

[48] Parham, "A Critical Analysis of the Tongues Question," *The Apostolic Faith*, June 1925, pp. 2-6.

[49] Parham, *Charles F. Parham*, pp. 389-420; Bloch-Hoell, *The Pentecostal Movement*, p. 54.

Chapter Six

PENTECOST COMES SOUTH

I went to the Holiness Church to services here today and heard Brother G. B. Cashwell preach. He has been to California and got Pentecost and speaks in an unknown tongue. Some seeking the experience here. (Dunn, N. C., December 30, 1906)　　—Thurman Carey

The news of the Azusa Street revival in Los Angeles had spread over the entire nation and to many parts of the world before the end of 1906. Members of the holiness churches were the ones most affected by the news from California. Seymour's paper, *The Apostolic Faith*, was sent without cost to thousands of ministers and laymen over the nation. Arresting and sensational articles about people speaking with tongues "just like the Apostles did on the day of pentecost" appeared in every issue. Copies of the roughly printed and irregularly issued paper were avidly read and passed from hand to hand. Holiness preachers from coast to coast read with wonder and great interest of the "pentecostal outpouring" at Azusa Street, where people not only spoke with tongues, but sang hymns and prophesied in foreign languages. Reports of supernatural interpretations of tongues, divine healing of diseases, visions of tongues of fire, and spectacular scenes of religious ecstasy exercised a peculiar attraction to most of those who read them.[1]

---

[1] Bloch-Hoell, *The Pentecostal Movement*, pp. 42, 43, 145-147. For the theologically minded it should be explained that the Greek term for speaking in unknown tongues is *glossolalia*. Also, pentecostal apologists

The holiness people of the South followed the progress of the meeting through the pages of *The Way of Faith*, the outstanding holiness periodical of the area. For many months during 1906 and 1907, Bartleman sent regular reports to editor J. M. Pike, who published them from his offices in Columbia, South Carolina. In the same building was located the "Oliver Gospel Mission," an urban holiness rescue mission for the poor and destitute. Pike had also allowed the Holmes Bible Institute to conduct classes in the building from 1903 to 1905. The prestige of Pike and his paper among the holiness community added weight to Bartleman's reports concerning Azusa Street. In August 1906 he wrote to *The Way of Faith* that "strong men lie for hours under the mighty power of God, cut down like grass. The revival will be a world-wide one, without doubt." It was this kind of report that holiness leaders around the nation read concerning the Azusa Street revival. To say the least, it was interesting reading to anyone with a strong holiness background.[2]

The scenes at Azusa Street as described by Seymour and Bartleman were nothing new to many holiness people. The "Fire-Baptized Way" was already well known, especially in the South and also in the Middle West. Many of the holiness people had felt that some physical evidence would often accompany one's sanctification to prove that he had "prayed through." Some thought that the best proof that one was thus baptized with the Holy Ghost was that he would perform the "holy dance." Others taught that "hallelujah earthquakes" would be felt by the newly baptized, while some thought that shouting in a drunken ecstasy like the disciples on the day of Pentecost was the best evidence. Tongues had

made a sharp distinction between tongues as the "evidence" that one had received the baptism with the Holy Spirit, and the "Gift of Tongues" which may be exercised throughout life for devotional purposes. No distinction is usually made between ecstatic utterances, known languages, or unknown tongues. For further theological discussion see: John Nichol, *Pentecostalism* (New York, 1966), pp. 12-13; Brumback, *What Meaneth This?* pp. 261-272; Wade H. Horton, ed., *The Glossolalia Phenomenon* (Cleveland, Tennessee, 1966), pp. 21-65 and *passim;* Joseph H. King, *From Passover to Pentecost* (Memphis, 1914), pp. 113-143.

2 *The Way of Faith*, August 1906. L. R. Graham, personal interview with the author, Memphis, Tennessee, 1966.

been experienced by many holiness people over the years, but they were considered to be only one of many "evidences" or "proofs" of sanctification. Before 1906 holiness writers felt that tongues should be part of "a normal gospel meeting," although most felt that the words "other tongues" referred to "the new language of new converts." W. B. Godbey, the outstanding Greek scholar in the National Holiness Movement, ignored tongues in his *Commentary on Acts*, calling instead for a return of "the old-time, knockdown power" to the church.[3]

Although most holiness people probably heard of speaking with tongues for the first time in connection with Azusa Street, the practice was well known to scholars of biblical and church history. According to the records, many periods of Christian history from St. Paul to Charles Parham had been punctuated by occasional outbreaks of glossolalia. Examples of the phenomenon had been known among the Montanists in second-century Italy, the Albigenses in twelfth-century France, and the Waldensians in thirteenth-century Italy. The Mormons and the Shakers had also experienced the phenomenon in eighteenth- and nineteenth-century America. The Irvingites had made tongue-speaking a cardinal doctrine of their "Catholic Apostolic Church" in England during the 1830's, while the great Welsh revival of 1904-05 had been characterized by striking examples of the practice. The 1906 outbreak of tongues at Azusa Street was clearly a recurrence of a well-known Christian phenomenon.[4]

The American South was the scene of several instances of

---

[3] W. B. Godbey, *Commentary on the New Testament* (Cincinnati, 1896), IV, 231-234; Thomas Waugh, *The Power of Pentecost* (Chicago, N. D.), p. 101; A. B. Simpson, *Emblems of the Holy Spirit* (Nyack, New York, 1901), pp. 1-128. None of these mention tongues as an evidence of the Holy Spirit.

[4] For a scholarly examination of tongues, both as a historical fact and a psychological phenomenon, see George Barton Cutten, *Speaking with Tongues* (New Haven, 1927), pp. 11-184. Other later works on the subject are: Ira J. Martin, *Glossolalia in the Apostolic Church* (Berea, Kentucky, 1960); Vivier, "Glossolalia"; John L. Sherrill, *They Speak with Other Tongues* (New York, 1964); and Nichol, *Pentecostalism*. Also see Gaddis, "Christian Perfectionism in America," pp. 37-222; and Philip Schaff, *History of the Christian Church* (New York: Charles Scribner's Sons, 1910), I, 423-462.

tongue-speaking during the nineteenth century. The Cane-Ridge camp meetings of 1800 saw examples of the practice in addition to many other frontier religious demonstrations. A great increase of glossolalia came in the 1890's, however, when the climax of the National Holiness Movement resulted in the formation of new denominations. One of the first faith-healing evangelists in America, Mrs. M. B. Woodworth Etter, reported occurrences of tongues in a mass healing revival in St. Louis in 1890. There a young girl was reported to have spoken and written "very intelligently" in a foreign language unknown to her. Beginning her ministry as a member of the United Brethren Church in the eighties, Mrs. Etter claimed that some people had "spoken in tongues all along through my ministry." In addition to tongues, Etter claimed to have the "gifts of healing, casting out devils, miracles, and visions."[5]

In the same year that Mrs. Etter was preaching in St. Louis, Daniel Awrey, a man who later became prominent in pentecostal circles, spoke in tongues in a prayer meeting in Delaware, Ohio. Later moving to the town of Benah, Tennessee, Awrey came in contact with the Fire-Baptized holiness movement. In 1899 in Benah, Awrey's wife along with a dozen others spoke in tongues when they received the "baptism of fire." Publicizing his experiences in the holiness press, Awrey became well known to holiness people and was present in 1898 at the organizational council of the Fire-Baptized Holiness Church in Anderson, South Carolina.[6]

Perhaps the greatest instance of speaking with other tongues before 1906 occurred in the Camp Creek revival in North Carolina in 1896. In this meeting many, including "men, women and children . . . spoke in tongues under the

5 Mrs. M. B. Woodworth Etter, *Marvels and Miracles; Signs and Wonders* (Indianapolis, 1922), pp. 68-70. In two other books entitled *Signs and Wonders God Wrought in the Ministry for Forty Years* and *The Acts of the Holy Ghost*, Etter recorded the most colorful and fantastic ministry in all pentecostal literature. Much of it, however, is open to serious question as authentic history.

6 Bailey, *Pioneer Marvels*, pp. 19-20; Kendrick, *The Promise Fulfilled*, p. 35; *The Pentecostal Holiness Advocate*, March 31, 1921, p. 11. Awrey later joined the Assemblies of God and died in Liberia as a pentecostal missionary.

mighty spirit of God." Many years later it was estimated by those who had been present that over one hundred persons were thus exercised in the meeting. This event preconditioned the members of the Church of God in nearby Cleveland, Tennessee, to accept the doctrine of tongues as the initial evidence of the reception of the Holy Spirit when the news of Azusa Street swept the South.[7]

The experiences of Parham and his Bible school students in Topeka and Houston from 1901 to 1905 were also important harbingers of the historic events that were to occur in Los Angeles in 1906. One historian has estimated that over one thousand persons in the United States had spoken with tongues before the Azusa Street revival, but the probability is that thousands more had done the same in the many camp meetings and revivals that reached high levels of fervor and enthusiasm after the Civil War.[8]

The importance of the Azusa Street revival was that it acted as the catalytic agent that congealed tongue-speaking into a fully defined doctrine. For years the phenomenon had been recognized but not singled out as a necessary evidence of the baptism with the Holy Ghost. It was Parham's insistence that tongues were necessary as the only "biblical evidence" of the Holy Ghost baptism that caused division within the holiness ranks. Now the adherents of the pentecostal doctrine had settled on one incontrovertible evidence which was uniform for all and supported by biblical references. In his first sermon on Pentecost in 1901, Parham offered tongues as a solution to the problem of evidences:

> Now all Christians credit the fact that we are to be recipients of the Holy Spirit, but each have their own private interpretations as to his visible manifestations; some claim shouting, leaping, jumping, and falling in trances, while others put stress upon inspiration, unction and divine revelation.... How much more reasonable it would be for modern Holy Ghost teachers to first

[7] Juillerat, *Book of Minutes*, p. 11; Homer Tomlinson, *Diary of A. J. Tomlinson*, I, 37; A. J. Tomlinson, *The Last Great Conflict* (Cleveland, Tennessee, 1913), pp. 200-215. Many in the Church of God bodies point to this event as the beginning of the pentecostal movement in the United States.

[8] Frodsham, *With Signs Following*, pp. 25-29; Parham, *Voice Crying in the Wilderness*, pp. 29-38.

receive a *Bible Evidence*, such as the Disciples, instead of trying to get the world to take their word for it.[9]

It was precisely this settlement, that tongues were the only initial evidence of the reception of the Holy Spirit, that gave pentecostalism its greatest impetus. It at once solved the problem of proving to one's self and to the world that one had received the experience. Pentecostalism thus succeeded in "doing what the Holiness Movement could not do" in that it offered the believer a "repeatable and unmistakable motor expression which, in effect, guaranteed his possession of the Spirit."[10] In addition to solving the problem of the evidence of the baptism, the attaching of tongues to the Holy Ghost baptism had a strong scriptural base in the New Testament, a fact which easily convinced many holiness people, practically all of whom interpreted the Bible literally.

Most of those who read of the meeting at Azusa Street in holiness papers reacted favorably to the "California Pentecost." In Falcon, North Carolina, at the campground headquarters of Crumpler's Holiness Church, preachers read each issue of *The Way of Faith* with great interest. One of the young preachers, George Floyd Taylor, reported that upon reading his first account of the revival, "my heart said amen."[11] Another of Crumpler's preachers, G. B. Cashwell, of Dunn, North Carolina, not only said "amen" at the news from Los Angeles, but decided to travel there to see for himself what was happening and, if possible, to receive his own pentecostal experience.

Cashwell, who was destined to become the "Apostle of Pentecost" to the South, was a large man of some 250 pounds. Blond-haired and fair-faced, he was in 1906 a middle-aged man who had forsaken the Methodist ministry to join the ranks of the Pentecostal Holiness Church in 1903. When the annual conference of the church met in Lumberton, North Carolina, in November 1906, Cashwell was con-

9 Parham, *Voice Crying in the Wilderness*, p. 27.

10 James N. Lapsley and John H. Simpson, "Speaking in Tongues," *The Princeton Seminary Bulletin*, LVIII (February 1965), 6-7.

11 G. F. Taylor, *The Spirit and the Bride* (Dunn, North Carolina, 1907), p. 39.

spicuously absent. The Chairman of the Conference, Crumpler, read the following letter to the puzzled delegates:

> If I have offended anyone of you, forgive me. I realize that my life has fallen short of the standard of holiness we preach; but I have repented in my home in Dunn, North Carolina, and I have been restored. I am unable to be with you this time, for I am now leaving for Los Angeles, California, where I shall seek for the Baptism of the Holy Ghost.[12]

Those present were greatly interested in Cashwell's journey. Many had felt quite sympathetic toward the Azusa Street meeting and some had already begun to pray for a similar outbreak to occur in the East, but Cashwell was the only one venturesome enough to cross the continent in quest of the pentecostal experience.

Upon his arrival in Los Angeles, Cashwell went directly to the Azusa Street Mission. What he saw there was somewhat unsettling to this Southern gentleman. With Seymour preaching and in general charge of the services and the majority of worshippers Negroes, he at first thought of leaving without participating in the service. After traveling such a great distance, however, he felt that he must attend, even if he did not participate. During his first service in the mission, a young Negro man walked over to him and placed his hands on his head, praying for him to be "baptized with the Holy Ghost." This caused "chills to go down my spine," Cashwell later reported. At first deeply prejudiced against Negroes, he saw his prejudice fading as interest in speaking with other tongues began to overwhelm him. After a few services he "lost his pride" and asked Seymour and several Negro boys to lay hands on his head in order for him to be "filled." In a short time he received the pentecostal experience and began to speak with other tongues.[13]

Cashwell did not tarry long in the "American Jerusalem" after his historic experience at Azusa Street. Returning to his

[12] *The Pentecostal Holiness Advocate*, May 29, 1930, p. 1; Bailey, *Pioneer Marvels of Faith*, p. 48.

[13] G. B. Cashwell, "Came 3,000 Miles for His Pentecost," *The Apostolic Faith*, December 1906, p. 3; L. R. Graham, one of Cashwell's early friends, personal interview with author, 1966; Frodsham, *With Signs Following*, pp. 41-42.

home in Dunn, North Carolina, he rented an old, three-storied building which had previously been used as a tobacco warehouse for a pentecostal meeting, which would be for the southeastern area of the United States what the Azusa Street meeting had been to the western area. On December 31, 1906, the meeting began which was to result in the conversion of most of the holiness movement in the Southeast to the pentecostal view.[14]

Before beginning the Dunn meeting, Cashwell had invited all the ministers of the Fire-Baptized Holiness Church, the Pentecostal Holiness Church, and the Free-Will Baptist Church to attend. The results far exceeded anything that had ever been seen in the Southern holiness movement. Thousands of people jammed the old warehouse to see and hear firsthand about the "tongues movement." Practically the entire ministerium of the Pentecostal Holiness and the Fire-Baptized Holiness Churches attended, most of them going to the altar and receiving the pentecostal experience that Cashwell preached. G. F. Taylor, one of the youngest ministers in Crumpler's church, was so intensely expecting to be "baptized" that in only five minutes after seeing the preacher who had been to Azusa Street "the Holy Ghost was talking" with the young minister's tongue.[15]

As the Dunn meeting continued, many Baptists, Methodists, and Presbyterians joined the holiness people at the services. For over a month the old warehouse resounded to Cashwell's preaching and the shouts of the newly baptized. Scores of holiness preachers "went down to the altar" and came up "speaking in tongues, singing in tongues, laughing the holy laugh, shouting and leaping and dancing and praising God," in scenes reminiscent of the Cane-Ridge camp meetings of a century before. One preacher of the Free-Will Baptist Church, H. H. Goff, attended the meeting and returned without receiving his "baptism." His children met him at the door saying, "Papa, Papa, have you got the tongues?" Replying in the negative, he added, "but I want it worse than

14 Campbell, *The Pentecostal Holiness Church*, pp. 240-241; Florence Goff, *Tests and Triumphs* (Falcon, North Carolina, 1923), p. 51.

15 Taylor, *The Spirit and the Bride*, p. 39.

anything in all the world." A few nights later he received "the tongues" in the warehouse among "a great multitude."[16]

Although many of the preachers of the Holiness Church and the Fire-Baptized Holiness Church attended the Dunn meeting, their leaders, Crumpler and King, were conspicuous by their absence. Crumpler had discussed the new doctrine of tongues with Taylor sometime before Cashwell's return to Dunn and had stated flatly that if Cashwell preached the pentecostal doctrine "he was going to oppose" him. For some reason, Crumpler had no confidence in Cashwell and for that reason decided to leave the state for the duration of the Dunn revival. Holding a revival of his own in Florida during January 1907, Crumpler was unaware that most of his ministers were in Dunn in complete support of Cashwell's doctrine. This trip was to be fatal to Crumpler's future control of the church.[17]

King spent the first days of January 1907 at his home in Toccoa, Georgia, not cognizant of the historic meeting in Dunn, although he already knew of the Azusa Street meeting. While preaching in a camp meeting at Thornbury, Ontario, in September of 1906, he had met an old friend, A. H. Argue from Winnipeg, Manitoba, who told him about the Azusa Street revival. As the conversation ended, Argue handed him a copy of Seymour's *Apostolic Faith* describing the new pentecostal experience. Placing it in his pocket, King forgot it until some days later while riding the train through Buffalo on his way back to Georgia. Reading the paper with great interest, he found that he agreed with everything printed therein. Seymour's teaching about receiving the baptism with the Holy Spirit subsequent to sanctification was what he had "believed and taught for a number of years." The claim of speaking with other tongues seemed to him a reasonable position since the paper did not claim it as the only evidence of the baptism. Arriving in Toccoa, he heard more reports

[16] Goff, *Tests and Triumphs*, p. 51; Campbell, *The Pentecostal Holiness Church*, p. 241; Thurman A. Carey, *Memoirs of Thurman A. Carey* (Columbia, South Carolina, 1907), p. 21.

[17] Campbell, *The Pentecostal Holiness Church*, p. 241. No evidence has been preserved describing the reasons for Crumpler's mistrust of Cashwell.

from California and was "pleased to learn of this mighty work." At the time the Dunn meeting was in progress, King was in his home in Toccoa engaged in ten days of "prayer and fasting for an outpouring of the Holy Spirit."[18]

The Dunn meeting came to a close at the end of January 1907, but services continued in the Dunn Pentecostal Holiness Church where Cashwell had preached before the revival was moved to the warehouse. Great excitement was generated throughout the Southeast by the Dunn meeting. Accounts of it were carried in the *Way of Faith* and spread throughout the South. Holiness people from Danville, Virginia, to Birmingham, Alabama, bombarded the evangelist with requests for similar revivals in their communities. As he traveled through the South from 1906-1909, Cashwell established himself firmly as the "pentecostal apostle to the South."[19]

From Dunn, Cashwell toured the South holding revivals in Memphis, Tennessee; West Union, Clinton, and Lake City, South Carolina; High Point, North Carolina; Danville, Virginia; Toccoa and Valdosta, Georgia; and Birmingham, Alabama. Wherever he went huge crowds gathered to hear him preach the new gospel of pentecost and tongues. Everywhere, holiness preachers either joined his cause or openly opposed him. His opening volley in every meeting would be, "Come on, preachers, bring your Bibles out." To those who came he taught that speaking with other tongues was the only biblical evidence of receiving the Holy Ghost. To the seekers at the mourner's bench he would say, "Keep on praying, He [the Holy Spirit] will testify when He comes in." In every meeting, scores testified to receiving the experience of speaking with other tongues. Of these meetings Taylor wrote excitedly in September 1907, "So a great revival is now upon us, and it is sweeping the world. This is the latter rain." With such

18 King and King, *Yet Speaketh*, pp. 111-113.

19 The best accounts of the Dunn revival are found in: Taylor, *The Spirit and the Bride*, pp. 44-95; F. M. Britton, *Pentecostal Truth, or Sermons on Regeneration, Sanctification, the Baptism of the Holy Spirit, Divine Healing, the Second Coming of Jesus, etc.* (Royston, Georgia, 1919), pp. 235-243; King and King, *Yet Speaketh*, pp. 111-114; Goff, *Tests and Triumphs*, pp. 49-53; and Campbell, *The Pentecostal Holiness Church*, pp. 240-242ff.

interest in his work, Cashwell began publication of a paper before the end of the year called *The Bridegroom's Messenger*. This periodical was intended by its editor "to take care of the pentecostal work of the South." Through the pages of this publication countless more learned of the pentecostal message.[20]

Convincing the masses and the pastors of the holiness churches was a relatively easy task for Cashwell, but converting the denominational leaders was a more difficult matter. His first confrontation with a church leader came in February 1907, when the Fire-Baptized Holiness congregation in Toccoa, Georgia, invited him to hold some special services. Attending this revival was King, the General Overseer of the Fire-Baptized Holiness Church and pastor of the Toccoa congregation. Although he had spent much of January praying and fasting for an "outpouring" of the Holy Spirit, King was not at all prepared to accept Cashwell's teaching as the fulfillment of the revival he was seeking. When Cashwell arrived in Toccoa, King, an astute student of the Greek New Testament, prepared to join him in a theological battle over tongues, a doctrine he still questioned. Taking Dean Alford's *Critical Notes on the New Testament in Greek*, Wesley's *Notes*, and a New Testament, he spent several hours examining the biblical texts dealing with speaking with tongues. To his astonishment, all that he read confirmed in his mind the correctness of Cashwell's views. After a great intellectual struggle, he arrived at the first service "with an open mind." Soon he found himself not only in agreement with the new pentecostal view, but at the altar seeking the experience. The next night, February 15, 1907, he received the experience, and thereafter became one of the nation's leading exponents of the pentecostal theology.[21]

The next holiness leader to accept the pentecostal view from Cashwell was N. J. Holmes, whose "Altamont Bible School" in 1906-1907 was located on Paris Mountain outside Greenville, South Carolina. On first hearing of the Dunn

[20] *The Pentecostal Holiness Advocate*, November 8, 1917, p. 8. L. R. Graham, personal interview with author, November 1966; Taylor, *The Spirit and the Bride*, pp. 39-59.

[21] King and King, *Yet Speaketh*, pp. 116-121; King, *From Passover to Pentecost*, pp. 167-182.

meeting, Holmes was doubtful about the "tongues baptism." In 1905 a student in the school had spoken with tongues in a prayer meeting, causing great wonder and excitement among the student body. The Azusa Street meeting and the Dunn revival had been reported in the *Way of Faith* and had been followed closely by faculty and students alike. In the spring of 1907, a student by the name of Lida Purkie attended one of Cashwell's services at West Union, South Carolina, and returned to the school a confirmed pentecostal. Completely stirred by this event, the student body voted to send Holmes to West Union to investigate the phenomenon. Holmes returned convinced that "God was in it," although he disagreed with Cashwell's theology. For several weeks thereafter many of the students received the experience and began to speak with other tongues. This outbreak became so intense that "neither Holmes nor the teachers knew what to do" about it. Eventually a study of the Scriptures convinced Holmes and his wife, as well as L. R. Graham, President Holmes' assistant, that the pentecostal doctrine was correct. By April 1907, Holmes and practically the entire faculty and student body had spoken with tongues. From that time forward Holmes' school became a bastion of pentecostal theology.[22]

Cashwell met with failure in his efforts to convert the leader of his own church, A. B. Crumpler, to the pentecostal view. Upon his return from Florida in February 1907, Crumpler wasted no time in opposing the new doctrine which seemed to be sweeping his church. In several articles in the *Holiness Advocate*, he had vigorously denounced Cashwell and his "jabbering" followers. But by that time the majority of his readers were pentecostal in sentiment if not in fact. Before the end of 1907 the subscription list had fallen so low, because of protest to his articles, that publication had to

---

22 Holmes, *Life Sketches and Sermons*, pp. 36-58; Thomas, *History of Holmes Theological Seminary*, pp. 13-14; L. R. Graham, personal interview with author, November 1966. Dr. Paul F. Beacham and Mrs. Nina Holmes, in a personal interview with the author, January 11, 1967, stated that Holmes first opposed Irwin's "baptism with fire" in 1898. His conversion to pentecostalism came as a result of his study of tongues in the Scriptures. Holmes Theological Seminary [the present name] was the first institution of higher learning to embrace the pentecostal view.

be suspended. For several months Cashwell's "pentecostal party" vied with Crumpler's "anti-pentecostal party" for control of the church. By 1908 it was apparent that a showdown would come in the convention of the church, which was scheduled to meet in Dunn, North Carolina.[23]

The climactic events in the controversy occurred in November 1908, in the Dunn Convention of the denomination. Both the pentecostal and the anti-pentecostal factions arrived in strength for the meeting. Crumpler's views were by then well known from both his articles in the *Holiness Advocate* and his scathing sermons in various churches. The pentecostal faction was led by Cashwell, who by 1908 considered himself the natural leader of the Southern pentecostals, and by G. F. Taylor, whose book *The Spirit and the Bride* had appeared in September 1907, in ringing defense of the new doctrine. Although the pentecostals were clearly in the majority, they voted to retain Crumpler as president on the first day of the convention.[24]

Before the first day of the convention ended, Crumpler realized that he had no hope of overcoming the pentecostal majority, so he withdrew from the church he had created. Leaving with him was one pastor and his church at LaGrange, North Carolina. The other fourteen churches and most of the other preachers remained with the pentecostals. With the defection of Crumpler, a member of the pentecostal party, A. H. Butler, was elected to the vacant president's chair. The work of the convention which followed was devoted to reforming the movement in the pentecostal image. Cashwell's paper, *The Bridegroom's Messenger*, was adopted as "the organ of this church until further arrangements" to take the place of Crumpler's now defunct *Holiness Advocate*. Cashwell was designated chairman of the committee to revise the *Discipline* of the church.[25]

[23] Campbell, *The Pentecostal Holiness Church*, pp. 241-244.

[24] *Proceedings of the Ninth Annual Convention of the Holiness Church of North Carolina* (Dunn, North Carolina, 1908), pp. 3-4; Taylor, "Our Church History," The *Pentecostal Holiness Advocate*, March 17, 1921, pp. 8-9. Taylor's *The Spirit and the Bride* was the first book-length defense of the new pentecostal theology.

[25] *Proceedings of the Holiness Church*, p. 4.

The *Discipline* was duly revised by the committee, which added a paragraph stating "that on receiving the baptism with the Holy Ghost we have the same evidence which followed in Acts 2nd, 10th, and 19th chapters, to wit: the speaking with other tongues as the Spirit gave utterance." To further insure the future pentecostal character of the church, the convention adopted a resolution offered by Cashwell and two of his friends:

> Resolved, that this convention request all pastors and officers of the churches to admit no preacher or teacher into any of our churches who preach or teach against the baptism of the Holy Ghost as taught in our revised *Discipline*.[26]

Thus the little denomination, which in 1908 included fifteen churches, all within the state of North Carolina, became officially a pentecostal church. The following year the group, which had been called "The Holiness Church of North Carolina" since 1901, voted to restore the prefix "pentecostal" to its name since it was now definitely a part of the fast-growing pentecostal movement.[27]

In the long run, the identification of the church with the pentecostal movement and the loss of Crumpler, its founder, caused little harm to the young church. When the final reckoning was made of gains and losses, it was found that only two churches refused to accept the new doctrine, while only "five or six preachers and a few scattered members" left with Crumpler. In only a short time, Crumpler returned to the Methodist Church, where he remained for the rest of his life.[28]

In the same area of North Carolina that saw the Pentecostal Holiness Church undergo its doctrinal revolution, the Free-Will Baptist Church also felt the winds of change. As has already been noted, a part of the Free-Will Baptist Church's membership had accepted the teaching of holiness before Crumpler's 1896 revivals, and many more during the height

26 *Ibid.*, pp. 6-7.

27 *Proceedings of the Tenth Annual Convention of the Pentecostal Holiness Church, 1909*, p. 6.

28 *The Advocate*, May 29, 1930, p. 1; December 27, 1917, p. 14; Campbell, *The Pentecostal Holiness Church*, p. 249.

of his preaching campaigns in the state. When Cashwell returned to Dunn from Los Angeles in 1906, many Free-Will Baptist ministers also accepted the pentecostal message. In time a controversy erupted between the pentecostal and non-pentecostal elements of the church, resulting eventually in the organization of the "Pentecostal Free-Will Baptist Church" with headquarters in Dunn, North Carolina. Many Southern Baptist members also became converts to the pentecostal religion, because of the efforts of traveling evangelists who made converts in private homes, brush arbors, and tent meetings throughout the area.[29]

One of the more ecumenical results of the Dunn pentecostal revival was the merger of the Pentecostal Holiness Church with the Fire-Baptized Holiness Church in 1911. Since the two denominations operated in practically the same territory and shared the same doctrines after 1906, it was felt that a merger of the two groups would be desirable. Accordingly, a motion offered by G. F. Taylor in the 1909 convention of the Pentecostal Holiness Church was adopted, which invited the Fire-Baptized Holiness Church and the pentecostal element of the Free-Will Baptist Church to join in a proposed merger. In the ensuing months the Fire-Baptized Holiness Church accepted the proposal and appointed a commission to negotiate with representatives of the Pentecostal Holiness Church. The Free-Will Baptists, however, voted not to participate in the merger proceedings.[30]

The convention that effected the merger of the Pentecostal Holiness and Fire-Baptized Holiness Churches took place in Falcon, North Carolina, during January of 1911. Meeting in the octagon-shaped tabernacle on the grounds of the historic Falcon Campgrounds, the two groups worked out the intricate problems of the merger in only a few days and the

[29] *Discipline of the Pentecostal Free-Will Baptist Church, Inc.*, pp. 8-16; Stewart, *History of the Free-Will Baptists*, pp. 411-416; Goff, *Tests and Triumphs*, pp. 49-65; an interview with H. T. Spence on November 11, 1966, described how a traveling "tongues" preacher brought the pentecostal message to his Baptist Church in Raleigh in 1908. After getting this new "funny religion" the entire Spence family joined the local Pentecostal Holiness Church.

[30] Campbell, *The Pentecostal Holiness Church*, pp. 251-255; *Proceedings of the Pentecostal Holiness Church, 1909*, p. 7.

consolidation was consummated on January 30, 1911, with only two dissenting votes out of a total of thirty-eight cast. The new organization voted to adopt the name of the younger and smaller group, the Pentecostal Holiness Church. Since J. H. King, General Overseer of the Fire-Baptized Holiness Church, was absent from the convention, being at the time on a world tour of the mission fields, another member of his church, S. D. Page, was elected to fill the newly created office of "General Superintendent." Elected as his assistants were King, who was given responsibility for foreign missions, and A. H. Butler, former head of the Pentecostal Holiness Church, as head of the "home missions" division. At the time of the consolidation, the new church had congregations in the states of North Carolina, South Carolina, Georgia, Florida, Virginia, Oklahoma, and Tennessee. The year following, a Negro convention was added to the denomination, but it was to be extremely short-lived, being dropped from the roll in 1913.[31]

In 1915 another merger was consummated which combined the Pentecostal Holiness Church with the Tabernacle Pentecostal Church of South Carolina. The latter church had been formed by N. J. Holmes in connection with his Bible College in Greenville, South Carolina, in 1910. First called the Brewerton Presbyterian Church, it later changed its name to the Tabernacle Pentecostal Church to designate its doctrinal position. Although Holmes and his college church in Greenville did not participate in the merger, several former Presbyterian Churches throughout South Carolina joined the Pentecostal Holiness Church in a meeting called for the merger at Canon, Georgia, in 1915.[32] These mergers, which

31 *Discipline of the Pentecostal Holiness Church, 1965,* pp. 6-7; *Minutes of the First General Convention of the Pentecostal Holiness Church, 1911,* pp. 1-4; Campbell, *The Pentecostal Holiness Church,* pp. 255-259; King and King, *Yet Speaketh,* pp. 142-294. On his world tour King traveled to Japan, China, India, the Near East, Europe, and Scandinavia. While on this tour he met the earliest pentecostal leaders in these lands and helped to shape the world pentecostal movement by his sermons and lectures.

32 *Manual of the Pentecostal Holiness Church, 1965,* p. 7; Campbell, *The Pentecostal Holiness Church,* pp. 263-266.

produced the present Pentecostal Holiness Church, illustrated the fact that the pentecostal movement, as well as the holiness movement, contained strong ecumenical tendencies.

After bringing the pentecostal message to the Eastern Seaboard through the 1906-07 Dunn revival, Cashwell received invitations to preach throughout the South. Word of his revival campaigns was spread through the pages of his *Bridegroom's Messenger* and the *Way of Faith*. From 1906 to 1909 his services were in great demand, as invitations came by the score for him to preach the pentecostal message in many states. Following the Dunn and Toccoa meetings, Cashwell was invited to Memphis and Birmingham to preach to interested groups who had read of his services in the East. In May 1907, he traveled to Memphis, where a meeting with glossolalia in evidence held in a tent caused a minor sensation. As a result of that meeting the first pentecostal church of Memphis was organized. Following the Memphis meeting, Cashwell journeyed to Birmingham, where another important pentecostal outbreak occurred. Two men who received the pentecostal experience in Birmingham were H. G. Rodgers and M. M. Pinson, former Methodist ministers. They later formed a Pentecostal Association in the Mississippi Valley, which eventually became a part of the Assemblies of God denomination. Cashwell's preaching tour through Western Tennessee and Alabama was the first instance of the pentecostal doctrine being taught in the mid-Southern region.[33]

Word of the pentecostal revival which was sweeping the South came to the leaders of the Church of God in Cleveland, Tennessee, through the preaching of Cashwell in Birmingham. Although many had spoken with tongues in the revival at Camp Creek, North Carolina, in 1896, the Church of God had not embraced it as a formal doctrine. The first direct contact Tomlinson had with the new doctrine was in a meeting with Pinson in Birmingham, Alabama, in June 1907.

[33] B. F. Lawrence, *The Apostolic Faith Restored* (Springfield, Missouri, 1916), pp. 90-95; Bailey, *Pioneer Marvels*, pp. 33-34. Pinson and Rodgers were two of the leading founders of the Assemblies of God, a church destined to become the largest pentecostal denomination in the United States.

While preaching there, the General Overseer was amazed to hear Pinson and others speaking in foreign languages. After a week of services with Pinson, he wrote in his *Diary* that "glorious results" came from the revival, adding the terse statement "speaking in tongues by the Holy Ghost." On his return to Cleveland, he found that many of his preachers had already received the experience. He then determined to invite Cashwell to Cleveland so that his churchmen could hear the doctrine from the lips of the Southern "Apostle of Pentecost" himself.[34]

Tomlinson and other Church of God leaders had been much interested in the spreading pentecostal revival throughout the year 1907. In January of that year Tomlinson had preached on "The Baptism with the Holy Spirit" to the General Assembly of the denomination and had seen several of his subordinates receive this experience with the accompaniment of tongues, while he himself had not received it. Several times he had unsuccessfully sought the experience.[35] Now, at the close of the General Assembly of January 1908, which met in Cleveland, Cashwell was present, preaching in a revival at the local Church of God. On Sunday, January 12, after the close of the General Assembly, Cashwell began to preach on the subject of Pentecost with Tomlinson listening intently. While Cashwell continued to preach, the General Overseer slipped out of his chair "in a heap on the rostrum at . . . Cashwell's feet." While lying there Tomlinson received the pentecostal experience and according to his own testimony, spoke in ten different languages. From that point on, the Church of God, and all its subsequent branches, became full-fledged members of the pentecostal movement.[36]

Following Tomlinson's baptism under Cashwell's preach-

34 Tomlinson, "Journal of Happenings," June 14, 1907; *Church of God Evangel*, March 8, 1916, p. 2.

35 Tomlinson, *Answering the Call of God*, p. 9.

36 Tomlinson, "Journal of Happenings," January 13, 1908; *Answering the Call of God*, pp. 9-10; Homer Tomlinson, *Diary of A. J. Tomlinson*, I, 27-36; Conn, *Like a Mighty Army*, pp. 84-85. Tomlinson's baptism is one of the most graphic and detailed in all pentecostal literature. See Tomlinson, *Diary of A. J. Tomlinson*, I, 27-29.

ing, the Church of God experienced one of its greatest advances under the impetus of the new pentecostal message. Congregations were begun in Chattanooga and in the city of Cleveland. A tent meeting held in September 1908 caused the Cleveland newspaper to report that "the Holiness people have practically captured all east and northeast Cleveland, and their strength is materially increasing."[37] The next month a local preacher wrote in panic that "our town and country is flooded with false pentecostal doctrine—satanic power and influence is taking its sway." It was evident from these meetings that the pentecostal doctrine struck a responsive chord in Southern Protestants and that the Church of God was beginning to move "like a mighty army" across the land.[38]

Following the lead of the larger group in Cleveland with the same name, the Church of God (Mountain Assembly) in Kentucky also received favorably the doctrine of speaking with tongues. Hearing of the Azusa Street meeting through various holiness periodicals in 1906, the leaders of this group, notably J. H. Bryant and J. H. Parks, introduced the doctrine to their church. A great deal of persecution followed during the years 1906 and 1907, with bands of rowdies interrupting services and trying to discourage the spread of the "holy rollers," but the little church survived the challenge. In the years following 1906 the church experienced a slow and tedious growth, mainly because of its isolation.[39]

Early in 1907 news of the pentecostal revival in Los Angeles came to the attention of the leaders of the Church of God in Christ in Memphis. The two dominant personalities in this infant holiness church, C. H. Mason and C. P. Jones, reacted differently to the stories from California. Mason, convinced from an early age that "God endowed him with supernatural characteristics, which were manifested in dreams and visions," felt strangely drawn to investigate the pente-

---

[37] *The* (Cleveland) *Journal and Banner,* September 17, 1908, p. 3; quoted in Conn, *Like a Mighty Army,* p. 87.

[38] *Ibid.,* October 29, 1908, p. 1.

[39] Gibson, *History of the Church of God, Mountain Assembly,* pp. 51-53.

costal services at Azusa Street. Jones, on the other hand, was cool to the idea of speaking with other tongues. In March 1907, Mason persuaded two of his fellow ministers, J. A. Jeter and D. J. Young, to travel with him to Los Angeles to investigate the Azusa Street revival. Arriving in California, the three went directly to Azusa Street where they were delighted to see Seymour, a fellow Negro, in charge of the services, which were by then largely attended by whites. During their five-week stay, all three men received the pentecostal experience of speaking with other tongues and returned to Memphis as convinced pentecostals.[40]

Upon their return to Memphis, Mason and his followers found that another Azusa Street veteran, Glenn A. Cook, a native of Los Angeles, had preceded them with the pentecostal message. Cook, a white man, had already made many pentecostal converts. The intrusion of pentecostal doctrine under Cook's and Mason's leadership alienated Jones, then "General Overseer" and "Presiding Elder." Soon the pentecostal faction, under Mason, and the non-pentecostal faction, under Jones, became locked in a struggle over leadership of the movement. In the General Assembly of the church that met in Jackson, Mississippi, in August 1907, the pentecostal controversy dominated the proceedings. After a "very lengthy discussion," the Assembly "withdrew from C. H. Mason and all who promulgated the doctrine of speaking with tongues the right hand of fellowship." Thereupon, Mason and a majority of the preachers and membership of the church withdrew from the Assembly. Jones, remaining in control of the non-pentecostal faction, changed the name of his group to "The Church of Christ (Holiness) U.S.A."[41]

Later in 1907 Mason convened another Assembly in Memphis, this one representing the pentecostal group that had been expelled in Jackson. In this first "General Assembly" of the new pentecostal church, the old name, "Church of God

40 Mason, *Bishop C. H. Mason*, pp. 18-22; Fidler, "Historical Review of the Pentecostal Outpouring in Los Angeles," p. 14; Kendrick, *The Promise Fulfilled*, pp. 197-198.

41 *Yearbook of the Church of God in Christ, 1960-1961*, p. 9; Kendrick, *The Promise Fulfilled*, p. 198; Mason, *Bishop C. H. Mason*, p. 22; Landis, *Yearbook of American Churches* (New York, 1965), p. 33.

in Christ," was retained and a pentecostal paragraph was added to the articles of faith. The doctrine of entire sanctification as a second work of grace was retained, thereby keeping the church in the holiness tradition. From its reorganization in 1907, the Church of God in Christ grew rapidly to become the largest Negro pentecostal group in the world. So great was Mason's prestige that many white pentecostal ministers accepted ordination at his hands. From 1907 to 1914 his church was interracial, many whites joining it because, as an incorporated denomination, the Church of God in Christ could obtain clergy permits for use on the railroads, and aid them in being bonded for weddings. Many of the men who founded the white "Assemblies of God" church in 1914, were thus ordained in the Church of God in Christ by Bishop Mason.[42]

With the conversion of Mason to the pentecostal position, the pentecostal invasion of the South was complete. In only a few months much of the holiness movement in the South had been converted to pentecostalism. Some holiness bodies, such as J. O. McClurkan's pentecostal mission in Nashville and the Wesleyan Methodist Church, refused to countenance the "new light" on Pentecost. The thousands of holiness devotees remaining in the Methodist Episcopal Church, South, remained largely untouched by the movement. Other leaders, such as A. B. Simpson, head of the Christian and Missionary Alliance, rejected the pentecostal view only after much investigation. The surviving members of the older, more conservative wing of the holiness movement sternly denounced the new movement. W. B. Godbey, L. L. Pickett, George A. Watson, and many others rejected "tongues" as unscriptural and even "demon-inspired." But by 1908 the die was cast, especially in the South. With the major Southern holiness bodies, the Church of God, the Pentecostal Holiness Church, the Fire-Baptized Holiness Church, and the Church of God in Christ, all now firmly in the pentecostal camp, future major

[42] *Yearbook of the Church of God in Christ, 1960-1961*, p. 9; Fidler, "Historical Review of the Pentecostal Outpouring in Los Angeles," p. 14; Kendrick, *The Promise Fulfilled*, p. 80. *The Yearbook of American Churches, 1965*, pp. 33-37, credits Jones' Church of Christ (Holiness) with having 7,621 members in 146 churches, while Mason's Church of God in Christ claimed 413,000 members in 4,100 churches.

growth in the South was to be on the side of the pentecostals, the term "holiness church" in many areas becoming
synonymous in the public mind with pentecostalism.[43]

The key to the amazing spread of the pentecostal movement into the South was the receptive attitude of the various
holiness leaders in the months from 1906 through 1908. The
winning of King, Tomlinson, and Mason was crucial to the
advance of Southern pentecostalism. All three were deeply
committed to the holiness movement and adhered to the
second work theory of sanctification. When the pentecostal
revival came, they merely added a "third experience" to the
first two. When doctrinal difficulties later brought the experience of sanctification into question, the Southern churches
held firmly to the perfectionism that they had inherited from
Methodism. By accepting the "radical" doctrine of speaking
with other tongues, they displayed their willingness to
change, while by retaining and staunchly defending the conservative doctrine of sanctification, they illustrated their un-
compromising orthodoxy.

Among the casualties of the new movement was the
"pentecostal prophet to the South" himself. After 1908,
Cashwell found that he would not be able to control the
movement that he had been so responsible for beginning. A
temperamental and egotistical man, he succeeded in making
enemies as well as friends for the movement. In 1909, he
defected from the Pentecostal Holiness Church and returned
to the Methodist Church, as Crumpler had done before him.
Before his death in 1916, Cashwell denounced the pentecostals and tried to disclaim the part he had played in their
beginning. But try as he might, he could not erase the fact
that his brief preaching tour of 1906 through 1908 had
resulted in bringing three holiness denominations into the

43 See Holmes, *Life Sketches and Sermons*, pp. 152-170; Taylor,
The Spirit and the Bride, p. 52. For the views of the Church of the
Nazarene, see Smith, *Called Unto Holiness*, pp. 319-320. The classical
holiness view also found strong expression in *The Pentecostal Herald*,
edited from Asbury College by Henry Clay Morrison from 1888 to
1942 and thereafter by J. C. McPheeters. Throughout this period, this
influential voice of the holiness movement expressed a staunch
anti-tongues position.

pentecostal movement and had profoundly affected the religious future of the South as well as the entire United States.[44]

[44] Cashwell's name was dropped from the roll of the Pentecostal Holiness Church in 1910; see the *Proceedings of the Pentecostal Holiness Church, 1910*, p. 4. Also see Bailey, *Pioneer Marvels of Faith*, pp. 48-49. Campbell states in his *The Pentecostal Holiness Church*, p. 241, that Cashwell "did grievously fail God and bring reproach on the cause of the full gospel. . . ," although he does not include the nature of his failure. Part of this information is based on H. T. Spence, interview with the author, November 11, 1966.

Chapter Seven

CRITICISM AND CONTROVERSY 1906-1920

Many Pentecostal people have run wild after that which is new and sensational in the last six years, such as "finished work," . . . rejection of the Trinity, anti-organization . . . and many other preposterous, nonsensical sensations. . . . —J. H. King (1917)

It was inevitable that the introduction of religious views as radical and emotionally divisive as the pentecostals' would cause criticism and controversy both without and within the holiness movement. Coming as a grand division within the older holiness movement, it was not surprising that some of the earliest and bitterest critics were members of those holiness churches which rejected speaking with other tongues. Yet it is one of the ironies of church history that those most responsible for a new religious movement often become the most hostile to the work of their own hands.

The pentecostal movement was first and foremost a product of the spiritual milieu of the National Holiness Movement. Preachers such as S. B. Shaw, George Hughes, and J. A. Wood had for years called for a "new pentecost" that would shake the world. Hughes, a leading member of the National Holiness Association, had in 1901 called for a "world-rocking revival of religion" which would "shake the very foundations of earth." This revival, which was to be "along pentecostal lines," would be "a fit opening of the 20th

Century."[1] As early as 1856 William Arthur, a Methodist
preacher of holiness, had called for a pentecostal effusion
which would be followed with "miraculous effects." Among
these effects was included a "baptism with purifying flames
of fire." His book, entitled prophetically *The Tongue of Fire*,
was republished in 1891 by L. L. Pickett and circulated
widely among holiness people.[2]

The thinking that produced *The Tongue of Fire* had influenced a new departure in holiness theology by 1875. This
development came about as a result of Vicar Harford-
Battersby's holiness conventions at Keswick, England. Although the Keswick conventions became the English counterpart of the American National Holiness Association, a difference of emphasis was to result in a different view of sanctification. The English view, heavily influenced by the Keswick
conventions, was that sanctification was in reality the "baptism with the Holy Spirit." Soon those with Keswick connections spoke of the second blessing as their "baptism" rather
than their sanctification. While the English drifted toward a
different terminology, the Americans continued to speak of
the second work as "sanctification" and continued to stress
the Wesleyan doctrines of perfection, purity, and cleansing.
Through a monthly paper entitled *The Christian's Pathway to
Power*, and numerous books and pamphlets as well, the
Keswick view of "Holy Ghost power" came to be as widely
known as Wesley's "Christian perfection." By the 1890's and
the early part of the twentieth century, this "Keswick terminology" had permeated much of the American holiness
movement and exercised great influence on religious innova-
tors such as Parham and Irwin.[3]

1 Shaw, *Echoes of the General Holiness Assembly, 1901*, p. 54.

2 William Arthur, *The Tongue of Fire, or the True Power of
Christianity* (Columbia, 1891), pp. 43-79, 100, 164-167.

3 Herbert F. Stevenson, *Keswick's Authentic Voice* (Grand Rapids,
Michigan, 1959), pp. 13-22; Smith, *Called Unto Holiness*, pp. 24-25; R.
A. Torrey, *The Holy Spirit* (New York, 1927), pp. 1-45. Since Wesley
never identified sanctification as the baptism with the Holy Ghost,
many pentecostals still claim to be fully Wesleyan. See Robert A.
Mattke, "The Baptism of the Holy Spirit as Related to the Work of
Entire Sanctification," *Wesleyan Theological Journal*, Spring 1970, pp.
22-32.

By the time of the Azusa Street revival of 1906 the theological foundations of the pentecostal movement had been well laid. It is not surprising, therefore, that many holiness people who had prayed for and predicted a pentecostal outbreak were ready to accept the events of 1906 in Los Angeles as the answer to their prayers. That many leaders such as King, Cashwell, Tomlinson, and Mason, accepted the pentecostal message, along with hundreds of Methodists, Baptists, and holiness preachers, shows how well the climate of the times favored the new theology.

In spite of the Keswick persuasion within the holiness movement at the turn of the century, many religious leaders not only rejected, but actively opposed, the emanations from Azusa Street. Criticism ranged from mild questioning about the emotional excesses of the pentecostal adherents to positive denunciations and ecclesiastical anathemas. Probably the earliest and bitterest critic was Alma White, leader of the "Pillar of Fire" church, which saw one of its congregations in Los Angeles taken over by pentecostal enthusiasts in 1906. Calling Seymour and Parham "rulers of spiritual Sodom," White called speaking with other tongues "this satanic gibberish" and pentecostal services "the climax of demon worship." Her polemic against the movement was published in 1936 in a volume entitled *Demons and Tongues.* This book was representative of the early old-school holiness criticism of the movement.[4]

Another early critic was the famous holiness preacher, W. B. Godbey, whose *Commentary on the New Testament* had become a classic in the holiness world. Visiting Los Angeles in 1909, he found the city "on tip toe, all electrified with the movement." Upon invitation he visited Azusa Street and preached to a "large audience" of pentecostals. When they asked if he had spoken in tongues, the scholarly Godbey responded with the Latin, *"Johannes Baptistes tinxit, Petros tinxet. . . ."* Upon hearing this, the pentecostals exclaimed that he had truly received his "baptism." Repelled by the noise and disorganization of Seymour's service, Godbey departed in complete disenchantment, calling the Azusa people "Satan's preachers, jugglers, necromancers, enchanters, magi-

---

[4] White, *Demons and Tongues,* pp. 43, 56, 82ff.

cians, and all sorts of mendicants." Dismissing the movement as a product of "spiritualism," he used his considerable influence in persuading a large portion of the holiness movement to reject the pentecostal message. Other leading preachers of the day also added their voices to the rising chorus of criticism. Dr. G. Campbell Morgan, one of the most respected preachers of the twentieth century, called the pentecostal movement "the last vomit of Satan," while Dr. R. A. Torrey claimed that it was "emphatically not of God, and founded by a Sodomite." Such criticism was accepted at face value by many observers who often knew little or nothing about the new movement.[5]

In his *Holiness, The False and the True*, H. A. Ironside in 1912 denounced both the holiness and the pentecostal movements as "disgusting . . . delusions and insanities." Characterizing pentecostal meetings as "pandemoniums where exhibitions worthy of a madhouse or a collection of howling dervishes are held night after night," he charged that such meetings caused a "heavy toll of lunacy and infidelity."[6] Surpassing Ironside in outspoken criticism was H. J. Stolee, who in his *Speaking in Tongues* summarized four decades of criticism. Attributing "mental instability," "mob psychology," "hypnotism," and "demon power" to pentecostal worship, he conjectured that the "general neurasthenia," or "nerve weariness," of twentieth-century life was responsible for most of the converts to the new religion. Using the language of psychology, he speculated that "tongues" were produced by "hallucinations," "melancholia," "paranoia," "megalomania," "hysteria," and "a cataleptic condition."[7]

Other observers such as Beverly Carradine, well known for many decades in the National Holiness Movement, condemned the new "tongues movement." Writing in 1910, he called the pentecostals speakers of "gibberish" rather than "the real gift of tongues." Wielding great influence on the other holiness denominations, Carradine helped stem the

5 *Ibid.*, pp. 120-127; Taylor, *The Spirit and the Bride*, p. 52; Ewart, *The Phenomenon of Pentecost*, p. 85.

6 See pages 38-39.

7 Stolee, *Speaking in Tongues*, pp. 77, 75-93. "Typical" pentecostal services are described on pages 65-84.

pentecostal tide which threatened to engulf the entire holiness movement. Another holiness leader, A. B. Simpson, head of the Christian and Missionary Alliance, rejected the pentecostal contention that *all* must speak in tongues as the evidence of their Holy Ghost baptism. After a highly emotional revival in his Missionary Training Institute in Nyack, New York, in May 1907, Simpson faced a doctrinal problem when many of his students and teachers began to speak with other tongues. After much thought, the president of the institution decided that tongues was only "one of the evidences" of the indwelling of the Holy Spirit. Tongues would be allowed in Christian and Missionary Alliance services, but would not be encouraged. Simpson's dictum "seek not—forbid not" eventually became known as the "Alliance position," a compromise unique in the early history of the movement.[8]

The Pentecostal Church of the Nazarene, largest of the holiness denominations, early became a bastion of antipentecostal thought. With the leader of the denomination, Bresee, pastoring the mother church of the movement in Los Angeles in 1906, it is not surprising that he and his church opposed the Azusa Street meeting, constituting as it did a direct threat to his own congregation. During the years 1906-1909, he actively opposed the rival center and placed his denomination in direct opposition to the new doctrine. Eventually the name "Pentecostal Church of the Nazarene" became an embarrassment, since many persons confused it with the new pentecostal or "tongues" movement. Accordingly, in the General Assembly of 1919 the denomination voted to drop the word "pentecostal" from the name in order to avoid confusion. From that time on the church has been known to the world simply as "The Church of the Nazarene." Following the lead of the Nazarenes, the Wesleyan Methodist Church, The Salvation Army, the Pilgrim Holiness Church, and the Free Methodist Church also dis-

[8] Beverly Carradine, *A Box of Treasure* (Chicago, 1910), pp. 78-85; Hollenweger, "Handbuch Der Pfingstbewegung," II, 408; Brumback, *Suddenly from Heaven,* pp. 88-97. For a summary of the Christian and Missionary Alliance view see J. T. McCrossan, *Speaking with Other Tongues, Sign or Gift, Which?* (Seattle, 1927), pp. 3-31.

sociated themselves completely from the pentecostal movement.[9]

The struggling pentecostals were not without their defenders, however, although few understood the full doctrinal or historical implications of their new movement. The first book-length apology for the movement appeared in September 1907, following the Dunn revival. Entitled *The Spirit and the Bride*, this volume was written by G. F. Taylor, the young follower of Cashwell and antagonist of Crumpler. With an introduction by J. H. King of the Fire-Baptized Holiness Church, it was issued against "determined and desperate opposition." In the crucial months following the introduction of pentecostalism to the South, Taylor's book exercised a powerful influence in aiding the pentecostal parties in gaining control of the Southern holiness churches. Another early work that circulated widely in the Western and Middle-Western areas was David Wesley Myland's *The Latter Rain Covenant and Pentecostal Power*, which appeared in 1910. Both Taylor and Myland held the view that the pentecostal movement was intended to prepare the church for the second coming of Christ.[10]

In 1914, King, one of the better educated leaders of the movement, published his theological defense of the new pentecostal doctrine in his *From Passover to Pentecost*. This volume became required reading for thousands of pentecostal ministers in the years following its appearance. Two years later B. F. Lawrence published another defense, entitled *The Apostolic Faith Restored*. This book was followed a decade later by the first serious history of the movement, *With Signs Following*, by Stanley H. Frodsham, an Englishman who had migrated to the United States. These earlier works were followed by a veritable flood of pentecostal literature as the

9 Redford, *Rise of the Church of the Nazarene*, pp. 39-42; S. L. Brengle, *When the Holy Ghost Is Come* (New York, 1914), pp. 20-31; Henry E. Brockett, *The Riches of Holiness* (Kansas City, 1951), pp. 108-121; Smith, *Called Unto Holiness*, pp. 319-320.

10 Taylor, *The Spirit and the Bride*, pp. 8, 122; Myland, *The Latter Rain Covenant and Pentecostal Power* (Chicago, 1910), pp. 100-121. Using charts of rainfall in Palestine from 1861-1901, Myland concluded that the second coming of Christ would occur soon after 1906.

growing denominations developed publishing houses after 1910.[11]

The budding pentecostal movement not only faced criticism from without, but also suffered from dissension and controversy from within. The years from 1906 to 1914 saw the most fundamental doctrinal cleavage that the movement was to experience, the schism over sanctification as a second work of grace. In the first stages of the movement's development the Wesleyan view was universally accepted among pentecostals. Since most of the first pentecostal leaders had been prominent in the holiness movement, it seemed natural for them to maintain the place of sanctification as a "second blessing" which cleansed the seeker from "inbred sin," thus preparing him for the reception of the Holy Spirit. Both Parham and Seymour adhered to this view consistently throughout the rest of their lives. The Southern holiness denominations, led by King, Mason, and Tomlinson, had been founded as a result of the second work controversy in Methodism and the idea of the "double-cure" was deeply ingrained in their doctrine and history. Indeed, entire sanctification had been the very reason for their foundation, making a departure from it virtually unthinkable.

The problem over the second work arose when large numbers of converts began to enter the movement from non-Wesleyan backgrounds, notably the Baptist Church. Not schooled in holiness theology, these men thought of Christian experience as involving only two steps, conversion and the baptism with the Holy Ghost. The man who became the leader of the group that was to question the necessity of the second blessing was W. H. Durham of Chicago, Illinois. Pastor of the well-known North Avenue Mission, Durham had traveled to Azusa Street in 1907 and had returned a convert to the new pentecostal doctrine. Although he had previously preached the Wesleyan view of sanctification, Durham determined never to preach it again after his trip to Los Angeles. By the end of 1907, Durham's mission church had become a mecca for Midwestern pentecostals, his ministry to that

[11] King, *From Passover to Pentecost* (Memphis, 1914); Lawrence, *The Apostolic Faith Restored* (Springfield, Missouri, 1916); Frodsham, *With Signs Following* (Springfield, Missouri, 1926).

region being similar to Cashwell's in the South. From 1906 to 1911 Durham's influence increased among pentecostals through his monthly periodical *The Pentecostal Testimony* and through his dynamic preaching. Called a "pulpit prodigy," he attracted thousands to his "pentecostal services" in the North Avenue Mission where many of his followers experienced a peculiar shouting experience known as the "Durham jerks."[12]

The controversy began with a sermon Durham preached at a Chicago pentecostal convention in 1910 in which he sought to "nullify the blessing of sanctification as a second definite work of grace." Calling his new doctrine "The Finished Work," Durham called for a new view which assigned sanctification to the act of conversion based on "the finished work of Christ on Calvary." Denying Wesley's concept of a "residue of sin" in the believer, he taught that one was perfectly sanctified at conversion and had no need of a "second change" later. This was, in effect, the Oberlin theology developed by Charles G. Finney in the years before the Civil War. Since Durham's teaching cut directly across the accepted view of the pentecostals with a holiness background, a great controversy ensued which ultimately divided the pentecostal movement into two theological camps.[13]

The problem was brought to an early crisis when Durham returned to Los Angeles for a preaching mission in February 1911. Coming first to the "Upper Room Mission," by then the largest pentecostal church in the city, Durham was invited to leave when his doctrine became known. He then returned to the fabled Azusa Street Mission, which by 1911 was essentially a local Negro church, still under Seymour's leadership. Since Seymour was in the East on a preaching tour, Durham was invited to preach in this the "Mother Church" of pentecostalism. With his dynamic personality and new message, Durham soon filled the old mission with crowds from other missions in the city. When Seymour heard of the "finished work heresy" being preached at Azusa

12 Brumback, *Suddenly from Heaven,* pp. 69-70. J. Roswell Flower, personal interview with the author on July 13, 1969.

13 *Ibid.,* pp. 98-106; Ewart, *The Phenomenon of Pentecost,* pp. 72-77.

Street, he hastily returned and bolted the doors of the mission to Durham, who then moved to another location to continue his revival. News of this event reverberated throughout the pentecostal movement and brought the crisis into the open.[14]

Those following Durham's teaching referred to sanctification as a "fictitious experience" which was not supported by the Scriptures. Opponents of the Chicago pastor charged that he was "attacking the doctrinal foundations of the movement." From 1910 to 1914 the battle raged with much acrimony and "carnality" being exhibited on both sides. In Baxter Springs, Missouri, Parham heard of the new view and rejected it, calling it an opening for "animalism" or "spiritualistic counterfeits" into pentecostal ranks. In Portland, Oregon, Mrs. Florence Crawford and her "Apostolic Faith" movement also rejected the doctrine. In the end, the "finished work theory" gained its greatest support among the urban independent and unorganized churches and missions, which by then numbered in the hundreds across the nation. So pervasive was the new view that most of the pentecostal denominations that began after 1911 incorporated it in their statements of faith.[15]

The "finished work" theory failed to move the Southern pentecostal groups, which were already steeped in the holiness movement. In the battle between "finished work" and "second work" the Church of God, the Pentecostal Holiness Church, and the Church of God in Christ stood firmly for the second work of sanctification. For these churches, the belief in entire sanctification as a second work of grace became a test of orthodoxy, and anyone professing to believe in the "finished work" was considered a "false teacher" or a

[14] Bartleman, *How Pentecost Came to Los Angeles*, pp. 145-146. While denouncing the doctrine of sanctification at Azusa Street, Durham was attacked by a young holiness girl who had worked as a prostitute before her conversion. She used a hat pin to register her "pointed opposition" to Durham's teachings. See Brumback, *Suddenly from Heaven*, pp. 99-100, 103.

[15] Parham, "A Critical Analysis of the Tongues Question," *The Apostolic Faith*, June 1925, p. 5; Bartleman, *How Pentecost Came to Los Angeles*, p. 150; Crawford, *A Historical Account of the Apostolic Faith*, pp. 69-70; Ewart, *The Phenomenon of Pentecost*, p. 74.

"deluded Yankee." In his *Passover to Pentecost*, King defended the second work as vigorously as he did the first and the third. Surprised and pained "almost beyond degree" that this new idea had penetrated pentecostal ranks, King described the new doctrine as "Antinomianism . . . dressed up in a Zinzendorfian garb and going through the land with all the intrepidity of a new resurrection."[16] The Church of God and the Church of God in Christ remained largely untouched by the controversy. Like the Pentecostal Holiness Church, their origins as holiness denominations dictated a close adherence to the "second work" view.[17]

As the "finished work" theory spread among the hundreds of independent pentecostal missions and "assemblies" throughout the nation, calls began to be heard for a unified organization which would provide a denominational home for all those with similar views. Pentecostal people in the North and West had been reluctant to join the Southern pentecostal groups in the years following 1906, although they were the only pentecostal denominations in existence. From 1907 to 1914 many white ministers had been ordained by C. H. Mason, since his group, the Church of God in Christ, was chartered by the state of Tennessee. Their affiliation with the Church of God in Christ, however, was purely nominal, extending only to ministerial credentials. As a rule, most of these white ministers preferred to gather informally in "state camp meetings" where their ecclesiastical affairs could be discussed freely without reference to Mason or any other church officials. Rapport was maintained between these ministers and churches by means of various indepen-

16 Antinomianism was the belief that a Christian could not commit sin after conversion since the laws of the Old Testament had no force in the New Testament age. Count Zinzendorf, a contemporary of John Wesley, denied that sanctification was a second work of grace.

17 King, *From Passover to Pentecost*, p. 81; Tomlinson, *Diary of A. J. Tomlinson*, pp. 238-239. For comments on the controversy from the periodicals of the various movements, see: *The Pentecostal Holiness Advocate*, September 13, 1917, p. 1; June 17, 1926, p. 1; *The Church of God Evangel*, January 10, 1914, pp. 1-3; March 28-June 27, 1914, a series of four major articles entitled "Perilous Times Have Come"; October 2, 1915, pp. 1-4; August 24, 1918, p. 1; *The Pentecostal Evangel*, September 4, 1920, p. 5; May 12, 1923, pp. 5-7; *Word and Witness*, August 20, 1912, p. 1; May 20, 1913, p. 1.

dent periodicals which began circulation after 1906. The most prominent of these was *The Apostolic Faith*, edited by E. N. Bell, formerly a Baptist pastor from Fort Worth, who had become a pentecostal convert under Durham's preaching in Chicago. This paper had no connection with Parham's or Seymour's publication of the same name. Other influential papers were J. Roswell Flower's *Christian Evangel*, published in Indianapolis, and M. M. Pinson's *Word and Witness*, issued from Arkansas. In these and other periodicals, announcements were made of camp meetings, conventions, and missionary assemblies.[18]

Since the early pentecostals outside the Southern churches felt that denominational organizations were to be avoided, partly because of Parham's anti-denominationalism, interchurch meetings were rare. In various parts of the nation, groups of ministers gathered in local "associations" for fellowship and mutual aid. The earliest of these was the "Apostolic Faith Movement," which began in Orchard, Texas, in April of 1906 under Parham's leadership. In 1909 this group broke with Parham and accepted the leadership of two Texas pentecostal ministers, E. N. Bell and Howard A. Goss. In 1911 the group dropped the name "Apostolic Faith Movement" and accepted credentials from Mason's "Church of God in Christ." At the same time that Bell's group was emerging in Texas, another group was developing in Alabama under the leadership of Cashwell's convert, H. G. Rodgers. Meeting in Dothan, Alabama, in 1909, this group adopted the name "Church of God" and issued ministerial credentials to its pastors. This name was adopted without knowledge of Tomlinson's church with headquarters in Cleveland, Tennessee. At the second meeting of the infant church in Slocumb, Alabama, in 1911, the group changed its name to "The Church of God in Christ" in deference to Mason's church. Thus by 1911, three groups operated under the name of Mason's church, the one in Texas led by Bell, the one in Alabama led by Rodgers, and Mason's own group in Memphis.[19]

[18] Brumback, *Suddenly from Heaven*, pp. 155-156; Kendrick, *The Promise Fulfilled*, p. 79; J. Roswell Flower, "History of the Assemblies of God" (n.p., n.d.), pp. 17-19.

[19] C. C. Burnett, . . . *In the Last Days . . . An Early History of the*

After 1911 a move was initiated by Bell and Rodgers to unite the Texas and Alabama groups, both of which were made up of whites who were becoming increasingly dissatisfied with the existing arrangement with Mason's church. At a meeting of both white groups in Meridian, Mississippi, in June 1913, a merger was effected which resulted in an all-white church with 352 ministers. Although the group continued to use the name "Church of God in Christ," it began to issue separate ministerial credentials which superseded those issued earlier by Mason. Later that summer, Pinson, editor of *Word and Witness*, and Bell, editor of *Apostolic Faith*, decided to join forces and issue one periodical. Bell was selected to edit the new *Word and Witness*, as it was called. Before the end of the year the idea of forming a separate white denomination on a national basis gained currency among the leaders of the group, since most of them saw the existing organization as "frail" and "inadequate" and felt the relationship to Mason's denomination to be somewhat ambiguous. Accordingly, a call was issued in the December 20th issue of the *Word and Witness* for a "General Council" of all "pentecostal saints and Churches of God in Christ" to meet the following April in Hot Springs, Arkansas, to discuss various problems common to all.[20]

The Hot Springs "General Council" met in the Grand Opera House on Central Avenue during the first week of April 1914. Although the three hundred ministers and laymen disclaimed any desire to inaugurate a new "sect" or "denomination," the delegates succeeded in doing just that. Adopting a document entitled "Preamble and Resolution of Constitution," the group created a new denomination with the name "General Council of the Assemblies of God." Following the keynote address by M. M. Pinson entitled "The Finished Work of Calvary," the new church adopted a statement of faith which included the usual pentecostal article

Assemblies of God (Springfield, Missouri, 1962), pp. 7-9; Brumback, *Suddenly from Heaven*, p. 154; Kendrick, *The Promise Fulfilled*, pp. 79-80; Nichols, *Pentecostalism*, pp. 109-110; Irwin Winehouse, *The Assemblies of God, A Popular Survey* (New York, 1959), pp. 28-30.

20 *Word and Witness*, December 20, 1913, p. 1. Also see Kendrick, *The Promise Fulfilled*, pp. 81-83; and Brumback, *Suddenly from Heaven*, pp. 156-157.

concerning speaking with tongues, while stating in another
article that "entire sanctification" should be "earnestly
pursued" as a "progressive" rather than an instantaneous
experience. The adoption of this statement placed the new
"Assemblies of God" outside the Wesleyan tradition, thus
creating the first formal doctrinal division in the pentecostal
movement. The Assemblies' of God Constitution became the
model of the subsequent "finished work" pentecostal denominations that were formed after 1914. The type of government adopted by the new church was essentially congregational in form whereas the earlier Southern pentecostal
groups had developed strongly episcopal forms. In general the
Assemblies of God represented the "Baptistic" type of pentecostal church while the older ones were of the "Methodistic"
type.[21]

The formation of the Assemblies of God was of the greatest importance to the future development of the pentecostal
movement. It represented the end of a notable experiment in
interracial church development. After 1914 the Church of
God in Christ became exclusively black while the Assemblies
of God continued as a predominantly white church. It also
ended the period of doctrinal unity which had existed from
1906. After 1914 the pentecostal movement was to continue
about equally divided between "holiness" advocates of the
"second work" and "assembly" advocates of the "finished
work." Because of this doctrinal variation, all hope was
ended of a merger of all pentecostals into one body. Since
the delegates to the Hot Springs Council had come from all
sections of the United States, the new church was from the
beginning one of the largest pentecostal denominations in the
country and therefore destined to wield a large influence on
the rest of the movement.

Despite its auspicious beginnings, the young Assemblies of
God Church was soon wracked by a "new issue" that threatened to destroy it in its infancy. This issue became known as
the "Jesus only" or "pentecostal unitarian" question and,

[21] *Word and Witness*, March 20, 1914, pp. 2, 3; April 20, 1914, p. 1;
May 20, 1914, pp. 1-3; *The Combined Minutes of the General Council
of the Assemblies of God*, April 2-12, 1914, pp. 4-8. M. M. Pinson,
"The Finished Work of Calvary," *The Pentecostal Evangel*, April 5,
1964, pp. 7, 26-27.

like the parent movement, it had its origins in Los Angeles. The occasion for this new "revelation" was a "world-wide" pentecostal camp meeting held in the spring of 1913 with hundreds of preachers from across the continent in attendance. The first mention of the doctrine, which was to shake the pentecostal movement from coast to coast, came during a baptismal service outside the large camp-meeting tent. The speaker, R. E. McAlister, casually mentioned that "the apostles invariably baptized their converts once in the name of Jesus Christ" and "that the words Father, Son, and Holy Ghost were never used in Christian baptism." Upon hearing these words, "a shudder swept the preachers on the platform," and one preacher even mounted the platform to warn McAlister to refrain from preaching that doctrine or it would "associate the camp with a Dr. Sykes who so baptized." Unknowingly, evangelist McAlister had fired a shot that would resound throughout the movement within a year.[22]

Others hearing McAlister reacted differently to his theory. One preacher, John G. Scheppe, "spent the night in prayer" and toward morning "was given a glimpse of the power of the name of Jesus." Awakening the campers, he ran through the camp shouting about his discovery. The following day the campers "searched the Scriptures" concerning the "name of Jesus." Deeply impressed by these happenings was one Frank J. Ewart, who began to discuss the question of baptism "in Jesus' name" with McAlister. Ewart, a native of Australia, had come to Los Angeles by way of Canada and had entered the Baptist ministry. An intense and fearless man, he had defied his church by accepting the pentecostal doctrine in Portland, Oregon, in 1908. Expelled from the Baptist Church, he had come to Los Angeles to become an assistant to William Durham in his last pastorate. Upon Durham's death, Ewart succeeded him as pastor of the pentecostal church on the corner of Seventh and Los Angeles Streets. By 1913, Ewart was one of the leading figures of the West Coast pentecostal movement.[23]

22 Fred J. Foster, *Think It Not Strange, A History of the Oneness Movement* (St. Louis, 1965), pp. 9, 51, 52; Ewart, *The Phenomenon of Pentecost*, pp. 75-77.

23 Ewart, *The Phenomenon of Pentecost*, pp. 6-7; Foster, *Think It Not Strange*, p. 43.

Ewart then spent a year formulating his new doctrine before preaching his first "Jesus Only" sermon in Belvedere, just outside Los Angeles, in 1914. According to Ewart's view there was only one personality in the Godhead—Jesus Christ—the terms "Father" and "Holy Spirit" being only "titles" used to designate various aspects of Christ's person. Therefore the idea of a "trinity" was a mistake which had been foisted on the church by the Bishop of Rome at the Council of Nicea in A.D. 325. Consequently, anyone who was baptized in the name of "the Father, the Son, and the Holy Ghost," was not truly baptized at all and was in error. One of Ewart's first converts was Glenn A. Cook, an Azusa Street veteran who had first preached the pentecostal message to Mason's Church of God in Christ in Memphis in 1907. To correct this historical oversight, Ewart and Cook set up a tank inside a tent and rebaptized themselves "in the name of Jesus" on April 15, 1914. Following their rebaptism they began a determined campaign to reconvert and rebaptize the entire pentecostal movement into their new "oneness" belief. Soon Ewart began spreading the message around the nation through a periodical he edited entitled *Meat in Due Season*. In a short time the story of the "Jesus only" or "oneness" belief had crossed the nation much as the Azusa Street story had done nine years before.[24]

One very important factor in the spread of the "oneness" doctrine was an Eastern preaching tour taken by Cook in 1915. Visiting the Assemblies of God Church of G. T. Haywood in Indianapolis, he converted this leading Negro pastor, rebaptizing him along with 465 followers according to the new formula. The news of Haywood's defection caused consternation among the Assemblies of God leaders, since Haywood pastored one of the largest churches in this movement and was their leading Negro preacher. By June 1915, Bell, the head of the church, and other leaders were so alarmed that a special meeting of church officials was called in Little Rock,

[24] Ewart, *The Phenomenon of Pentecost,* pp. 50-51; Nichols, *Pentecostalism,* pp. 90, 91; Gordon F. Atter, *The Third Force* (Peterborough, Ontario, 1962), pp. 91-93. The pentecostal unitarians accept the term "oneness" but reject the appellation "Jesus Only," the name given by other pentecostals. Members generally prefer to be known as the "Jesus Name" movement.

Arkansas, to combat this new "heresy." For some weeks thereafter Bell published several articles in *Word and Witness*, now the official periodical of the Assemblies of God Church, denouncing the unitarian concept and defending the Trinity. But Bell's opposition was short-lived. In a camp meeting at Jackson, Tennessee, hosted by H. G. Rodgers, both Bell and Rodgers shocked the denomination by accepting the "Jesus Name" theory and submitting to rebaptism by a visiting "oneness" preacher named L. V. Roberts. After Bell's and Rodger's defection the "new issue" became "the issue" in the Assemblies of God Church. For the next year the new doctrine spread, "leaping from church to church and assembly to assembly" until it seemed that the entire denomination would be engulfed by the new view. The rebaptism of H. H. Goss in August and McAlister, whose preaching sparked the movement in Los Angeles in November, seemed ominous to trinitarian partisans.[25]

By the end of 1915 this controversy, so ancient in its origins, proliferated in the ranks of the pentecostal movement, threatening to take it over completely. Greatest resistance to the doctrine was met in the Southeastern states where the Churches of God and the Pentecostal Holiness Churches, with their strong holiness backgrounds, were largely undisturbed by the controversy.[26] From the beginning of the "oneness" movement in 1913, there were leaders in the newly formed Assemblies of God who sternly opposed it. The youthful General Secretary of the denomination, J. Roswell Flower, and John W. Welch, a member of the "Executive Presbytery," organized a resistance movement and rallied the trinitarians for a last-ditch stand. To the Third

25 See *Word and Witness*, May 1915, p. 4; *The Weekly Evangel*, June 5, 1915, pp. 1-3; July 3, 1915, p. 1; July 17, 1915, p. 1; August 14, 1915, p. 1; September 15, 1915, pp. 1-2; Foster, *Think It Not Strange*, pp. 54-57; Ewart, *The Phenomenon of Pentecost*, pp. 99-100; Brumback, *Suddenly from Heaven*, pp. 191-210; Winehouse, *The Assemblies of God*, pp. 43-46.

26 *The Church of God Evangel*, May 26, 1923, p. 1; December 14, 1929, p. 1; December 5, 1936, p. 3; August 23, 1947, pp. 3-13. *The Pentecostal Holiness Advocate*, September 6, 1917, p. 10; May 2, 1918, p. 3; Campbell's *Pentecostal Holiness Church* and Conn's *Like a Mighty Army* make no reference to the controversy.

General Council of the Assemblies of God, which met in St. Louis in October 1915, unitarians and trinitarians both sent large delegations, each hoping to win the church to its side. Although dissension was strong, the council adopted doctrinal statements adverse to the unitarian view. The delegates then adjourned the meeting with great apprehension, knowing that the issue would be settled finally in the Fourth General Council which was to meet the following year.[27]

This General Council, which met in October 1916 in St. Louis, became the historic meeting that finally settled the place of the unitarians in the pentecostal movement. In the months preceding the council meeting the controversy had become acute, with every church and preacher forced to take a stand on the "new issue." Charges of "Sabellianism" and "oneism" were countered with accusations of "three-Godism" and "Popish slavery." The trinitarians were able with the help of Flower, Welch, and Pinson to gain the advantage before the council gathered. A decisive stroke was the winning of Bell, still the most powerful man in the church, back to the trinitarian view. By the time the council convened in October it was apparent that the trinitarians were in complete control of the church. Although the young denomination had vowed never to adopt a formal creed, a committee was appointed to prepare a "Statement of Fundamental Truths" to guide the church in the future. Members of both factions listened as the committee read its report a few days later, a strongly trinitarian document which declared the propriety of calling the Godhead a "trinity or as one Being of three persons." The unitarians, seeing that they had failed to win the argument, left the meeting in disgust and made plans to meet later to form their own sect. In the end, the eighteen-month-old Assemblies of God denomination lost 156 preachers out of 585 and over one hundred congregations, but the "sad new issue" was settled. After this climactic meeting it was apparent that the Assemblies of

[27] *The Weekly Evangel,* July 3, 1915, p. 1; July 17, 1915, p. 1; *Minutes of the General Council of the Assemblies of God,* October 1915, pp. 4-6, 8. See Brumback, *Suddenly from Heaven,* pp. 194-197; and Foster, *Think It Not Strange,* pp. 65-67, for contrasting views of the council.

God, and with them the majority of all pentecostals, would remain trinitarian.[28]

This "new issue" among pentecostals was confined to the North American continent. England, Scandinavia, and the other European nations were largely untouched by the controversy. The thriving national pentecostal groups in Latin America also remained untouched by the issue. The pentecostal unitarians were thus entirely an American phenomenon, with their greatest strength in the Middle and Far West.[29]

After failing to capture the older pentecostal denominations, the unitarians decided to establish their own separate denomination. Led by the Negro minister, Haywood of Indianapolis, most of them joined in forming the "Pentecostal Assemblies of the World" in a convention in Indianapolis later in the year. With roughly equal numbers of white and Negro ministers and churches, the new group was completely interracial in character. Its unitarian beliefs were written into its statement of faith and published in the new church Manual. A requirement for baptism was that the formula contain the words "in the Name of the Lord Jesus Christ."[30]

The Pentecostal Assemblies of the World continued as an interracial church until 1924 when the white ministers withdrew to form a separate white denomination, explaining that the "mixture of races prevented the effective evangelization of the world." Accordingly, later in the year a group called the "Pentecostal Ministerial Alliance" was formed, an organization exercising authority over its ministerial members but not over churches. In a short time this body developed into a

[28] *Minutes of the General Council of the Assemblies of God,* October 1916, pp. 8, 10-13; *The Weekly Evangel,* March 4, 1916, p. 6; October 21, 1916, pp. 4-5, 8; November 25, 1916, p. 8. Also see *The Latter Rain Evangel,* May 1915, pp. 2-9; Foster, *Think It Not Strange,* p. 68; Winehouse, *The Assemblies of God,* pp. 202-206; and Carl Brumback, *God in Three Persons* (Cleveland, Tennessee, 1959), pp. 11-17ff.

[29] Gee, *The Pentecostal Movement,* pp. 124, 125.

[30] Everett Leroy Moore, "Handbook of Pentecostal Denominations in the United States" (Unpublished Master's thesis at Pasadena College of Religion, Pasadena, California, 1954), pp. 242-252.

formal denomination known as the "Pentecostal Church, Incorporated."[31]

Yet another "oneness" church was organized in 1913 called the "Pentecostal Assemblies of Jesus Christ." This group developed separately from the others and by 1936 had 16,000 members in 245 churches. These congregations were located in twenty-seven states, with their greatest concentration being in Illinois, Louisiana, and Texas. The "Pentecostal Church, Incorporated" had in that same year 168 churches and 9,681 members in twenty-three states.[32] Since these two groups were identical in doctrine and were located in practically the same territory, a move for merger gained strength through the following decade. This move resulted in a union of the two denominations in a special General Conference called for this purpose in St. Louis in 1945. The newly constituted group adopted the name "The United Pentecostal Church," becoming by merger the largest unitarian pentecostal denomination in the United States.[33]

In addition to the older and larger denominations, several smaller "oneness" groups were formed in the years after 1916, developing separately from the other churches. In 1916, the "Apostolic Overcoming Holy Church of God" was founded by the Reverend W. T. Phillips, a Negro Methodist preacher. Originating in Mobile, Alabama, this group adopted a unitarian statement of faith, but operated without close ties with the rest of the pentecostal denominations. By 1965 this body claimed a total membership of 75,000 in 300 churches. Most of its congregations were located in Alabama, Illinois, Kentucky, Oklahoma, and Texas.[34]

[31] *Ibid.*, p. 254; Kendrick, *The Promise Fulfilled*, pp. 172, 173; Foster, *Think It Not Strange*, pp. 73-78, indicates that the schism was caused by the indignation of Northern Negro ministers at the segregation policies of the Southern white members.

[32] *Religious Bodies: 1936* (Washington: United States Government Printing Office, 1941), II, ii, 1323, 1330.

[33] Moore, "Handbook of Pentecostal Denominations"; Elmer T. Clark, *Small Sects in America* (New York, 1956), p. 170; Kendrick, *The Promise Fulfilled*, p. 173; Foster, *Think It Not Strange*, pp. 78-81. The "Pentecostal Assemblies of the World" continued to function as the largest Negro unitarian group in the nation.

[34] Landis, *Yearbook of American Churches, 1965*, pp. 14, 15; Moore, "Handbook of Pentecostal Denominations," pp. 269-281.

Another large "oneness" group was the "Church of Our Lord Jesus Christ of the Apostolic Faith," another Negro group, which was founded by R. C. Lawson in Columbus, Ohio, in 1919. The headquarters of this group was moved to New York City early in its history. With churches in twenty-seven states, this denomination by 1954 claimed to have 45,000 members in 155 churches. The membership claims of this church, along with those of some of the other Negro groups, may be excessive, although it is possible that those denominations serve vast numbers in urban ghettos where Negroes are concentrated in heavily populated districts.[35]

Other smaller splinter groups of these churches were founded after 1916 for which information and statistics are either lacking or difficult to obtain. Among these are: the Full Salvation Union, founded in 1934 in Lansing, Michigan, by James F. Andrews; the Apostolic Church, founded by the Reverend R. L. Blankenship in Texas in 1945; and the "Jesus Church," founded by Sam Officer in Cleveland, Tennessee, in 1953.[36] In addition to these groups, there sprang up hundreds of independent congregations throughout the United States which held to the unitarian view, but which did not affiliate themselves with any nationally organized denomination. It would be impossible to gather complete and accurate information on these churches, many of which practice such oddities as snake-handling and free love. These fringe groups were generally rejected by the more orthodox pentecostals, who regarded them as heretics. It has generally been estimated by pentecostal leaders that the independent congregations approximated the number of the organized ones. A conservative estimate of the total number of pentecostal unitarians in the United States in 1964 was placed at 500,000, over half of whom were Negroes.[37]

The pentecostal unitarians have generally been considered

35 Mead, *Handbook of Denominations, 1965*, p. 86.

36 Moore, "Handbook of Pentecostal Denominations," pp. 290-313. Officer's "Jesus Church" is the only "oneness" group to issue from the holiness-pentecostal tradition, all the others having come from the "finished work" wing of pentecostalism.

37 Morton T. Kelsey, *Tongue Speaking* (New York, 1964), pp. 242-243.

to be an integral part of the pentecostal movement as a whole, although the trinitarian groups tended to view them as simple, ignorant, innocent, but deluded people. As of 1965, the "Jesus only" denominations were not admitted to membership in the "Pentecostal Fellowship of North America," an ecumenical organization that consisted of sixteen of the "respectable" pentecostal denominations. However, when pentecostal leaders have cited statistics to show the overall size and growth of the movement, the unitarian groups have always been included.

By the middle of the twentieth century, observers both within and outside of the pentecostal movement began to see a trend among the unitarians toward a more trinitarian view of the Deity. Some have predicted that in time they will be wholly within the fold of traditional trinitarian Protestantism. Non-pentecostals have tended to see little difference between the trinitarian and unitarian branches of the pentecostal movement, since both were intensely evangelical. The pentecostal "unitarians" also have always made a sharp distinction between themselves and the older Unitarian-Universalist movement which has no connection whatever with the pentecostal groups.[38]

The advent of the "oneness" unitarian controversy caused other pentecostal groups to reassess their doctrinal stand concerning the Trinity. In 1917 the Pentecostal Holiness Church added a paragraph to its *Discipline* which strongly supported the traditional trinitarian view. This was significant since previous editions of the *Discipline* after 1900 had failed to mention the Trinity at all. For several years following 1916 the *Advocate* sternly opposed pentecostal people who had "run wild after that which was new and sensational." In 1917 the "heresies" which had plagued pentecostalism were listed by the Pentecostal Holiness Church as "finished work, one name baptism, rejection of the Trinity, anti-organization . . . and many other preposterous nonsensical sensations. . . ." It was obvious by such articles as these that the

[38] *Ibid.*, pp. 85, 86; Kendrick, *The Promise Fulfilled*, p. 4; M. J. Wolff, "We Are Not Unitarians," *The Pentecostal Herald*, March 1967, p. 5.

pentecostal movement suffered serious convulsions in its early years.[39]

The conflict between the "three God people" and the "Jesus only" pentecostals continued, especially among the independent congregations. In the late 1940's Archie Robertson found congregations in rural Tennessee that were bitterly divided over the issue. Even among snake-handling partisans in the Appalachian Mountains "cross-ups" persisted into the 1950's over "baptism in one or three names." By this time, however, the major pentecostal denominations had firmly institutionalized their positions as either trinitarian or unitarian.[40]

By 1920 the great theological controversies which formed the major cleavages within the pentecostal movement had been fought out and settled along the general lines that exist today. Although minor questions of church government and interchurch relations caused problems in the ensuing years, the "finished work" and "Jesus only" questions emerged as the primary issues that divided the movement. The Southern pentecostal groups maintained a surprising solidarity in doctrine and polity throughout these controversies. The three major Southern churches—Tomlinson's Church of God, Mason's Church of God in Christ, and King's Pentecostal Holiness Church—rejected both questions, remaining in the Wesleyan "second work" and the trinitarian traditions. Their theologies never varied from that taught in the Azusa Street revival. Seymour also rejected the "finished work" and "Jesus only" theories, as did Parham, the doctrinal father of the entire movement.

In the end, the pentecostal movement split into equal factions over the question of sanctification with about one-half of the churches and members siding with the "finished work" partisans and the other half maintaining the traditional Wesleyan "second work" view. About one-fourth of all the pentecostals in the United States eventually sided with

39 *The Pentecostal Holiness Discipline, 1917*, pp. 5-14, 17-18; *The Pentecostal Holiness Advocate*, September 6, 1917, p. 10; May 2, 1918, p. 3.

40 Archie Robertson, *That Old-Time Religion* (Boston, 1950), p. 173.

the unitarian faction. These proportions have tended to remain about the same since 1920.[41]

Like all new religious movements, the pentecostal movement experienced the twin challenges of criticism from without and controversy from within during its formative period. Both challenges resulted in a strengthening and diversifying of the movement. Criticism from the outside only succeeded in consolidating it, as pentecostal converts rose to defend their new-found theology through sermons and publications.

Controversy from within the movement also succeeded in expanding the scope of pentecostalism. Each new doctrinal variation produced new denominations, which in turn spawned new families of denominations through further schisms. The outcome of these controversies was the creation of a national movement composed of many submovements. Pentecostalism succeeded in creating at least twenty-five separate denominations within fourteen years. In fact, by the middle of the twentieth century, some Protestant observers were referring to pentecostalism as the "Third Force in Christendom" rather than being only another cluster of new denominations arising in the traditional manner of the past.[42]

[41] The assertion that only "a few diehards" who are "inconsequential" retained the second work theory of sanctification is obviously not based on fact since 50 percent of all pentecostals can still be classified thus. See Ewart, *The Phenomenon of Pentecost*, p. 74; and James S. Tinney, "A Wesleyan-Pentecostal Appraisal of the Charismatic Movement," *The Pentecostal Holiness Advocate*, January 7, 1967, pp. 4-10.

[42] Henry P. Van Dusen, "Third Force in Christendom," *Life*, June 9, 1958, pp. 113-124; Gordon Atter, *The Third Force* (Peterborough, Ontario, 1962), pp. 1-9, *passim;* McCandlish Phillips, "And There Appeared to Them Tongues of Fire," *The Saturday Evening Post*, May 16, 1964, p. 31.

Chapter Eight

THE NEGRO
PENTECOSTALS

Glory to God! Makes me feel good to see White and
Colored praisin' God together.

—Archie Robertson,
That Old-Time Religion

A little-known aspect of the modern pentecostal movement is the important role Negroes have played in its growth
and development from the beginning. This striking interracial
phenomenon occurred in the very years of America's most
racist period, those from 1890 to 1920. In an age of Social
Darwinism, Jim Crowism, and general white supremacy, the
fact that Negroes and whites worshipped together in virtual
equality among the pentecostals was a significant exception
to prevailing racial attitudes. Even more significant is the fact
that this interracial accord took place among the very groups
that have traditionally been most at odds, the poor whites
and the poor blacks.

In the period when most holiness and pentecostal groups
were forming into recognizable denominational bodies, the
racial lines were often very indistinct, with Negroes serving as
officials, preachers, and church members. Only after the
various movements began to coalesce into formal denominations did divisions occur along racial lines. The reasons for
these later separations on the basis of race may be found in
the existing pattern of race relations in the United States
when the pentecostal movement began in 1906. As a glaring

exception to the social pattern of the nation, and particularly of the South, the interracial pentecostal groups were subjected to great social pressure to conform to the pattern of segregation which with the beginning of the twentieth century dominated most aspects of American life.[1]

By 1900 the racial lines in American religious life had already been clearly drawn by the harsh realities of the post-Civil War era. The freeing of the slaves had caused a grand division of Protestantism along racial lines. One of the most cherished dreams of the Negro slave was to have his own church where he could worship in the manner most congenial to his nature. With the end of the war came freedom from white surveillance of the Negro worship services which had been one of the slaveholders' major concerns. Although worship services continued to be integrated immediately after 1865, deep problems soon arose which led to all-white and all-Negro denominations. Increasingly the whites began to resent the presence of large numbers of Negroes in their churches, which in many cases formed a large majority of the local congregations. On their part, the Negroes resented white domination of the services. Moreover, the Negroes desired to worship in their own more emotional manner under the direction of their own ministers. Consequently, several all-Negro denominations were formed in the years following the Civil War. In 1870 the Colored Methodist Episcopal Church was founded as a schism from the Methodist Episcopal Church, South. Ten years later the National Baptist Convention was organized. The Primitive and Free-Will Baptists, along with the Cumberland Presbyterians, also experienced similar divisions. This trend continued until reports showed that by 1929, 90 percent of all Negro Christians belonged to churches restricted to their own race.[2]

The holiness movement in America paralleled these racial developments in time. The National Holiness Association was

[1] Richard Hofstadter, *Social Darwinism in American Thought* (Philadelphia, 1945), pp. 86-102, 146-173.

[2] Richard H. Niebuhr, *The Social Sources of Denominationalism* (Hamden, Connecticut, 1929), pp. 239-263; W. D. Weatherford, *The American Churches and the Negro* (Boston, 1957), pp. 25-222; Gross Alexander, *History of the Methodist Episcopal Church, South*, pp. 133-140.

founded in 1867, when the movement for racial separation of the churches was beginning. The decade of the 1890's saw the founding of several holiness denominations in all parts of the nation. Unfortunately, this decade witnessed the beginnings of Negro disfranchisement in the South and of Jim Crow segregation throughout most of the United States. Because of the racial attitudes of the times, the holiness movement divided with few exceptions along racial lines.

Of the numerous holiness denominations that were formed, two were Negro groups that would later become pentecostal. The first was the "United Holy Church," which began in 1886 near Wilmington, North Carolina, in the town of Method. Other small bodies joined this church until 1902, when the formal organization of the denomination was effected with the help of W. H. Fulford, a Negro Elder of the Fire-Baptized Holiness Church. This church generally followed the lead of the white holiness churches of North Carolina, adopting after 1906 a statement of faith which placed the group in the pentecostal family. This move evidently was taken as a result of Cashwell's revival in Dunn in 1906-1907. Although identical in doctrine with the Pentecostal Holiness Church and the Church of God, the United Holy Church developed separately with a minimum of contact with its white sister denominations.[3]

The church which was destined to become the largest Negro body of either the holiness or pentecostal movements was the Church of God in Christ. As has already been noted, this church had its origins in Mississippi, Tennessee, and Arkansas in 1897. Although the founders, Jones and Mason, had been Baptists, they adopted the Wesleyan view of sanctification. After Mason's trip to the Azusa Street revival in Los Angeles in 1907, the church suffered a division over the newly arrived pentecostal doctrine. With the withdrawal of Jones and the non-pentecostal faction, Mason became the undisputed leader of the church, which grew rapidly after 1907. At the time of Mason's death in 1963, his denomi-

---

[3] H. L. Fisher, *History of the United Holy Church of America* (n.p., n.d.), pp. 1-8. In 1949 representatives of this group attended the General Conference of the Pentecostal Holiness Church, but no affiliation was effected. See the *Minutes of the Eleventh General Conference of the Pentecostal Holiness Church, 1949*, p. 27.

nation numbered over 400,000 members in the United States.

Although the United Holy Church and the Church of God in Christ were functioning denominations in 1906, neither played a direct role in the beginning of the pentecostal revival at Azusa Street. As has been seen, the leading figure in the Azusa Street meeting was Seymour, a Negro, who belonged to Parham's Apostolic Faith Movement with headquarters in Baxter Springs, Kansas. That the one outstanding personality in bringing about the pentecostal revival in Los Angeles was a Negro is a fact of extreme importance to pentecostals of all races. All pentecostals acknowledge their debt to Seymour, although few are willing to recognize him as the "founder" of the movement. Negro pentecostals refer to him as the "Apostle and Pioneer" of the movement and often attempt to demonstrate that the pentecostal movement began as a Negro phenomenon, later accepted by whites.[4]

Despite some controversy over the matter, it can safely be said that Parham and Seymour share roughly equal positions as founders of modern pentecostalism. Parham laid the doctrinal foundations of the movement, while Seymour served as the catalytic agent for its popularization. In this sense, the early pentecostal movement could be classed as neither "Negro" nor "white," but as interracial.

There can be no doubt that in its early stages the pentecostal movement was completely interracial. The Azusa Street meeting was conducted on the basis of complete racial equality. Pentecostals point out that just as the first Pentecost recorded in Acts 2:1-11 included "men out of every nation under heaven," the modern "pentecost" at Los Angeles included people of every racial background. Participants in the meeting reported that "Negroes, whites, Mexicans, Italians, Chinese, Russians, Indians," and other ethnic groups mingled without apparent prejudice on account of racial origins. The fact that Cashwell was forced to reform his racial prejudices after arriving at the Azusa Street Mission indicates that the trend in early pentecostal services was toward racial unity in contrast to the segregationist trends of

4 Fidler, "Historical Review," pp. 3, 4; Bloch-Hoell, *The Pentecostal Movement*, pp. 42-53.

the times. Photographs of the leaders of the Azusa Street Mission taken in 1907 show whites and Negroes united in the operation of the church without any apparent distinctions on account of race.[5]

This interracial period was to continue during the years from 1906 to 1924 when the last separation over the issue of race occurred. The Church of God in Christ played a unique role from 1907 to 1914 by giving ordination to hundreds of white ministers of independent congregations, as has been observed. During these years the only organized pentecostal denominations were the Church of God in Christ, the Church of God (Cleveland, Tennessee), and the Pentecostal Holiness Church. Of these, only Mason's was legally incorporated, this having been done in Memphis in 1897. Since most white pentecostal churches outside the South were independent and had no recognized ecclesiastical body to ordain their ministers, they suffered by their inability to obtain bonding for performing marriages and other ministerial duties. They also were not able to obtain reduced clergy rates on the railroads. Since the Church of God in Christ was an incorporated religious denomination, scores of white ministers sought ordination at the hands of Mason. Large numbers of white ministers, therefore, were to obtain ministerial credentials carrying the name of the Church of God in Christ. One group in Alabama and Texas eventually made an agreement with Mason in 1912 to use the name of his church, but to issue ministerial credentials signed by their own leaders. The white leaders of this group were H. A. Goss, D. C. O. Opperman, H. G. Rodgers, and A. C. Collins. Although technically using the name of the Church of God in Christ, these white ministers were joined to Mason's group by only a "gentleman's agreement" with the understanding that credentials would not be given to any who were "untrustworthy."[6]

[5] A picture in *The International Outlook*, January-March 1963, p. 4, shows three Negroes and eight whites who lived together in the Mission and supervised its activities. Also see Nichols, *Pentecostalism*, pp. 61-62; Brumback, *Suddenly from Heaven*, pp. 84-85; Campbell, *The Pentecostal Holiness Church*, pp. 240-242; Bartleman, *How "Pentecost" Came to Los Angeles*, p. 29.

[6] Ethel A. Goss, *Winds of God* (New York, 1958), p. 163; Flower, "History of the Assemblies of God," pp. 16-19.

By 1914 these white ministers became dissatisfied with this arrangement and called for a convention of pentecostal leaders to meet in Hot Springs, Arkansas. The purpose of this convention was the formation of a national pentecostal denomination which would include all the white ministers and churches. Invitations were sent to King of the Pentecostal Holiness Church and to Tomlinson of the Church of God, but they refused to attend because of the "finished work" theory of sanctification that was openly espoused by most of the independent ministers who formed the majority of the Hot Springs delegates. As has already been seen, this Hot Springs Convention resulted in the formation of the Assembly of God denomination, which within ten years became the largest pentecostal denomination in the United States. As far as is known, no Negroes were invited to the convention.[7]

With the advent of the "oneness" issue in 1914, the young Assemblies of God group was wracked by the most serious controversy of its history. In the end this "new issue" came to have deep racial overtones, resulting in the formation of one of the most fully interracial church bodies in the United States. The father of the "pentecostal unitarian" movement was a white minister from Los Angeles, Frank J. Ewart. As has been seen, his movement for rebaptism "in Jesus name" swept over the pentecostal movement from 1914 to 1916. Of the hundreds of pentecostal ministers who accepted rebaptism according to Ewart's formula, none was more important in the long run than the Negro pastor from Indianapolis, G. T. Haywood. This man had founded one of the largest congregations in the new Assembly of God organization. Although composed of a majority of Negroes, his church was interracial. A powerful speaker, Haywood exercised a great influence in the councils of the church.

7 Brumback, *Suddenly from Heaven*, pp. 151-161; Kendrick, *The Promise Fulfilled*, pp. 73-93; Nichols, *Pentecostalism*, pp. 108-114. Although race was not mentioned as a basis for forming the Assemblies of God group, it is evident from the record that white ministers using credentials from Mason's Church of God in Christ were dissatisfied with the arrangement. Although the "Call" issued in Bell's *Word and Witness* for the Hot Springs Convention included "all the Churches of God in Christ," none of Mason's group appeared. See Brumback, *Suddenly from Heaven*, p. 157; and *The Pentecostal Evangel*, April 1964, pp. 1-32.

When Cook, one of Ewart's converts, took his fateful Eastern tour from Los Angeles in 1914, one of his first stops, it will be recalled, was at Haywood's church in Indianapolis. One Assembly of God official, J. Roswell Flower, became disturbed upon hearing of Cook's doctrine and attempted to prevent his progress by warning pastors of his coming. Writing Haywood in alarm after hearing Cook in St. Louis, Flower warned him that the touring evangelist was coming to his city "with an erroneous doctrine." Haywood answered, "Your warning came too late. I have already accepted the message and have been baptized." With the winning of Haywood, many Negro pentecostals were destined to become pentecostal unitarians.[8]

When the issue reached a climax in the 1916 General Council of the Assemblies of God, it has been observed how the trinitarian party of the denomination forced the adoption of a strongly worded trinitarian statement and that a large minority of dissenting "Jesus Name" ministers thereupon withdrew from the church to form a new group based on unitarian principles. The leader of these dissenters was Haywood, his large congregation in Indianapolis becoming a focal point for the new movement. In January 1916, the dissenters met in Eureka Springs, Arkansas, to effect a new denomination which could issue ministerial credentials. One factor adding urgency was the threat posed by the federal military draft law to young ministers of draft age. Therefore, a hastily formed group called "The General Assembly of the Apostolic Churches" was created with former Assembly of God leaders Opperman and Goss the top officials.[9]

This new organization soon found that it could not secure government recognition, and with World War I threatening, the group searched for an incorporated church with which they could merge. Such a group was found on the West Coast which used the name "Pentecostal Assemblies of the World." Founded in 1914 by a "oneness" minister named Frazier, it already had the prized government recognition. In late 1917 a merger was consummated between these two groups and the name "Pentecostal Assemblies of the World" was adopted

[8] Foster, *Think It Not Strange*, p. 54.
[9] *Ibid.*, p. 73.

to designate the entire church. The chairman of the newly merged denomination was a white man, C. W. Doak, and the secretary was the Negro, Haywood.[10]

For nine years the Pentecostal Assemblies of the World operated as a completely interracial church with roughly equal numbers of Negroes and whites serving as both officers and members. One participant, S. C. McLain, a Southern white minister, described this interracial period as a "unique fellowship." "Throughout the north and east," he said, "there seemed to be very little, if any, race prejudice. I, being southern born, thought it a miracle that I could sit in a service by a colored saint of God and worship, or eat at a great camp table, and forget I was eating beside a colored saint. But in spirit and truth God was worshipped in love and harmony." A great problem existed, however, in the Southern states because "ministers laboring in the South had to conform to law and customs."[11]

In the end it was the Southern system of segregation that destroyed the fellowship of the races and split the church along racial lines. Due to Southern laws during the time of this fellowship, no racially integrated meetings could be held below the Mason-Dixon Line because of Jim Crow laws governing convention and hotel facilities. Therefore from 1916 to 1924 all church conventions were held in Northern cities. Another complication was the fact that most of the Northern ministers were Negroes while most of the Southern ones were whites. With the church conventions held in the North, fewer Southerners could attend and consequently were outvoted on most vital issues. When the Southerners insisted on a convention in a Southern city, "a spirit of agitation began to arise" between the Negroes and the whites. A further complication arose in 1921 when the white ministers conducted a "Southern Bible Conference" in Little Rock that was notable because of the absence of any Negro participants. This move appeared ominous to Haywood and the other Negro ministers.[12]

The climax of the problem came at the General Confer-

10 *Ibid.*, p. 74.

11 *Ibid.*

12 *Ibid.*, pp. 75-76.

ence of the Church that met in St. Louis in 1924. Meeting early in the week, the whites held a separate conclave which they called "a continuation of the Southern Bible Conference." This was the final wedge that drove the races apart. In an "atmosphere of tension," the white ministers deserted the main hall of the conference when it convened and conducted an *ad hoc* meeting in the basement of the church. Here it was decided that the white ministers would withdraw from the denomination and leave the church under the direction of Haywood, who would henceforth head an all-Negro communion. The white ministers would then organize "another association to meet the needs of the South." Those leaving the church met later and formed the all-white "Pentecostal Ministerial Alliance" in Jackson, Tennessee, in February 1925. Thus ended a striking and unique period of interracial accord.[13]

The two major Southern white pentecostal denominations, the Church of God and the Pentecostal Holiness Church, also began as interracial communions. The Church of God had Negro members in its fellowship from its earliest days. As the church expanded into several Southern states after 1906, the problem of the Negroes' status in the church grew proportionately. By 1912 Tomlinson faced the problem of ordaining Negro clergymen and fitting them into the church. Although Tomlinson was an Indiana Quaker by upbringing, he bowed to the Southern system to solve his problem. On June 4, 1912, he wrote:

> Had a conference yesterday to consider the question of ordaining Edmund Barr (colored) and setting the colored people off to work among themselves on account of the race prejudice in the South.[14]

As the Church of God continued to develop, the Negro churches began to demand more self-government and independence from the white-dominated General Assembly. In 1926 a committee of Negro ministers appeared before the General Assembly and requested the privilege of conducting their own separate General Assembly. This right was granted

[13] *Ibid.*, p. 76; see Nichols, *Pentecostalism*, pp. 116-119.
[14] Tomlinson, "A Journal of Happenings," June 4, 1912.

to the Negro constituency with a provision which required that the "General Overseer" of the Negro churches always be a white man. This arrangement continued to be the Negro policy of the Church of God until 1966. This church is the only predominantly white pentecostal denomination that maintained a Negro branch as an integral, yet separated, part of the church.[15]

The Pentecostal Holiness Church also had a Negro branch in its early years. The Fire-Baptized Holiness Church, which later merged with the Pentecostal Holiness Church, had a Negro at its founding convention in Anderson, South Carolina, in 1898. This Negro minister, W. E. Fuller, was a dynamic preacher who for several years served on the Executive Committee of the denomination. Most of his time was spent in organizing Negro congregations. This he did with great success. In 1904 he claimed five hundred "conversions" while organizing four Negro congregations in South Carolina and Georgia. After ten years as full members of the Fire-Baptized Holiness Church, the Negroes held a separate convention in Anderson, South Carolina, in 1908. In this meeting the Negro churches voted to separate from the parent body and form their own denomination "because of criticism from the communities of the South against integrated church meetings." In 1926, this group voted to change its name to the "Fire-Baptized Holiness Church of God of the Americas." By 1959 this church had over 6,000 members in 60 churches and over 300 missions.[16]

Another Negro group separated from the Pentecostal Holiness Church in 1913. The churches forming this group had been a part of the Pentecostal Holiness Church in North Carolina before the 1911 merger with the Fire-Baptized Holiness Church. In the 1913 General Conference of the denomination which met in Toccoa, Georgia, the Negro churches requested through their delegates that they be separated from the main body of the church in order to "carry out a better

15 Conn, *Like a Mighty Army*, pp. 132, 182, 201-203; *Church of God Evangel*, November 15, 1919, p. 2.

16 *Discipline of the Fire-Baptized Holiness Church of God of the Americas, 1962* (Atlanta, Georgia), pp. 9-12; Bertha Teasley, personal interview with the author, September 12, 1963; Kendrick, *The Promise Fulfilled*, p. 4; W. E. Fuller, *Live Coals*, January 11, 1905, p. 2.

program" among their own people. They departed with the "good wishes" of the General Conference. The Negro Pentecostal Holiness Churches have remained quite small since their separation from the parent body in 1913, their churches being scattered throughout the Southeast.[17]

In addition to the foregoing Negro bodies, several other Negro pentecostal denominations sprang up in other sections of the United States outside the mainstream of the movement. Probably loosely organized, these churches are not included in the usual histories of the pentecostals. Some were creations of dominating men who built entire denominations around their personalities. Often their statistical reports were obviously exaggerated, as seen in the "National David Spiritual Temple of Christ Church Union," which claimed 40,000 members in only 47 churches in 1959.[18] Other churches in this category are the "Apostolic Overcoming Holy Church of God," the "Church of Our Lord Jesus Christ of the Apostolic Faith," and "Christ's Sanctified Holy Church, Colored." Some of these groups adopted names that were bewilderingly long and defied theological classification. One such group presented itself to the world with the fantastic name of "The House of God, The Holy Church of the Living God, The Pillar and Grounds of the Truth, House of Prayer for All People."[19]

Some Negro sects have been classified as pentecostal because of a seeming similarity in some practices of worship. Especially is this true of the sects which deified their founders, calling them "God," "Christ," "Daddy Grace," or "Father Divine." The most prominent of these are "Daddy Grace's House of Prayer" and "Father Divine's Peace Mission" with churches called "Heavens" in several large Northern cities. Although these groups often demonstrated charismatic or emotional phenomena which resembled pente-

---

[17] *Minutes of the Second General Convention of the Pentecostal Holiness Church, 1913* (Toccoa, Georgia), p. 5.

[18] Elmer T. Clark, *Small Sects in America* (New York, 1956), p. 119; Landis, *Yearbook of American Churches, 1965*, pp. 76-77.

[19] Clark, *Small Sects in America*, pp. 85-132, gives a compendium of these sects and their beliefs. Classification is extremely difficult because of a lack of literature in most groups, and because of chaotic statements in those with literature.

costal worship, they have never been recognized as part of the pentecostal movement as a whole.[20]

Probably the first "black supremacy" religious movement in America was the "Church of the Living God, Christian Workers for Fellowship," which began in Wrightsville, Arkansas, in 1889. Founded by William Christian, it continued into the twentieth century under the leadership of Christian's wife and later his son. According to the catechism of this church, Abraham, Isaac, Jacob, David, and Jesus were members of the Negro race. Quoting Scriptures for support, this document went on to say that "it is as natural to be black as the leopard to be spotted," although it was wrong to "make a difference between people because they are black."[21]

Added to all these sects are literally thousands of independent Negro pentecostal congregations that dot the major cities of America from coast to coast. With the mass migration of Negroes to the large cities, storefront versions of their home churches were created. By the 1960's it was impossible to investigate and properly classify these multifarious groups, which often carried names that defied description. Another result of the Northern Negro migration was the fact that in the 1960's the largest congregations of such "Southern" denominations as the Church of God in Christ, the United Holy Church, and the Fire-Baptized Holiness Church, were located in New York, Chicago, Detroit, and Philadelphia, rather than in the South.[22]

There are many reasons why Negroes have adopted the pentecostal religion in such great numbers. Some of them may be found in the nature of pentecostal worship, and others in the nature and condition of the Negro in the United States. In general, the emotional nature of pentecostal worship has always held a strong appeal to the Negro, who was already accustomed to highly charged modes of worship in the Baptist or Methodist churches from which he came.

20 *Ibid.*, pp. 122-127.

21 *Ibid.*, pp. 120-121; Landis, *Yearbook of American Churches, 1965*, p. 40. It is possible that the "Black Muslims" and other Negro supremacist groups received early inspiration from this movement.

22 *1960-61 Yearbook of the Church of God in Christ*, pp. 47-52, 64-68, 78-82, 88-90; *Discipline of the Fire-Baptized Holiness Church of the Americas*, pp. 13-21; Fisher, *The United Holy Church*, pp. 25-39.

DuBois' statement that the religious goal of the Negro was "to be mad with supernatural joy" seems to apply to most Negro Protestant churches, pentecostal and non-pentecostal alike.[23] When the traditional churches began to add more form and decorum to their services, the emotionally inclined Negro gravitated to the pentecostal churches. At least 80 percent of the members of Negro pentecostal churches came from other churches, particularly from Baptist and Methodist denominations.[24]

Once in the pentecostal fold, these members often criticized the "coldness" and "formality" of the older churches. However, in reality there has been little difference in manner of worship between the Negro pentecostals and the rest of Negro Protestantism with the exception of speaking in unknown tongues. In recent years, there has been a tendency for emotionalism to decline in the traditional Negro churches with a consequent exodus of members to pentecostal churches where they feel more "at home."[25]

Another attraction to the Negro is the fact that the pentecostal movement is essentially a religion of the socially disinherited and the economically underprivileged. For the most part, pentecostals come from the lower socio-economic levels of society and in many cases serve a class of people neglected by the larger, more traditional denominations. As the older churches became more middle class in constituency and in mentality, groups like the pentecostals held a strong appeal for the poverty-stricken masses who felt alienated within their own churches. In the early period of its history, the pentecostal movement was confined almost exclusively to the laboring classes of the nation. In the South the greatest growth occurred among the millhands in the cities and the sharecroppers in the rural areas.[26]

Since the Negro in the South, and indeed throughout the

[23] From *Souls of Black Folk*, quoted in Frederick Morgan Davenport, *Primitive Traits in Religious Revivals, A Study in Mental and Social Evolution* (New York, 1905), p. 54.

[24] Liston Pope, *Millhands and Preachers* (New Haven, 1942), p. 133.

[25] Ruby F. Johnson, *The Development of Negro Religion* (New York, 1954), pp. 81-132. See also Ruby Johnson, *The Religion of Negro Protestants* (New York, 1956), p. 142.

[26] Pope, *Millhands and Preachers*, p. 136.

entire nation, occupied the bottom rung of the social system, it was inevitable that large numbers would be drawn to pentecostalism, representing as it did the religion of the poor and underprivileged. Also contributing to the popularity of pentecostal religion was the fact that educational standards for the ministry were almost non-existent. The Negro "call to preach" continued to come, as Booker T. Washington described it, with the seeker "falling on the floor as if struck by a bullet." This emotional "call" led to an "oversupply" of ministers in most churches, an example of this tendency being a local church of two hundred members which reported a supply of eighteen "regular" preachers.[27] The low educational standards for the ministry among the pentecostals attracted many Negroes who felt that they would have a greater opportunity to preach there than in the older denominations.

Another attraction of pentecostalism to the Negro was the interracial character of the movement in its beginnings. With one of their own race playing a dominant part in the birth of the movement at Azusa Street, many Negroes thought the pentecostal movement to be primarily a Negro phenomenon. To spokesmen of the Church of God in Christ, the movement began as an interracial revival "first received and propagated by a colored man, Elder W. J. Seymour, and by a handful of other colored worshippers" in Los Angeles. This historic fact is a source of great pride to Negro pentecostals around the world.[28]

The eventual division of the movement into Negro and white branches, as has been seen, followed a pattern that had already been set by the older Protestant denominations before the beginning of the pentecostal movement. Although some Negroes accepted these divisions as normal and inevitable with some even requesting them, the majority felt that they were "sinful and embarrassing." In many cases the divisions were blamed on the racial "customs" and "prejudices" of the South, but never on the prejudices of the whites. It is probably safe to assume that the Negro pente-

27 Davenport, *Primitive Traits*, p. 56.
28 Editorial in *The International Outlook*, October-December 1963, p. 14.

costals as a whole resent the fact that the movement bowed to the pressures of the times and became divided. To some Negroes the "pentecostal problem" is the "cleavage of the races," which must be solved before the movement can "shake the world."[29]

The Negro pentecostals have turned their racial separateness to a distinct advantage in recent years in the conduct of their foreign missions programs. The Church of God in Christ experienced a phenomenal growth in mid-century in their African and Latin American fields. A large factor in this success has been the fact that Negro missionaries do not bear the stigma of preaching the "white man's religion." With 400,000 members in the United States, this church claimed a constituency of over 2,000,000 the world over by 1964. In many cases they were much more successful than white missionaries working in the same areas.[30]

In general, Negroes have been an integral part of the pentecostal movement from its beginning and have contributed much to its distinctive character. With over 1,000,000 members in the United States in 1965, they comprised 5 percent of the total Negro population. This was more than twice the national percentage of all pentecostals, which was only 2 percent. These figures reveal that the Negro pentecostals have grown much faster than their white co-religionists in the United States.[31]

In spite of the phenomenal growth of the Negro branches of the movement, little recognition of this record has been acknowledged by the white churches. Little or no contact has been maintained between these groups since the interracial period which began in 1906 ended in 1924. When the "Pentecostal Fellowship of North America" was formed in 1948 at Des Moines, Iowa, to "demonstrate to the world the essential unity of Spirit-baptized believers, fulfilling the prayer of the Lord Jesus 'that they all may be one . . . ,' " not a single

29 *Ibid.*, p. 15.

30 *Ibid.*, pp. 1-15; Nichols, *Pentecostalism*, p. 104; Landis, *Yearbook of American Churches, 1965*, p. 37.

31 Kendrick, *The Promise Fulfilled*, p. 16; Bloch-Hoell, *The Pentecostal Movement*, pp. 56-64, points out that in 1936 Negroes constituted 14.54 percent of the pentecostal movement but only 9.7 percent of the population.

Negro denomination was invited to join. Beginning with eight
denominations in 1948, the Pentecostal Fellowship of North
America added other groups until in 1965 it numbered seven-
teen denominations—all white. No explanation has been
offered as to why the Negro churches have not become a part
of the organization. Negroes, however, have been members of
the "World Pentecostal Conference" since its organization in
Zurich, Switzerland, in 1947.[32]

Extremely difficult to determine is the attitude of the
white pentecostal community toward the Negro in both the
early and later years of its history. Some prejudice was
displayed in the early stages of the movement in spite of the
interracial aspects. Parham once criticized the Azusa Street
meetings because of their "disgusting" similarity to "Southern darkey camp meetings." Although Seymour was his most
famous disciple, Parham spent the later years of his life as an
avid supporter of the Ku Klux Klan, praising its members for
their "fine work in upholding the American way of life." In
1927, in a speech to the Klan in Saginaw, Michigan, he stated
that:

> Only by being "saved" could the Klan "ever be able to realize
> their high ideals for the betterment of mankind, and so I am
> making a general call to all the members of the invisible empire of
> the Ku Klux Klan . . . to the restoration of the old-time reli-
> gion."[33]

Most Pentecostals, however, repudiated the Klan, even in
the South. In 1946 when the Klan was being revived in
Georgia, the *Pentecostal Holiness Advocate* opposed it as
being an "anti-American organization—essentially evil and
anti-Christian." The Southern pentecostals generally har-
bored a deep suspicion of the Klan because from the earliest
years the Klan persecuted "holiness people" along with
Negroes, Catholics, and Jews. A long-remembered part of
Church of God history was the fact that Klan "night raiders"
had attacked their original congregation at Camp Creek,

32 R. O. Corvin, "The Pentecostal Fellowship of North America,"
Pentecost, December 1949, p. 2; Kendrick, *The Promise Fulfilled,* pp.
210-212; Nichols, *Pentecostalism,* pp. 215-218.
33 Charles F. Parham, *The Apostolic Faith,* March 1927, p. 5.

North Carolina. Although some pentecostals joined the Klan as individuals and others accepted offerings from the hooded members of the "Empire," their aversion for the Klan remained constant over the years.[34]

Although disclaiming kinship with the Klan, most Southern pentecostals stood firmly with their region in the post-World War II racial controversy. Some church spokesmen referred to "anti-South agitation from the North" as the source of the South's problems. The Church of God and the Pentecostal Holiness Church, being the most "Southern" of the white pentecostal churches, expressed the Dixie viewpoint through the early part of the century, but later, as they became national churches, they tended to drop political and racial topics altogether from their periodicals.[35]

Official statements pertaining to race are extremely rare in pentecostal literature. Since the larger denominations either had Negro branches or had congregations in Northern states, their racial policies were generally unstated and unpublished. Throughout all the racial turmoil following the 1954 desegregation decision of the Supreme Court, the voices of the larger pentecostal churches were conspicuous for their silence. Occasionally a smaller Southern denomination would speak out in defense of the Old South. In 1965, the Emmanuel Holiness Church, one of the splinter sects of the old Fire-Baptized Holiness movement, declared ambivalently,

> We welcome all nationalities of people into the Emmanuel Holiness Church in their respective Conference bodies. So be it resolved, that we are opposed to the act of integration of the races.[36]

All denominational statements for or against integration of the races failed to obscure one important fact, the practical

---

[34] G. H. Montgomery, "Editorial," *The Pentecostal Holiness Advocate*, September 19, 1946, p. 3; Conn, *Like a Mighty Army*, p. 35.

[35] G. H. Montgomery, "Christianity, the South, and Race Agitation," *The Pentecostal Holiness Advocate*, September 5, 1946, p. 3; Conn, *The Evangel Reader*, pp. 158-251.

[36] *Minutes and Discipline of the Emmanuel Holiness Church Annual State Assemblies of Alabama, Florida, Georgia, North Carolina, and South Carolina, 1965*, p. 6.

integration of the poor whites and Negroes in backwoods pentecostal revival services. Probably the major instances of complete interracial worship in the South in the twentieth century occurred regularly among the rural devotees of divine healing and snake-handling. Among these radical fringe elements of pentecostalism, interracial worship was the rule rather than the exception. In a typical snake-handling service near Chattanooga, one observer reported that fully half the congregation under the lamplit tent were Negroes. After the singing of white and Negro spirituals, the white preacher said to his mixed audience:

> Glory to God! Makes me feel good to see whites and colored praisin' God together.[37]

Far from being an isolated case, this interracial service of the "Dolly Pond Church of God" represents a type of race-mixing that has occurred in the South since before the Civil War. Interracial worship in revivals, tent meetings, camp meetings, and pulpit exchanges has been the rule rather than the exception among the pentecostals of the South. Although much of it disappeared after 1954 when the Civil Rights movement brought social ostracism to the whites who practiced it; interracial worship and even interracial congregations continued into the 1960's among the divine healers of the large urban areas. In 1967 one of the largest pentecostal churches in Washington, D. C., was white pastor John L. Meares' congregation which was predominantly black.[38]

By 1964 there were signs that the major pentecostal denominations were officially supporting the Negroes' drive for civil rights. In that year the Cleveland Church of God adopted a resolution on "human rights" which declared that "Christian love and tolerance are incompatible with race prejudice and hatred." It further declared that "no American should, because of his race, or religion, be deprived of his right to worship, vote, rest, eat, sleep, be educated, live, and

---

[37] Robertson, *That Old-Time Religion*, pp. 169-181.

[38] J. Floyd Williams and Bishop J. A. Synan, interviews with the author, May 17, 1967.

work on the same basis as other citizens." This resolution is remarkable in that it was adopted during the political furor created by the passage of the 1964 Civil Rights "public accommodations" act.[39]

In order to implement its "declaration on human rights," the Church of God in 1966 abolished its separate "colored assembly" and totally integrated its Negro churches into the main body of the denomination. All references to "colored" status of churches, ministers, or members were deleted from the official minutes and records of the church. This action was taken and the process completed while the Methodist Church was still debating the fate of its Negro "Central Jurisdiction." In this case, the pentecostals actually surpassed the performance of the more traditional Protestant denominations.[40]

Although not all pentecostal groups have taken steps comparable to those of the Church of God, the trend in recent years has been for them to join the march of events in regard to the race question. In 1965 the General Conference of the Pentecostal Holiness Church directed its General Executive Board to "seek to establish communication with sincere religious leaders among American Negroes; that an effort be made to form Negro Associate Conferences, and that, in general, sincere action be focused toward constructively assisting our Negro friends with the moral and spiritual problems which are so prevalent and so pressing."[41] By 1967, most pentecostal colleges had complied with the racial requirements for receiving federal aid, and most of them were actively recruiting Negro students and athletes.

With a shorter history and less tradition than the older Protestant denominations, it seemed that the pentecostal bodies might possibly be more flexible and better able to meet the racial challenges of the twentieth century. Begin-

[39] *Minutes of the 50th General Assembly, 1964*, pp. 67-68. This church has more members living in the old Confederacy than any other pentecostal denomination.

[40] *Minutes of the 51st General Assembly, 1966*, p. 62.

[41] *Minutes of the Fifteenth General Conference of the Pentecostal Holiness Church, 1965*, p. 72.

ning as an interracial fellowship, the only effective one in American Christianity, they had bowed to the social pressures of the times in dividing on racial lines, but as they entered the last half of the century, there were signs that the pentecostals might once again set the pace in ecclesiastical race relations.

Chapter Nine

THE PENTECOSTALS
IN SOCIETY

It is becoming increasingly evident that the pente-
costal movement we are witnessing . . . is an authentic,
reformation-revival of historic significance, equal with
those other great movements of centuries past.
　　　　　　　　　　　　—Charles S. Sydnor, Jr.,
　　　　　　　　　　　　　The Presbyterian Survey

　　The history of the pentecostal people in American society
is in many respects similar to that of the Methodists and
Baptists of the eighteenth and nineteenth centuries. Beginning as total outcasts, they were to gain a status of suspicious
toleration, followed eventually with full acceptance by the
community. The early history of the pentecostals in society
was in reality a story of mutual rejection. The pentecostals
rejected society because they believed it to be corrupt,
wicked, hostile, and hopelessly lost, while society rejected
the pentecostals because it believed them to be insanely
fanatical, self-righteous, doctrinally in error, and emotionally
unstable. In such an atmosphere it was inevitable that much
prejudice, hostility, and suspicion would mar the relationship
of the early pentecostals to society at large.[1]

　　[1] While little has been written on the pentecostals in society, the
following sources are helpful: Duncan Aikman, "The Holy Rollers,"
American Mercury, XV (October 1928), 180-191; Anton Boisen,
"Religion and Hard Times," *Social Action*, V (March 1939), 8-35;

An important reason for the widespread hostility to the early pentecostals was the suspicion that everything odd and erroneous was believed and practiced by them. Whenever a pentecostal meeting took place in a community, rumors were rife about "magic powders," "trances," "wild emotion," and "sexual promiscuity." Although generally untrue and wildly exaggerated, these rumors eventually entered the folklore of the nation and stamped anyone claiming to be "holiness" or "pentecostal" with the epithet "holy roller." Those who engaged in this "religion of knockdown and dragout" were considered to be uncultured and uneducated "poor white trash" who inhabited the outer fringes of society. A member of one of the traditional churches who joined a pentecostal church was generally considered to have "lost his mind" and to have severed his normal social connections. Within this framework, it is not surprising that the relationship of the pentecostals to society has been marked with mutual hostility and even violence.[2]

Much of the opprobrium directed toward pentecostals, of course, was brought on by extremists within the sect whose actions added a "grain of truth" to the falsehoods already in circulation. Probably no other religious movement of recent times has attracted so many adherents with unorthodox and "odd" opinions about religion. Probably the most damaging practice has been the rite of "snake-handling," carried out by mountain sects which have no connection with the major pentecostal denominations. Basing their belief on a literal interpretation of Mark 16, these people have traditionally felt it their religious duty to "take up poisonous serpents" in order to prove their spiritual superiority.[3]

Charles S. Braden, "Sectarianism Run Wild," *Protestantism: A Symposium* (Nashville, 1944); Nils Bloch-Hoell, *The Pentecostal Movement*, pp. 172-176; Nichols, *Pentecostalism*, pp. 70-93; Stolee, *Speaking in Tongues*, pp. 83-113; and Pope, *Millhands and Preachers*, p. 139.

[2] "The Hypnotic Holy Ghost," *The Roanoke Times*, December 5, 1909, quoted in B. E. Underwood, *Fiftieth Anniversary History of the Virginia Conference of the Pentecostal Holiness Church* (a sketch) (Dublin, Virginia, 1960), p. 3.

[3] Mark 16:17-18 declares, "And these signs shall follow them that believe; In my name shall they cast out devils; they shall speak with new tongues; They shall take up serpents; and if they drink any deadly

The cult of snake-handlers began in 1909 near the town of Grasshopper, Tennessee, when a Church of God preacher, George Hensley, became convinced that the handling of snakes was a duty of all the "redeemed." Organizing the "Church of God With Signs Following," Hensley soon created havoc in Tomlinson's branch of the Church of God as the practice spread throughout its congregations. The issue remained unclear within the Church movement for many years with some ministers practicing it and others denouncing it. Those who refused to handle snakes were called "backslidden" and "powerless" by those who followed the cult. The practice became the most widespread in parts of Kentucky, Alabama, and Tennessee. In time the controversy was ended when the Cleveland, Tennessee, branch of the Church of God formally denounced it as "fanaticism," and forbade its practice within the church. The Pentecostal Holiness Church also denounced snake-handling, although it never seems to have been practiced in that church.[4]

Other spectacular practices that brought public criticism and misunderstanding were speaking in tongues, interpretation of tongues, the "holy dance," the "holy laugh," and the "laying on of hands" for divine healing. To an outsider, the sound of someone speaking with unknown tongues often sent chills of fright rather than conviction of sins. Equally as sensational was the practice of "interpreting" the message in "tongues" into English. Taylor, the minister who founded Emmanuel College in Franklin Springs, Georgia, at one time claimed to be able to interpret any message in tongues, whether written or spoken. For several years he received mail from throughout the United States for interpretation. Also a common practice was for some pentecostals to sing songs in other tongues. Although these practices were considered by pentecostals to be sure signs of "possession" by the Holy

thing, it shall not hurt them; they shall lay hands on the sick, and they shall recover."

4 Robertson, *That Old-Time Religion*, pp. 169-181, describes a typical snake-handling service. Also see Conn, *Like a Mighty Army*, p. 191; *The Pentecostal Holiness Advocate*, August 8, 1918, pp. 8-10; *The Church of God Evangel*, July 1, 1916, p. 1; July 1, 1922, p. 2; February 5, 1949, pp. 8-9; *The Christian Evangel*, August 9, 1919, p. 5.

Ghost, they were seen as signs of madness and fanaticism by the unbelieving public.[5]

Another pentecostal practice that varied from the norm of other churches was that of allowing women to preach. The holiness movement had long allowed women to preach, basing its action on the prophecy in Joel 2:28: "Your sons and your daughters shall prophesy. . . ." Most felt that woman had brought sin into the world through Eve, and should therefore help to take it out again. One writer declared that all great spiritual awakenings featured women preachers who would not "cut off their hair, put on bloomers or rompers, but just prophesy and pray as a woman."[6] Another felt that "when we get our eyes on churches, creedism, and slack up, we elbow the women preachers off." As a result of this thinking, the pentecostals by the middle of the twentieth century probably had more women preachers than any other branch of Christianity.[7]

The first woman preacher to gain fame in the United States was Mary Woodworth Etter, whose divine healing campaigns of the 1890's led her through Florida, South Carolina, Indiana, Iowa, and Missouri. In sensational "campaigns" in churches, tents and auditoriums, Mrs. Etter claimed to have cured cancer, dumbness, tumors, deafness, . . . etc." Joining the pentecostal movement after 1906, she continued her spectacular ministry to the sick. One of Mrs. Etter's "trophies" was a man who reported that, "I had the following diseases: cancer, tumor, heart disease, asthma, catarrh of bronchial tubes, rheumatism, and kidney trouble . . . am now perfectly well." Obviously, Mrs. Etter was a champion, and not even Aimee Semple McPherson a genera-

[5] L. R. Graham, in a personal interview with the author, November 10, 1966; *The Pentecostal Holiness Advocate*, July 5, 1917, p. 15; Stolee, *Speaking in Tongues*, pp. 65-66; *The Pentecostal Evangel*, June 16, 1920, p. 8.

[6] S. D. Page, *The Apostolic Evangel*, June 1, 1918, p. 14; A. J. Tomlinson, "Women Preachers," *Church of God Evangel*, August 28, 1915-September 18, 1915 (series).

[7] *The Pentecostal Holiness Advocate*, July 11, 1918, p. 6. In 1966 the Pentecostal Holiness Church had 473 women ministers out of a total of 2,638; *Yearbook of the Pentecostal Holiness Church, 1966*, I, 6.

tion later could match her claims as a faith healer. A thorough feminist, Mrs. Etter did much to further the cause of her sex long before the climax of the woman's suffrage movement around 1920.[8]

The emphasis on healing that Mrs. Etter and Alexander Dowie of Zion, Illinois, popularized became one of the major attractions of the pentecostal religion. Everywhere pentecostal preachers claimed sensational cures ranging from "bad colds" to "raising the dead." Parham, the mentor of Seymour, was a faith healer prior to his "pentecostal" discovery in 1901. Carrying the idea of sanctification and perfection to its ultimate conclusion, he taught that "sanctifying power reached every part of our body, destroying the very root and tendency to disease." Just as John Wesley taught the possibility of entire cleansing from sin, Parham taught such an "entire cleansing from disease" in the experience of sanctification. In the early years of the movement, pentecostals felt that it was a sin to take medicine or to visit the doctor. One pentecostal preacher, F. M. Britton, once refused medical aid for one of his sons, and reported later that he "died without drugs." Some years later his wife also died after "refusing medicine." Although threatened with jail for refusing medical attention for his family, Britton never wavered in his views. Another striking case was that of Walter Barney, a Church of God preacher from Wytheville, Virginia, who was tried and convicted for "manslaughter" in 1915 for refusing medical care for a daughter who later died. His conviction, however, was later overturned by a pardon from the Governor of Virginia. Rather than an exception, these cases were the rule for many early pentecostals, and no revival meeting could be termed a "success" without several cases of healing.[9]

[8] Mrs. M. B. Woodworth Etter, *Marvels and Miracles; Signs and Wonders* (Indianapolis, 1922), pp. 213-223, 303-314. Mary Baker Eddy popularized healing through her "Christian Science" movement during this same period. There is no evidence that Mrs. Eddy was ever influenced by Etter or Dowie, or that the pentecostals' emphasis on healing was connected with her teaching.

[9] Parham, *Voice Crying in the Wilderness,* pp. 39-52; Britton, *Pentecostal Truth,* pp. 244-246; Conn, *Evangel Reader,* p. 97; *Church of God Evangel,* December 1, 1910, pp. 1-2; January 23, 1915, p. 2; November 19, 1949, pp. 12-13; August 19, 1950, pp. 8-9.

Other pentecostal beliefs that ran counter to the practices of society brought further criticism to the movement. There was hardly any institution, pleasure, business, vice, or social group that escaped the scorn and opposition of pentecostal preachers. Included in their catalog of "social sins" were: tobacco in all its forms, secret societies, life insurance, doctors, medicine, liquor, dance halls, theaters, movies, Coca Cola, public swimming, professional sports, beauty parlors, jewelry, church bazaars, and makeup. Anyone attending pentecostal services who indulged in any of the foregoing practices was sure to be branded as a "sinner." Furthermore, no member of a pentecostal church was permitted to practice them either, and the back door was always open to dismiss anyone who might "backslide." Needless to say, this stringent "holiness standard" kept the rolls of the churches small and restricted to only the "sanctified few."[10]

In addition to these variations, the pentecostals occasionally claimed to have experienced miracles that strained the credibility of the most sympathetic observers. Everything from preachers floating free of gravity to balls of supernatural fire were claimed as "proofs" of divine approval. Some testified to having "bloody crosses" appear on their foreheads, while others claimed supernatural "Holy Ghost Oil" on the palms of their hands. Of course, most church officials disavowed these extravagant claims, but many critics accepted them as further proof of pentecostal fanaticism.[11]

Since the pentecostals so completely rejected society, it is not surprising that society rejected the pentecostals. This period of rejection lasted roughly from 1906 to 1923, when Aimee Semple McPherson with her "Foursquare Gospel"

10 *Live Coals,* July 25, 1906, p. 3; *Living Words,* April 1903, pp. 13-16; Milton Tomlinson, *Basic Bible Beliefs* (Cleveland, Tennessee, 1961), pp. 97-128; *Discipline of the Pentecostal Holiness Church, 1961,* pp. 65-68; Juillerat, *Book of Minutes,* pp. 296-300; C. F. Wimberly, *Are You a Christian?* (Louisville, 1917), pp. 5-32; *The Pentecostal Evangel,* December 23, 1922, p. 5.

11 Gibson, *Church of God, Mountain Assembly,* p. 6, reports that a preacher "rose to the ceiling of the church when a hostile mob entered." On two occasions, Church of God ministers reported "balls of fire" over churches and tents which mystified the public. See *The Church of God Evangel,* November 15, 1910, pp. 4-5; August 26, 1916, p. 1.

movement gave pentecostalism its first "celebrity" and its first taste of acceptance by the public. It was during this time that the sobriquet "holy roller" was attached to the movement. Unlike the Methodists, Quakers, and Shakers, the pentecostals refused to accept this appellation. In 1915 Tomlinson's Church of God moved to "disclaim and repudiate the title Holy Rollers in reference to the Church of God." Other pentecostal denominations have consistently made similar disavowals.[12]

At times public opposition to the rise of the budding pentecostal movement took the form of obstructionism and even physical violence. Nowhere was this violence more extreme and damaging than in the South. One early pentecostal-holiness preacher reported the following incidents on his Southern preaching tours:

> [He] had three tents burned by angry people. Once a group of excited people sought to murder him but were unable to locate his hiding place. At another time he was run out of a certain city; at another he was beaten by an angry man. At another time the police had to give him protection.[13]

Other preachers reported instances of being beaten, gagged, shot with shotguns, thrown in jail, or threatened with death and mutilation. Others reported having churches burned and tents toppled. One Church of God preacher in Mississippi claimed that in 1917 two men "covered him with revolvers, gagged him and dragged him . . . through the woods where they beat him black and blue with a buggy trace, struck him a blow over the eye with a revolver, and broke two of his ribs by kicking him in the side. . . . After they had beaten him, they led him to the railroad and with severe threats compelled him to run."[14] J. W. Buckalew, another Church of God preacher, earned the nickname "Old Rough and Ready" because of his willingness to literally fight for his

[12] Juillerat, *Book of Minutes*, p. 201; Nichols, *Pentecostalism*, pp. 2, 77; see Allene M. Sumner, "The Holy Rollers on Shin Bone Ridge," *The Nation*, CXXI (July 29, 1925), 138.

[13] W. H. Turner, "The Tongues Movement: A Brief History" (Unpublished Master's thesis, The University of Georgia, 1948), p. 45.

[14] Conn, *Evangel Reader*, p. 158.

religion. Because of his many altercations with "anti-holiness" toughs, Buckalew earned a reputation among pentecostals that rivaled that of Peter Cartwright among the early Methodists.[15]

There are indications that the unpopularity of pentecostalism seriously hampered its growth in its early years. For every community that accepted a pentecostal church, there was another which would not. In the western area of Virginia, eight pentecostal-holiness churches were organized in 1913, all of which died because of opposition and lack of interest. In the course of fifty years only a hundred new churches survived while sixty others were abortive.[16] Yet the opposition and persecution that the pentecostals experienced served as a consolidating force within the movement, and brought sympathy from a part of the public that deprecated such violence. Although most violent opposition had ceased by 1925, instances of it continued throughout the middle of the twentieth century.

While the pentecostals and American society were engaged in rejecting each other, the years 1914 to 1925 might accurately be called the period of schism and realignment. The "finished work" and "Jesus Only" schisms of 1914 to 1919 were mainly over doctrinal and theological issues, while the schisms of the 1920's were caused primarily by personality clashes. After 1925 the pentecostal movement had attained the general outlines that it was to follow to the present time.

One of the first schisms caused by personality clashes occurred in the Georgia Conference of the Pentecostal Holiness Church in 1920, resulting in the organization of the "Congregational Holiness Church." The controversy producing this schism began over the doctrine of divine healing. Two ministers, Watson Sorrow and Hugh Bowling, held a

[15] For references to violence see Conn, *Evangel Reader*, pp. 144-175; J. W. Buckalew, *Incidents in the Life of J. W. Buckalew* (Cleveland, Tennessee, *circa* 1920); Watson Sorrow, *Some of My Experiences* (Franklin Springs, Georgia, 1954), pp. 60-72; Conn, *Like a Mighty Army*, pp. 29-37, 106-112; Tomlinson, "Journal of Happenings," pp. 1-30; Nichols, *Pentecostalism*, pp. 70-80; and Bailey, *Pioneer Marvels*, pp. 6-15.

[16] Underwood, *Fiftieth Anniversary History of the Virginia Conference*, p. 4.

view on healing that varied from the generally accepted ideas of the church at that time. The faction led by Sorrow and Bowling held that it was not sinful to use remedies and medicines to aid in the healing of sickness. Another faction led by F. M. Britton and G. F. Taylor held that "the provision in the Atonement for the healing of the body was all-sufficient, and that it was unnecessary to supplement any human means to assist God in effecting a cure." For several months a debate on the issue raged throughout the church and in the pages of *The Advocate.*[17]

The controversy, which began as a doctrinal dispute, became in time a power struggle between personalities. In 1920, events came to a head in a trial which resulted in the expulsion of Sorrow and Bowling from the church. What the leader of the Pentecostal Holiness Church, J. H. King, described as a "terrible blow" to the denomination, came on January 29, 1921, when the Congregational Holiness Church was organized in High Shoals, Georgia. The adoption of the term "Congregational" displayed the opposition of the new group to the episcopal form of government that was practiced in the mother church. The new Congregational Holiness Church remained a small group confined to the states of Georgia, Alabama, Florida, North Carolina, and South Carolina. In 1965, it claimed 5,212 members in 151 churches.[18]

Similar schisms split the Church of God at Cleveland, Tennessee, in 1919 and 1923, resulting in the creation of two new denominations carrying variations of the name "Church of God." The first of these resulted from the strict tithing system that the church had adopted in its General Assembly in 1917. Under this plan, 10 percent of all the income of the

[17] Campbell, *The Pentecostal Holiness Church*, p. 277; B. L. Cox, *History and Doctrine of the Congregational Holiness Church* (Greenwood, South Carolina, 1959), p. 7; Sorrow, *Some of My Experiences*, p. 65.

[18] King and King, *Yet Speaketh*, p. 316; Cox, *Congregational Holiness Church*, pp. 7-11; Sorrow, *Some of My Experiences*, pp. 65-67; Landis, *Yearbook of American Churches, 1965*, p. 41. *The Pentecostal Holiness Advocate* in its 1920-1921 issues chronicles the controversy in detail with each side given ample space to air its views. See also B. L. Cox, *My Life's Story* (Greenwood, South Carolina, 1959), pp. 40-42.

local churches would be sent to the headquarters of the denomination to help equalize the salaries of the ministry.[19]

A small group of ministers led by J. L. Scott protested against this policy, feeling that paying tithes should be based on free will rather than coercion. Therefore, this group of dissenters organized the "Original Church of God" with headquarters in Chattanooga, Tennessee. This group also remained small, having in 1965 only 6,000 members in 35 churches, most of them in Tennessee.[20]

A more fundamental and far-reaching cleavage occurred in the Church of God in 1923 as a result of a power struggle between the church's leader and dominant figure, A. J. Tomlinson, and other leaders who constituted the "Supreme Council" of the church. Tomlinson, who had served as General Overseer of the denomination for over a decade, had by 1920 gained almost complete control of the entire operation of the church. Overworked and fatigued by his heavy responsibilities, he began to see himself as holding theocratic authority in the church. This authority was threatened, however, when the church adopted a constitution in 1921 which created new positions curtailing his power.[21]

Dissatisfied with the constitution, Tomlinson called for its abrogation in the Assembly of 1922, but the church was in no mood to accept his suggestions, largely because of charges of misappropriation of funds which had been made during the previous months. With Tomlinson "under a cloud" of suspicion, the Assembly voted to create more offices to further decrease his authority. In addition, a commission was appointed to investigate his financial administration of church funds. These restraints were more than the formerly all-powerful Overseer could take, so he tendered his resigna-

19 Juillerat, *Book of Minutes*, pp. 293-296; *Church of God Evangel*, May 4, 1918, p. 1.

20 Landis, *Yearbook of American Churches, 1965*, pp. 34-35; Nichols, *Pentecostalism*, p. 137; Tomlinson, *Diary of A. J. Tomlinson*, I, 262-263.

21 Simmons, *History of the Church of God*, p. 38; Duggar, *A. J. Tomlinson*, pp. 188-194; *Minutes of the Sixteenth Annual Assembly, 1921*, p. 27.

tion, but upon the insistence of friends consented to remain in office another year.[22]

During the following year the "committee on better government" investigated the church's finances and charged Tomlinson with misappropriating some fourteen thousand dollars. In impeachment proceedings which Tomlinson described as "unjust and illegal," the "Council of Elders" in July 1923 relieved the General Overseer of his office for "mishandling church funds." With his connection with the church now completely severed, Tomlinson "walked out on a street corner in Cleveland, Tennessee, under the starry sky with the Church of God banner and started building again." In what he described as "a revolution to save the Church of God from wreck and ruin," he began a new movement which eventually took the name of "The Tomlinson Church of God." In the year that followed, law suits were filed in the Chancery Court of Bradley County, Tennessee, to decide which group could claim funds arriving in Cleveland addressed to the "Church of God" headquarters. In a decision that was later sustained by the Tennessee Supreme Court, the group that had impeached Tomlinson gained the right to the use of the name "Church of God."[23]

All went well with the "Tomlinson Church of God" until the death of its founder in 1943, when a power struggle developed between his two sons, Milton and Homer, for control of the church. In a bewildering set of moves and countermoves, the younger brother Milton, who was not a minister but a printer, was elected as "General Overseer." After Milton's accession to power, Homer was inexplicably expelled from the church. Following this development, Homer went to New York City where he founded a third denomination which he christened "The Church of God,

[22] Tomlinson, *Answering the Call of God*, p. 38; Conn, *Like a Mighty Army*, p. 174; *The Church of God Evangel*, December 9, 1922, p. 1; *Minutes of the Seventeenth Annual Assembly, 1922*, pp. 17-58.

[23] Tomlinson, *Answering the Call of God*, p. 23; Tomlinson, "A Journal of Happenings," entry for September 10, 1923; Conn, *Like a Mighty Army*, pp. 175-190; Kendrick, *The Promise Fulfilled*, pp. 192-193. Tomlinson's side of the controversy is given by his son Homer in the *Diary of A. J. Tomlinson* (New York, 1953), II, 98-112. See also *The Church of God Evangel*, July 14, 1923, pp. 1-4.

World Headquarters." In March 1953, the former "Tomlinson" Church of God with Milton as Bishop and General Overseer changed its name to "The Church of God of Prophecy," which, it is claimed, designates it as the one, true "Church of God."[24]

In recent years, Milton's "prophecy" church has distinguished itself as the developer and custodian of the "Fields of the Woods" shrine in Cherokee County, North Carolina, where over two million dollars has been spent to memorialize the spot where A. J. Tomlinson "prevailed in prayer" in 1903 and thereby founded "the Church of God" of prophecy. Here a vast array of monuments mark the spot on Burger Mountain where all the nations of the world, it is claimed, will one day recognize the authority of the Church of God and be brought within the fold. Called the "Biblical Wonder of the Twentieth Century," this shrine is supported by the "Church of God of Prophecy Marker Association."[25] Indicative of the progress that the church has made in recent years is the fact that a new junior college was authorized in 1964 to be located in Cleveland, Tennessee, and known as "Tomlinson College."[26]

The "World Headquarters" Church of God under Homer Tomlinson has been known chiefly because of the activities of its leader, who since 1943 has run for President of the United States several times as the candidate of his own "Theocratic Party." In addition to his other duties, he crowned himself "king" of all fifty states and every sovereign nation of the world, including Soviet Russia. By 1965 "Bishop Homer" had also proclaimed himself "King of the World," as well as "the son of God" and "heir to the throne of David." In 1966 he set up his "world headquarters" in Jerusalem and in his 74th year made preparations to "rule

24 Homer Tomlinson's version of these events is given in Clark, *Small Sects in America*, pp. 102-104; also see Nichols, *Pentecostalism*, pp. 139-143; *Minutes, 60th Annual Assembly of the Church of God of Prophecy, 1965*, pp. 30, 31; and *Cyclopedic Index of Assembly Minutes, 1906-1949* (Cleveland, Tennessee, 1950), pp. 150-159, 370-375.

25 See *Biblical Wonder of the Twentieth Century* (Cleveland, Tennessee, 1964), pp. 3-37.

26 *Minutes of the 60th Annual Assembly, 1965*, pp. 77-78, 127-131.

the world in righteousness" from his room in that city's Imperial Hotel. This dream, unfortunately, came to a sudden end with the death of the self-proclaimed Bishop and King in 1969.[27]

In the same year that the elder Tomlinson was expelled from the Church of God in Cleveland, Tennessee, a young lady, Aimee Semple McPherson, founded yet another pentecostal body in Los Angeles known as the "International Church of the Foursquare Gospel." Born on a farm in Ontario, Canada, in 1890, Aimee Kennedy was raised by strict Methodist parents. As a teenager, Aimee met Robert Semple, a pentecostal preacher, and was converted to pentecostalism. Attracted to Semple, she married the young preacher and with him entered the evangelistic ministry. On a missionary trip to China, Semple died and was buried in Hong Kong, leaving Aimee and their young daughter to return to the United States alone.[28]

In 1917, after her marriage to Harold McPherson, Aimee began the evangelistic work that was to make her one of the most celebrated and controversial evangelists of twentieth-century America. Since her early training for the ministry was with Pastor William Durham in Chicago, Mrs. McPherson adopted the "finished work" view of sanctification that Durham championed. For several years she was listed as a minister of the Assemblies of God Church, but her burgeoning ministry, which caught the public fancy around 1920, made it inevitable that she would become the founder of a separate denomination.[29]

[27] An article in Tomlinson's paper *The Church of God*, October 15, 1966, pp. 1-2, proclaimed that Tomlinson had set up the "Throne of God" in Jerusalem whence he had forgiven "one and all" of all their sins.

[28] Aimee Semple McPherson, *The Story of My Life* (Los Angeles, 1951), pp. 15-79. Other autobiographical works detailing her life and ministry are: *This Is That, Personal Experiences, Sermons and Writings of Aimee Semple McPherson* (Los Angeles, 1923); *In the Service of the King* (New York, 1927); and *The Foursquare Gospel* (Los Angeles, 1946). A critical biography is Lately Thomas, *The Vanishing Evangelist* (New York, 1959). The best sympathetic account is Nancy Bon Mavity, *Sister Aimee* (New York, 1931).

[29] Kendrick, *The Promise Fulfilled*, p. 154; *The Pentecostal Evangel*, November 15, 1919, pp. 6-10; May 29, 1920, pp. 8-9; June 10, 1922, p. 9.

In 1921, while preaching about the vision in Ezekiel 1:1-28 concerning the beast with the four faces—those of a man, a lion, an ox, and an eagle—Mrs. McPherson conceived the idea of a "Foursquare Gospel." The four corners represented salvation, the Holy Ghost baptism attested by tongues, divine healing, and the second coming of Christ. The center for her activities became the vast "Angelus Temple," which was built in Los Angeles in 1923 at a cost of one and a half million dollars. With a seating capacity of over 5,000 persons, she kept the "Temple" full for every service. Her sermons were highly dramatic. In one service it was reported that "Sister, in football togs, carried the ball of the Foursquare Gospel for a touchdown, Jesus ran interference." On another occasion the congregation watched in amazement as the evangelist arrived dressed in policemen's clothes, riding a motorcycle:

> She drove recklessly to the front of the auditorium, slammed on the brakes, blew a screech on a police whistle, raised a white gloved hand to the congregation, and shouted: "Stop you're going to hell!"

With such histrionics and dramatics, Mrs. McPherson soon was a familiar figure to newspaper readers from coast to coast.[30]

Even more dramatic and controversial was her famous "kidnapping incident" in 1926. In May of that year, the famous leader of "Foursquaredom" disappeared for several weeks after being last seen on a beach in Southern California. After her return she claimed that she had been kidnapped and held for ransom in Northern Mexico. Her friends staunchly defended her when critics tried to prove that she had in reality gone to a "love nest" with Kenneth G. Ormiston, a radio announcer from her station in Los Angeles. After much controversy in the press and a court trial which attempted unsuccessfully to prove the kidnapping story a hoax, "Sister" Aimee returned to the "Temple" to continue her ministry. In spite of other troubles both public and

[30] Bach, *They Have Found a Faith*, pp. 57-87; McPherson, *In the Service of the King*, pp. 239-248; McPherson, *The Foursquare Gospel*, p. 22; *The Pentecostal Evangel*, June 5, 1926, pp. 1-3.

domestic, Mrs. McPherson incorporated on December 28, 1927, the "International Church of the Foursquare Gospel" with herself as lifetime president.[31]

Although Mrs. McPherson gained a nationwide following and built a major denomination in her own lifetime, many pentecostal and non-pentecostal spokesmen rejected her ministrations. Alma White, the most critical anti-pentecostal writer of the century, described Mrs. McPherson as a "necromancer, familiar with the black arts," who spoke with the "mutterings of a witch." Others opposed her on more theological grounds. When invited to speak in a Pentecostal Holiness Church in Roanoke, Virginia, in 1926, Mrs. McPherson was refused permission to preach by J. H. King, General Superintendent of the denomination, because of her "finished work" theory of sanctification. Many other ministers and church officials became hostile to her because of the kidnapping incident.[32]

One permanent outcome of the adverse publicity surrounding the alleged kidnapping of the famous woman evangelist was the creation of yet another pentecostal denomination. One of Mrs. McPherson's most successful campaigns was conducted in Des Moines, Iowa, in 1927 and 1928. In a short time three large congregations were formed under the banner of the Foursquare Church. The pastor sent to minister in one of the largest was a Californian with a powerful personality and great organizational ability, Rev. J. R. Richey. Largely as a result of the kidnapping incident, in addition to questions concerning Mrs. McPherson's strict ecclesiastical polity, Richey decided to lead a break with the church in 1932. In the end, the Iowa and Minnesota District of the Foursquare Church voted to separate and form a new group under Richey's leadership which took the name "Open Bible Evangelistic Association."[33]

[31] Thomas, *Vanishing Evangelist*, pp. 1-319, traces the story of the kidnapping incident and the subsequent trial. Mrs. McPherson defends herself in *The Story of My Life*, pp. 208-221. A contemporary account is given in Mavity, *Sister Aimee*, pp. 77-320.

[32] White, *Tongues and Demons*, pp. 112-115; McPherson, *Story of My Life*, pp. 122-142. The story of Mrs. McPherson's funeral was given wide coverage in *Life* magazine (October 20, 1944), pp. 85-89.

[33] Kendrick, *The Promise Fulfilled*, pp. 164-165; Nichols, *Pentecostalism*, pp. 144-145.

In a short time, the Open Bible group made contact with a similar group in Oregon known as the "Bible Standard Church," which had split off the Apostolic Faith group of Mrs. Florence Crawford in Portland in 1919. Led by Fred Hornshuh and A. J. Hegan, this group had objected to the exclusiveness of Mrs. Crawford's group as well as its stern views on divorce and remarriage. In 1935 these two groups merged to form a new pentecostal denomination which later adopted the name "Open Bible Standard Churches, Incorporated" with headquarters in Des Moines. A striking fact of the merger was that both branches were schisms from denominations founded and controlled by women preachers.[34]

The advent of Aimee Semple McPherson marked a turning point in the history of the pentecostal movement in the United States. Being the first well-known pentecostal person to the public at large, she did much to add interest and toleration to a religion that had been considered of interest only to the lowest levels of society. Indeed, "Sister Aimee" proved that the pentecostals were capable of producing preachers who could appeal to the public as strongly as did the evangelists of the more traditional churches. In fact, the twentieth century has seen pentecostal preachers who strongly paralleled the appeal of the older type of evangelists in the tradition of Charles G. Finney and Dwight L. Moody. Just as Billy Sunday shared headlines with Mrs. McPherson during the twenties and thirties, Billy Graham has shared top billing with another pentecostal, Oral Roberts, in the fifties and sixties.

By 1930 there were many signs that indicated the trends that the pentecostal movement would follow in the future. It was clear by that time that the great appeal of the pentecostal religion would be to the lower classes, but that as the lower classes rose on the economic scale, the pentecostals would rise with them. The advent of pentecostal churches as middle-class institutions would come, not by converting members of the middle class, but by entering it *en masse* from below. The major characteristics of pentecostal worship, which included emotional fervor, informality, lay

---

[34] Kendrick, *The Promise Fulfilled*, pp. 166-171.

clergy, millenarianism, and strict ethical standards, exercised a strong appeal to the laboring classes. The experience of the pentecostals closely fulfilled the dictum of Ernst Troeltsch that "the really creative, church-forming, religious movements are the work of the lower strata." Some writers have charged that the rise of sects is only a religious guise for a more deep-seated protest against prevailing social and economic conditions. Others feel that this development is an overt "protest against the failure of religious institutions to come to grips with the needs of marginal groups, existing on the fringes of cultural and social organization." To some extent, all of these generalizations are true in the case of the pentecostals, and they help to explain the great attraction this type of religion has had for the lower classes.[35]

There are some weaknesses, however, in explaining the rise of the pentecostals as primarily an economic and social protest movement. It has been shown that the greatest growth of the pentecostals (1910-1950) occurred when the laboring and farming classes were rapidly declining as a percentage of the total population. Obviously, the doctrines and mode of worship of the pentecostals were appealing to many who could not be classed as "economically deprived." Although some observers have emphasized psychological and cultural factors as being more important than the economic and doctrinal ones, it would appear that to large numbers of people, pentecostalism represented a continuation of the "old-time religion" as formerly practiced by the more traditional Protestant churches.[36] The pentecostals, from their beginnings, have occupied the lowest position on the social scale. In spite of a tremendous growth in wealth, fine church buildings, better educated ministers, and nationally known

[35] Richard H. Niebuhr, *The Social Sources of Denominationalism*, pp. 29-30; Liston Pope, *Millhands and Preachers*, p. 140; N. J. Demerath III, *Social Class in American Protestantism* (Chicago, 1965), pp. 40-42.

[36] W. S. Salisbury, *Religion in American Culture, A Sociological Interpretation* (Homewood, Illinois, 1964), p. 455; Demerath, *Social Class in American Protestantism*, p. 42; John B. Holt, "Holiness Religion: Cultural Shock and Social Reorganization," *American Sociological Review*, V (1940), 740-747; David O. Moberg, *The Church as a Social Institution* (Englewood Cliffs, N. J., 1962), p. 228.

ministers such as Mrs. McPherson and Roberts, the pentecostals remained in the social cellar through the middle of the
century. In Gastonia, North Carolina, in 1939, it was reported that in the cotton mills:

> Presbyterian workers feel superior to those belonging to the
> Methodist and Baptist churches, while members of the latter two
> denominations regard themselves as definitely higher in the social
> scale than Wesleyan Methodists. All, in turn, despise the Church
> of God and deprecate the social status of its members.[37]

Other studies have indicated that this attitude has continued into the sixties, with the Episcopal Church having the
highest social status and the pentecostal groups the lowest. A
1964 survey of American social attitudes indicated that
among traditional Protestants, the churches mentioned as
being "least like one's own" were the pentecostal types and
the Catholic Church.[38] Another survey published in the same
year revealed that only the Jehovah's Witnesses were ranked
lower than the pentecostal and holiness churches.[39]

Despite their lowly social position and lack of economic
power, the pentecostals have experienced fantastic growth
during the twentieth century. Liston Pope, in his survey of
Gaston County, North Carolina, found that between 1910
and 1939 there were thirty-six pentecostal-type churches
organized in the county while the total for all other denominations combined was only eighteen, three of which were
closed. This example is typical of the mushroom-like growth
of pentecostal congregations throughout the nation. A
symbol of things to come was the fact that by 1965 the
Church of God (Cleveland, Tennessee) with three hundred
churches had passed the Presbyterian Church as the third
largest denomination in Georgia in the number of congregations. In many states, the number of pentecostal churches

[37] Pope, *Millhands and Preachers*, p. 138.

[38] W. Widick Schroeder and Victor Obenhaus, *Religion in American
Culture* (London, 1964), pp. 71-74.

[39] Salisbury, *Religion in American Culture*, p. 454. For interesting
attitudes toward pentecostals in the South see William W. Wood,
Culture and Personality Aspects of the Pentecostal Holiness Religion
(The Hague, 1965), pp. 11-67.

combined, easily ranked them closely behind the Baptist and
Methodist Churches.[40]

The statistics indicate that the pentecostal churches have
experienced phenomenal growth since the twenties. The
following table, although not complete, is representative of
this growth in the United States during the past fifty years:

Church	Churches 1926	Members 1926	Churches 1970	Members 1970
Assemblies of God	671	47,950	8,570	626,660
Church of God in Christ	733	30,263	4,500	425,500
Church of God (Cleveland, Tenn.)	644	23,247	3,834	243,532
Pentecostal Holiness	252	8,096	1,355	66,790
Pentecostal Assemblies of the World	126	7,850	550	45,000[41]

One of the most important reasons for this growth was the
fact that the pentecostals followed the migration of population to the cities. As has been shown, the pentecostal movement began as a city phenomenon, with many major events
occurring in Los Angeles, Chicago, Topeka, St. Louis, Dunn,
North Carolina, Portland, and Indianapolis. Aimee Semple
McPherson's settling in Los Angeles foreshadowed dozens of
"Temples" and "revival centers" which came to dot the
nation's largest cities. An outstanding city church in the
South was the famous "Garr Auditorium," which was built in
1931 in Charlotte, North Carolina. Beginning as a tent revival

[40] Pope, *Millhands and Preachers*, p. 97; Charles S. Sydnor, "The
Pentecostals," *Presbyterian Survey*, May 1964, p. 31. Sydnor states
that the pentecostals number almost a million in the South, or
"approximately the size of our Presbyterian Church, U. S."

[41] These figures were compiled from the U. S. Bureau of the Census,
Religious Bodies: 1926 (Washington: Government Printing Office,
1929), I, 60-1091; and Constant H. Jacquet, Jr., *Yearbook of American
Churches, 1970* (New York, 1970), pp. 18-59.

in 1930, Garr's group was able to rebuild a year later the old Charlotte city auditorium into a vast church edifice seating over 2,000. By the time of Garr's death in 1944, he had inaugurated a school of theology, a periodical known as *The Morning Thought*, and an ambitious missionary enterprise in Brazil.[42]

Another example of a "storefront" church that succeeded was Ralph Byrd's "Faith Memorial" Assembly of God Congregation in Atlanta. Beginning in 1935 as an itinerant evangelist in a tent meeting, Byrd had built within ten years a congregation of over 1,000. Moving from the tent, he constructed a wooden tabernacle which soon was too small. He eventually bought a large church building on fashionable Ponce de Leon Avenue where he continued to serve a large urban congregation.[43]

The pentecostals were particularly active in serving the millions of poorer migrants to the larger cities. The Northern urban ghettos were by the 1960's experiencing a startling growth of pentecostal storefront churches. The Southern Negro who went North generally carried his religion with him and re-established centers for worship in any space available, including store buildings and church edifices formerly owned by white congregations who had themselves migrated to the suburbs. Another interesting development was the rise of a large number of Spanish-speaking pentecostal churches among the Puerto-Rican population in New York City. With only 25 such churches in 1937, New York City had no less than 250 by 1967, a 1000 percent increase.[44]

Another key to the growth of pentecostalism was its relative youth and resultant flexibility on some issues that convulsed the rest of American Christianity during the twentieth century. While the rest of Protestantism wrestled with the great fundamentalist controversy over Darwin's evolu-

[42] *Twentieth Anniversary of the Garr Auditorium* (Charlotte, 1950), pp. 3-16.

[43] Ralph M. Riggs, "Those Store-Front Churches," *United Evangelical Action* (Cincinnati), IV (August 1, 1945), 4-5. See also William G. McLaughlin, *Modern Revivalism* (New York, 1959), pp. 468-469.

[44] Robert D. Cross, *The Church and the City, 1865-1910* (New York, 1967), pp. 262-266; Nichols, *Pentecostalism*, pp. 133-136.

tionary theory during the twenties, the pentecostals observed the fray from the outside. Although "fundamentalist to a man," the pentecostals did not play an active part in the controversy. The leading fundamentalist spokesmen were such Baptists, Presbyterians, and Methodists as William Jennings Bryan, Gerald Winrod, and Bob Jones. Since most of these fundamentalist leaders were strict Calvinists, the pentecostals with their equally strict Arminian theology were unwilling to become too closely allied with the movement. Because they were never an integral part of the fundamentalist party, the pentecostals emerged without the deep anti-intellectual bias that distinguished much of conservative Protestantism after 1925.[45]

The relationship between the pentecostals and the fundamentalists has been of some interest since both movements rose to prominence during the same period of time. A popular misconception has persisted that the pentecostals were the "ultrafundamentalists" of American religious life.[46] Although most pentecostals thought of themselves as fundamentalists, the feeling was not reciprocated by the leaders of organized fundamentalism. By the time the fundamentalist movement hit its crest in the 1920's, it had already effectively barred the door to fellowship with the pentecostals. In a 1928 convention of the "World's Christian Fundamentals Association," a group organized in 1919 to be the major voice of the movement, the pentecostals were soundly condemned. The resolution which disfellowshipped the entire movement read:

[45] *The Pentecostal Evangel,* October 24, 1925, p. 5; November 7, 1925, pp. 4-5. Although much has been made of the "Holy Roller" aspects of fundamentalism, the evidence suggests that most pentecostals were either unaware or uninterested in the controversy. There is certainly no literature extant to show a deep pentecostal involvement with the controversy, since the fundamentalists generally downed pentecostals along with Darwinists and Roman Catholics. See Robertson, *Old-Time Religion,* pp. 88-96; L. L. Pickett, *God or the Guessers, Some Scriptures on Present Day Infidelity* (Louisville, 1926), pp. 7-83, with its "holiness" view of evolution; and Smith, *Called Unto Holiness,* pp. 315-321, which indicates that the Calvinist context of fundamentalist thought repelled Arminian pentecostal and holiness thinkers.

[46] Mead, *Handbook of Denominations,* p. 167.

> Whereas; the present wave of modern pentecostalism, often referred to as the "tongues movement," and the present wave of fanatical and unscriptural healing which is sweeping over the country today, has become a menace in many churches and a real injury to sane testimony of Fundamental Christians,
>
> Be it resolved, that this convention go on record as unreservedly opposed to Modern Pentecostalism, including the speaking in unknown tongues, and the fanatical healing known as general healing in the atonement, and the perpetuation of the miraculous sign-healing of Jesus and His apostles, wherein they claim the only reason the church cannot perform these miracles is because of unbelief.[47]

There were several reasons for this rejection by the fundamentalists. One was the probable failure to discriminate between the moderate, mainline pentecostals and those that bordered on the cultic. There were, of course, always the snake-handlers and the cults of Father Divine and Daddy Grace, which had been repudiated by most pentecostals themselves. Perhaps the bizarre fringe had frightened them. The fundamentalists had also been captured by a rather new biblical view known as "Scofieldian dispensationalism," which viewed the pentecostalist practices of glossolalia and divine healing as signs heralding the "dispensation of Grace," destined to cease with the apostles of the New Testament. The pentecostals were therefore in grave error and beyond the pale of orthodox fundamentalism.[48]

As a result of this rejection, the pentecostals remained isolated from the rest of American Christianity as well as from each other until after World War II. It was, strangely enough, another rejection by fundamentalists that brought the pentecostals into the mainstream of evangelical Protestantism and into closer fellowship with themselves. During World War II, there was a move to unite evangelical Christians into a nationwide fellowship outside the aegis of the more liberal National Council of Churches. First in the field was the American Council of Christian Churches headed by Carl McIntire, which began in 1941. This group, however, rep-

[47] *The Pentecostal Evangel,* August 18, 1928, p. 7.

[48] William W. Menzies, "The Assemblies of God: 1941-1967, The Consolidation of a Revival Movement" (Unpublished Ph.D. dissertation, The University of Iowa, 1968), pp. 51-54.

resented the old militant, belligerent spirit of rancor and disruption that had characterized the fundamentalist versus modernist wars of the 1920's and 1930's. Furthermore, the ACCC continued the fundamentalist rejection of the pentecostals.[49]

In order to create an evangelical alliance without the unfortunate overtones of the now discredited fundamentalists, a new organization called the National Association of Evangelicals was formed in 1943. Several attempts were soon made to merge the ACCC with the younger NAE, but negotiations always broke down because of the fact that several pentecostal bodies had been founding members of the NAE. In his *Christian Beacon*, McIntire bitterly assailed the pentecostals and the NAE by saying:

> "Tongues" is one of the great signs of the apostasy. As true protestant denominations turn from the faith and it gets darker, the Devil comes more into the open, and people who are not fed in the old line denominations go out to the "tongues" movement, for they feel that they have some life.
>
> The dominance of the "tongues" groups in the NAE "denominations" and their compromise in regard to the Federal Council will not, we believe, commend this organization to those who desire to see a standard lifted in behalf of the historic Christian faith. . . .[50]

Following this volley, the NAE was forced to choose between the pentecostal groups already within the fellowship and the ACCC of Carl McIntire. In the end, they chose the pentecostals, the split between the NAE and the ACCC continuing to this day. For the pentecostals, these moves meant that the future course of the movement would be a moderate position between the left-leaning National Council of Churches and the right-leaning American Council of Christian Churches. Thus without strong ideological fetters from either extremes of the right or left, the pentecostals were in a fortunate position for greater theological and intellectual acceptance in the years to come.[51]

[49] *Ibid.*, pp. 56-58; Conn, *Like a Mighty Army*, p. 258.

[50] Carl McIntire, *Christian Beacon*, April 27, 1944, p. 8.

[51] Menzies, "The Assemblies of God, 1941-1967," pp. 59-61; *The*

A historic by-product of the pentecostal participation in the NAE was the formation of a nationwide fellowship between the larger pentecostal denominations in the late 1940's. From the beginning of the movement in 1906 until World War II, the pentecostals had remained isolated from each other and somewhat aloof, particularly because of doctrinal differences such as the problem of sanctification. The meetings of the NAE provided the first opportunities for the various pentecostal leaders to meet together. It was in the lobbies between sessions of the NAE meetings that the idea of a national organization of pentecostals was born. Many old antagonisms were forgotten as a feeling of kinship began to replace the older suspicions. Another stimulus toward unity was the suggestion made by the first World Pentecostal Fellowship, which met in Zurich, Switzerland, in 1947, that the pentecostals of North America combine into a closer fellowship. The climate of togetherness seemed to be worldwide among pentecostals in the mid-twentieth century.[52]

The first step toward uniting American pentecostals came at the close of the May 1948 meeting of the NAE in Chicago. Here "exploratory" plans were laid for the inauguration of a fellowship which would encompass the continent of North America. A second exploratory conference was held in Chicago on August 3 and 4, 1948, which included representatives of twelve pentecostal denominations. Here a name was proposed, the "Pentecostal Fellowship of North America," a common statement of faith suggested, and a statement of aims proposed. The conference closed by calling for a constitutional convention to be held in Des Moines, Iowa, at the headquarters of the Open Bible Standard Church in 1948.

The Des Moines Convention, which met from October 26 to 28, 1948, was composed of two hundred delegates from a dozen bodies. In short order a constitution was adopted and the PFNA became the voice of about one million pentecostals in North America representing over 10,000 local churches. Founding members of the fellowship included the

Church of God Evangel, May 21, 1949, pp. 12-15; The Pentecostal Evangel, June 19, 1943, p. 8.

52 Menzies, "The Assemblies of God, 1941-1967," pp. 80-81; Gee, The Pentecostal Movement, p. 122; Nichols, Pentecostalism, pp. 211-216.

Assemblies of God, The Church of God, the Pentecostal Holiness Church, the International Church of the Foursquare Gospel, and the Open Bible Standard Church. By the time of the second meeting in 1949, membership had grown to include fourteen groups, including the Pentecostal Assemblies of Canada. Notable for their absence were the Negro pentecostal bodies, the unitarian pentecostals, the Tomlinson branches of the Church of God, and churches such as the Pentecostal Church of God whose divorce views were considered too liberal for the founding bodies. In essence, the PFNA represented the mainstream of respectable, white, orthodox pentecostalism in North America.[53]

The growth of pentecostalism into a large worldwide family of churches also resulted in a new generation of Bible schools and colleges to serve the movement. Beginning with Holmes Bible College at Greenville, South Carolina, in 1898, the pentecostal movement saw the founding of a score of colleges between that year and 1950. The first denominationally owned college was Lee College, founded in 1918 by the Church of God in Cleveland, Tennessee. The following year the Pentecostal Holiness Church founded Emmanuel College in Franklin Springs, Georgia. The Assemblies of God founded their first denominational school, called Central Bible Institute, in Springfield, Missouri, in 1922. It was not until 1955, however, that that denomination opened its first liberal arts college, Evangel College, also located in Springfield.[54]

In the early days, there were many pentecostals who feared liberal arts education as a possible Trojan horse that might eventually cool the fires of revival ardor that had produced the movement. But by the fifties and sixties, no efforts were being spared in the upgrading of denominational

[53] The Church of God Evangel, April 15, 1944, p. 3; September 28, 1948, pp. 4-5; The Pentecostal Evangel, November 20, 1948, p. 13; The Pentecostal Holiness Advocate, May 27, 1948, pp. 2-6; November 11, 1948, pp. 3-11.

[54] See Thomas, Holmes Theological Seminary; Mauldin Ray, "A Study of the History of Lee College, Cleveland, Tennessee" (Unpublished Doctoral dissertation, Houston University, 1964); Vinson Synan, Emmanuel College—The First Fifty Years (Washington, D.C., 1968); and Brumback, Suddenly from Heaven, pp. 326-330.

schools and having them gain regional accreditation. One
event that seemed to promise much for the future of pentecostalism was the creation of a school billed as the first
distinctly pentecostal university in the nation—Oral Roberts
University in Tulsa, Oklahoma. Founded by two Pentecostal
Holiness preachers, Oral Roberts and R. O. Corvin, this
institution began classes in 1965 with plans for a hundred-
million-dollar campus that would house a first-rate university,
offering, in time, doctoral programs in several fields. One of
its first schools was the Graduate School of Theology, headed
by Corvin, which was accepted as the first pentecostal
seminary to offer postgraduate degrees. Symbolic of increasing acceptance by the traditional churches of the pentecostals was the fact that Billy Graham assisted in the act of
dedication in April of 1967.[55]

Soon after the dedication of the new university, however,
Roberts shocked the religious world by joining the Methodist
Church in March 1968. He also transferred his ordination
vows as an ordained minister. The world's best-known pentecostal since Aimee Semple McPherson, Roberts had since
1947 built a tremendous faith-healing empire from his headquarters in Tulsa. The overwhelming source of his support
during his earlier years had been from the pentecostals. But
by the 1960's a larger share of his income had been from
people in the more traditional churches. These people, most
of whom had experienced speaking with other tongues, were
dubbed "neo-pentecostals" by old-line members of the pentecostal movement. Roberts' defection from the church in
which his father and mother had been pioneer ministers, and
from the pentecostal movement in general which had brought
him to prominence, puzzled many. At any rate, the dream of
Roberts' university becoming an intellectual center for the
pentecostal world was shattered by this event.[56]

55 *Abundant Life*, June 1967, pp. 1-32, gives the story of the
founding and dedication of the school. See also the *Oral Roberts
University Bulletin, 1966-1967* (Tulsa, Oklahoma, 1967); and *Oral
Roberts University Outreach*, Winter 1967, pp. 1-24.

56 Oral Roberts, *My Twenty Years of a Miracle Ministry* (Tulsa,
Oklahoma, 1967), pp. 61-84; *Abundant Life*, February 1970, pp. 5-8.
For reaction to Roberts' conversion see *Christianity Today*, April 12,
1968, p. 34; and *The Pentecostal Holiness Advocate*, April 27, 1968, p.
13.

The fact that Roberts was accepted by the Methodist Church, although he vowed never to change his pentecostal doctrines, was indicative of the new acceptance pentecostalism was experiencing in American society by the middle of the twentieth century. Perhaps one reason for this new acceptance was the fact that the pentecostals were by then the fastest-growing segment of evangelical Christianity around the world. Their growth rates in the United States were also far above those of the more traditional denominations. As a result of these facts, a great deal of interest was increasingly being shown toward the pentecostals by the more liberal elements of both Protestantism and Catholicism. These new pentecostals called their movement the "Charismatic Movement" to distinguish themselves from the older mainline pentecostals. By the end of the 1960's, this movement was growing to such proportions that several denominations were forced to take official cognizance of the phenomenon. This reaction ranged from the denunciation of the pentecostals in the Episcopal Diocese of California by Bishop James Pike, to the acceptance of glossolalia by the Presbyterian Church, U.S.A., as an approved practice within the church.[57]

An even more arresting instance of the pentecostal penetration into other church bodies was the outbreak of glossolalia among many Roman Catholics in the United States. Beginning with a startling outbreak at Duquesne University in 1966, the movement rapidly spread to Notre Dame University where a major occurrence of tongues was in evidence among both students and faculty members by 1967. Although there were those who questioned the propriety of the meetings where the pentecostal phenomenon occurred, most observers were in agreement that the movement was beneficial and caused the participants to be more loyal to the Catholic Church. Some saw in the movement hope for a spiritual renewal which would "stir up afresh the grace of

[57] Frank Farrell, "Outburst of Tongues: The New Penetration," *Christianity Today*, September 13, 1963, pp. 3-7. See also "Fanning the Charismatic Flame," November 24, 1967, pp. 39-40. A survey of the new penetration of pentecostalism in the traditional churches is given in Morton T. Kelsey's *Tongue Speaking* (New York, 1964), and McCandlish Phillips, "And There Appeared Unto Them Tongues of Fire," *Saturday Evening Post*, May 16, 1964, pp. 30-40. Also see *Christianity Today*, June 19, 1970, p. 31.

baptism and confirmation." Far from condemning the phenomenon, Catholic theologians and ecclesiastical authorities called for an investigation of the possible value of glossolalia to the church. Of interest to those who studied the movement was the fact that the preponderance of Catholic pentecostals were from the intellectual groups "such as university and college teachers and their wives." The chief apologist for this new pentecostal wave among the Catholics was Kevin Ranaghan, a theology professor at Notre Dame University. In his book, *Catholic Pentecostals*, published in 1969, Ranaghan observed that the movement lacked the emotionalism of traditional pentecostal meetings, but was resulting in deepened loyalty to the church and reverence for the rosary and the mass. By 1970 it was reported that the movement was "spreading like wildfire" among Catholics and that over 30,000 had experienced the other tongues within the last two years. Taking cognizance of the new move, the U. S. Catholic hierarchy declared in November 1969 that the movement "should at this point not be inhibited but allowed to develop."[58]

A sign of the penetration of pentecostal practice into the traditional Protestant churches was the conversion of the widely read interdenominational monthly periodical, *Christian Life*, to the pentecostal view. Reported on its pages were many stories of Baptists, Methodists, Presbyterians, and others who had received the pentecostal experience. Among them were reports of some Methodist pastors and congregations that had experienced revivals of the phenomenon. To Wesleyan-oriented pentecostals, this was taken as a sign that the pentecostal movement was making the full cycle and finding a place in the church that had mothered the holiness-pentecostal movement in the first place.[59]

58 Kevin and Dorothy Ranaghan, *Catholic Pentecostals* (New York: Paulist Press, 1969), pp. 6-57; Edward O'Conner, "A Catholic Pentecostal Movement," *Ave Maria, A National Catholic Weekly*, June 3, 1967, pp. 7-30; "Catholic Pentecostalism," *Jubilee*, June 1968, pp. 13-17; *Christianity Today*, January 2, 1970, pp. 41-42; Kilian McDonnell, *Catholic Pentecostalism: Problems in Evaluation* (Pecos, New Mexico, 1970); J. Massingberd Ford, *The Pentecostal Experience: A New Direction for American Catholics* (New York, 1970).

59 Marvin Buck, "When the Holy Spirit Came to a Methodist Church," *Christian Life*, January 1962, pp. 34-36.

Among the holiness denominations that had bitterly rejected pentecostalism after 1906, there was a perceptible change of attitude by the late 1960's as a result of the neo-pentecostal movement in the other churches. The older view, that "pentecostalism is the holiness movement gone to seed," was rapidly being changed. By 1965, the best minds of the National Holiness Association were declaring that "the pentecostal movement is one of the unpaid debts of the holiness movement." To be sure, the older and quite negative attitude persisted among many, but a new strand of tolerance was being seen among younger leaders of the movement. Illustrative of the new openness was the fact that the National Holiness Association, by the end of its first century of existence in 1967, was admitting to its membership bodies that practiced speaking in tongues. An example of this practice was the membership of the Bethany Fellowship of Minneapolis. Dr. Frank Bateman Stanger, President of Asbury Theological Seminary, supports the contention that "there is a new climate of understanding emerging between holiness and pentecostal people" and that this has been engendered in large measure by common participation in such evangelical agencies and enterprises as the National Association of Evangelicals.[60]

A further probable reason for this new interest has been the fact that the pentecostal movement has far outgrown the older holiness movement around the world. Indeed, by the middle of the twentieth century, the pentecostals were burgeoning into what some called "the third force in Christendom." Surveys of the worldwide Christian scene were revealing that three-fourths of all Protestants in Latin America were pentecostals, that two-thirds of all non-Catholics in Italy were pentecostals, and that the majority of all Christians in South Africa were pentecostals. Furthermore, the largest free churches in Russia, Scandinavia, and France were pentecostal and the growth rates indicated vastly greater growth for the future. These startling facts have led some experts on church growth, such as Walter Hollenweger, Secre-

[60] John Peters, *Christian Perfection and American Methodism*, p. 195; Kenneth E. Geiger, *et al.*, *The Word and the Doctrine: Studies in Contemporary Wesleyan-Arminian Theology* (Kansas City, 1965), pp. 317-351.

tary of Evangelism of the World Council of Churches, to predict that the Christians of Africa and Latin America would outnumber the Christians on the other three continents by the year 2000. Of this vast body of new Christians, "the majority or at least a very considerable part of this Christianity will belong to the spontaneous non-literary pentecostal type." Because of this mushroom-like growth, the World Council of Churches has taken increased interest in the movement.[61]

By 1970 it was impossible to give precise figures of the size of the pentecostal movement in the United States and the world. This uncertainty was due to the fact that the pentecostals were averse to keeping accurate statistics and also to the fact that there existed so many independent groups that it was impossible to make a definitive count. The best-informed guesses were that by 1970 there were about four million persons in the United States who could be classified as being pentecostal. About half of these were in the mainline organized denominations and the other half in the thousands of independent storefront churches and missions that dotted the nation's cities and countryside. In addition there were uncounted thousands of "neo-pentecostals" in the traditional denominations who were pentecostal in experience and belief and generally designated themselves "the Charismatic movement."[62]

The worldwide size of the movement was even more difficult to estimate than that of the United States. Using various standards of defining exactly what constituted a "pentecostal" and educated guesses concerning statistics, estimates of the world constituency of the movement have ranged from 12,000,000 to 35,000,000. The pentecostals themselves accept a figure in the range of 12,000,000 to 15,000,000, while officials of the World Council of Churches tend toward the 35,000,000 figure. Whatever the actual number might be, it is evident that the movement has experienced phenomenal

61 Henry P. Van Dusen, "The Third Force," *Life*, June 9, 1958, pp. 122-124; Walter Hollenweger, "Pentecostalism and the Third World," *Pulse, Evangelical Committee on Latin America*, IV, 6 (December 1969), 11-13.

62 Kelsey, *Tongue Speaking*, pp. 242-243; Atter, *The Third Force*, p. 227; Kendrick, *The Promise Fulfilled*, p. 4.

growth since its first faltering days at the beginning of the century.[63]

Regardless of its eventual size or influence in the religious world, it is also clear that the pentecostal movement is one of the few major religious movements to originate in America and subsequently become a major force beyond the borders of the nation. Whether the movement deserves to be ranked alongside Catholicism and traditional Protestantism as a "third force" in Christian history remains to be seen, but the statement by the Presbyterian writer Charles S. Sydnor, Jr., that the pentecostal movement "is an authentic reformation-revival movement of historic significance, equal with those of other great movements of centuries past," seems to be well founded.[64]

[63] Hollenweger, "Pentecostalism and the Third World," p. 12; Atter, *The Third Force*, pp. 226-229.

[64] Charles S. Sydnor, Jr., "The Pentecostals," *The Presbyterian Survey*, June 1964, p. 37.

Chapter Ten

A SUMMARY

The appearance of over a score of pentecostal denominations in the United States in the twentieth century is a development of great significance in the social and religious life of the nation. Although the pentecostal movement began in the United States, itself a significant fact, its theological and intellectual origins were British. The basic premises of the movement's theology were constructed by John Wesley in the eighteenth century. As a product of Methodism, the holiness-pentecostal movement traces its lineage through the Wesleys to Anglicanism and from thence to Roman Catholicism. This theological heritage places the pentecostals outside the Calvinistic, reformed tradition which culminated in the Baptist and Presbyterian movements in the United States. The basic pentecostal theological position might be described as Arminian, perfectionistic, premillennial, and charismatic.[1]

Basically, the pentecostal and holiness churches are attempting to propagate the historic message of Methodism, although with some doctrinal and governmental changes. Indeed, the recorded accounts of the early Methodist camp meetings are strikingly similar to descriptions of modern-day pentecostal meetings. The religious experiences of the pentecostals also bear a striking resemblance to the experiences of

[1] Examples of pentecostal theological concepts are found in: Frank W. Lemons, *Our Pentecostal Heritage* (Cleveland, Tennessee, 1963); J. H. King, *From Passover to Pentecost* (Franklin Springs, Georgia, 1914); R. M. Riggs, *The Spirit Himself* (Springfield, Missouri, 1949); and J. A. Synan, *Christian Life in Depth* (Franklin Springs, Georgia, 1964).

Wesley, Finney, Moody, and other religious leaders of the past. Although all these did not speak with tongues, their "baptism with the Spirit" was as ecstatic and esoteric as any experienced by the later pentecostals. The fact that Finney once wept and "bellowed out the unutterable gushings" of his soul, whereas Moody in 1871 "dropped to the floor and lay bathing his soul in the divine" while his room "seemed ablaze with God," indicates that pentecostal-like religious experiences are nothing new.[2]

The rise of the modern holiness-pentecostal sects came only after this enthusiastic type of religious experience was rejected by its chief propagator—the Methodist Church. The Civil War, and its resultant moral letdown, caused a de-emphasis of holiness teaching in Methodism. The organization of the National Holiness Association in 1867 was an attempt to revive an interest in holiness teaching and practice, primarily within the Methodist churches, but also within much of American Protestantism. From 1867 to 1894 the extra-ecclesiastical "holiness associations" were able to revive the doctrine temporarily, but in the end failed to permanently influence the Methodist Church. After the 1894 denunciation of the holiness advocates by the bishops of the Southern Methodist Church, holiness-oriented ministers and laymen began to form denominations devoted to this theology, which they considered to be the original Methodism as taught by Wesley.

This period of schism occurred when the Methodist churches formed the largest Protestant denominational family in the United States, and during the decade from 1890 to 1900 when American Protestantism experienced its greatest growth.[3] A series of schisms in the nation's largest Protestant denomination, when it was at the height of its national influence, was a development of importance in American history. These schisms came when Methodism was attempting to come to grips with the challenges of the industrial, intel-

2 William R. Moody, *The Life of Dwight L. Moody* (New York, 1900), pp. 146-147; Charles G. Finney, *Memoirs of Charles G. Finney* (New York, 1876), pp. 17-18.

3 Robertson, *That Old-Time Religion*, pp. 79-111; U. S. Bureau of the Census, *Historical Statistics of the United States; Colonial Times to 1957* (Washington, 1961), pp. 226-228.

lectual, and social revolutions which were vitally changing the life of the nation. As Methodism began to accept the premises of the social gospel and the findings of higher criticism, the most conservative elements of the church, those who wished to preserve the traditional Methodist values, expressed their protest by joining the holiness revolts. The holiness crusade also pointed to the great reservoir of conservatism that continued to dominate much of organized Methodism at the turn of the century. This conservatism found its strongest voices in such men as Bishops Candler and Cannon who led the Methodist conservatives in the two decades that followed.

The holiness-pentecostal movement was also part of a larger protest movement which permeated the social and intellectual life of the nation from the Civil War to the First World War. Included in the long list of reformers and protesters were the feminists, prohibitionists, socialists, single-taxers, trade unionists, populists, and progressives. Along with these social and political reformers, America also saw a larger group of religious reformers during the same period. Mary Baker Eddy, with the "Christian Science" movement, vied for attention with the social gospel ideas of Gladden and Rauschenbusch. Revivalists such as Sam Jones and Billy Sunday offered their solutions to the problems besetting society, while the Roman Catholic Church consolidated the gains achieved by decades of massive immigration. An integral part of this massive response to the problems created by an industrialized, modern American society was the holiness-pentecostal movement, which added its voice to the general protests against what it considered to be the evils of the times.

The fact that the holiness schisms occurred at the same time and were concentrated in the same areas of the populist revolt suggests the social and intellectual origins of the movement. Representing as it did a conservative movement to preserve a religious way of life of an earlier era, the holiness break constituted the religious counterpart of the political and economic revolt of the populists. To the populistic mind the "eastern monopolies" included not only the moguls of Wall Street and the railroad interests, but the bishops of the Methodist Church as well.

The pentecostal movement, with beginnings from 1901 to 1906, represented a theological division within the holiness movement. This division was essentially caused by a controversy over the evidence required to prove that one had been baptized with the Holy Spirit. The pentecostals, following the teaching of such men as Parham and Seymour, held that speaking with other tongues met this evidentiary demand. The factions that refused to accept this interpretation continued the classical holiness movement as it had been taught since the days of Palmer and Inskip, while the pentecostals developed divergent modes of worship and theological interpretation. Essentially, however, the pentecostal movement began as a somewhat more emotional and theologically more experimental wing of the holiness movement, and it was to remain so. Attesting to these traits is the fact that all pentecostal groups were still being classified as late as 1970 according to their views of sanctification. Indeed, all holiness and pentecostal denominations have continued to include in their creedal statements references to "sanctification" or "holiness" that have served to identify their theological positions.

Other theological divisions occurred within the pentecostal movement from 1906 to 1923. The first of these was the "finished work" theory which denied the ancient premise of a "second work of grace" that brought "Christian perfection" to the believer. As a result of this controversy the Assemblies of God denomination was formed in 1914 as a pentecostal, but not holiness, group. Consequently, most of the pentecostal groups that were formed thereafter incorporated the "finished work" view of sanctification. This represented the first divergence from the original pentecostal doctrine as taught by Parham, Seymour, and Cashwell.

A second theological division occurred in 1916 when the infant Assemblies of God denomination was split over the "Jesus Only" or unitarian controversy. With their view that God the Father and the Holy Spirit were only "titles" referring to Jesus Christ, who alone constituted the Godhead, the pentecostal unitarians insisted on baptism or rebaptism in the name of Jesus only. This represented the most radical theological departure from orthodox Christian thought in the history of the holiness-pentecostal movement. As a result of this doctrinal rejection of the Trinity, a new generation of pentecostal denominations arose that was to be dedicated to the "Jesus Only" or "Jesus Name" view. Outstanding among these groups were the Negro "Pentecostal Assemblies of the World" and the white "United Pentecostal Church."

That the Pentecostal Assemblies of the World was initially an interracial church, with roughly equal numbers of Negroes and whites as both officials and members, points to the interracial character of the early pentecostal movement. Since the years from 1901 to 1924 were years of growing racism in the United States, this phenomenon of interracial worship by the lower classes of whites and Negroes was a significant exception to the racial mores of the times. Striking proof of this fact was the position of Seymour as the leader of the Azusa Street Mission in Los Angeles, the mother church of the movement. Although the pentecostal movement claims no single person as its founder, Seymour comes as close as any man to qualifying for the role.

The interracial period lasted from 1905, when Seymour was admitted to Parham's Bible School in Houston, until 1924, when the last interracial denomination divided on racial lines. In the interim, The Negro Church of God in Christ, led by Bishop C. H. Mason, served as the home of scores of white ministers who later organized the Assembly of God group. One by one, the pentecostal churches divided into white and Negro branches after 1906, the Fire-Baptized Holiness Church dividing in 1908, the Pentecostal Holiness Church in 1913, the Church of God in Christ in 1914, and the Pentecostal Assemblies of the World in 1924. The Cleveland Church maintained its Negro branch as a separate entity under white leadership until 1966 when the Negro churches and ministers were completely integrated into the structure of the church. This action indicated that even the most "Southern" pentecostal groups were taking steps to keep abreast of the Negro Civil Rights movement of the sixties.

The fundamentalist controversy which so bitterly divided American Christendom in the twenties left the pentecostal groups largely untouched. Since they did not participate in the leadership of the movement, which consisted largely of Baptists, Presbyterians, and Methodists, the pentecostals acted mostly as spectators. Because the decade of the twenties was also a period of controversy and schism within the pentecostal movement itself, few leaders had time or

opportunity to engage in the wider fundamentalist controversy. The "finished work" and "Jesus Only" schisms were
the major theological concerns of the pentecostals during the
decade. With these theological battles being fought and doctrines in the process of being consolidated, the pentecostals
had little interest in theological battles outside their own
movement. The fact that the fundamentalists themselves rejected the pentecostals, along with Darwinists, modernists,
and others, tended to alienate pentecostals who otherwise
might have supported them. Also, the heavy Calvinist orienta-
tion of fundamentalism tended to repel pentecostals, most of
whom were Arminian in theology. The lack of involvement in
the fundamentalist controversy spared the pentecostals much
of the anti-intellectualism that was one of the main residues
of the controversy.

The twenties also saw the last major period of schism
within the pentecostal movement. These splits, which occurred chiefly from 1920 to 1930, were based mainly on
personality conflicts and not on doctrinal issues. The dominating personalities of Aimee Semple McPherson, A. J. Tomlinson, and Florence Crawford resulted in the formation of
the Foursquare Church, the Church of God of Prophecy, and
the Open Bible Standard Churches. With the creation of these
groups, the period of sect-formation and schism in the movement ended, a period that had lasted roughly from 1906 to
1932. After 1932, no other major pentecostal groups were
formed in the United States, the movement having assumed
roughly its present form.

As occupation with controversy and schism lessened, the
pentecostal groups entered a period of institutional development that was to last until the present. By 1918 the Church
of God had begun its first college, which eventually became
known as Lee College. The Pentecostal Holiness Church
followed a year later with Emmanuel College. The Assemblies
of God created their first Bible school in 1922 in Springfield,
Missouri, but waited until 1955 before founding their first
liberal arts college. In addition to these institutions of higher
education, the pentecostal churches had by 1970 created
dozens of Bible colleges, high schools, printing presses, orphanages, retirement homes, and urban rescue missions.

Whether these institutions would bring to the movement

problems about formalism, ritualism, indifference, and "respectability" remained to be seen. However, by the early twenties the institutions of the movement were only in their incipient stages and hence not able to greatly influence the development of the denominations. But the fact remained that these institutions would eventually have a profound effect on the movements that created them. At any rate, it was clear that as the period of formal organization ended around 1930, the stage of massive growth and development began, and along with it, a growth of church institutions and ecclesiastical machinery that had been almost non-existent in the earlier years of the movement.[4]

Basically, the pentecostal movement is an heir of the frontier, enthusiastic type of religion that has been indigenous to the American religious experience. It is probably the only large group in the United States that continues to exhibit the fervor and enthusiasm so common during the Great Awakening, the Kentucky revivals, and the Methodist camp meetings. It also is an attempt to perpetuate the doctrine of perfectionism which dominated Protestantism during the nineteenth century, as well as the tradition of revivalism that loomed so large in the last century and the early part of the twentieth century.

By 1970 it was generally conceded that "the pentecostal churches are almost certainly the fastest growing Christian communities in the world."[5] It also was becoming increasingly apparent that they were appealing to an ever widening spectrum of America's citizens. Because of this phenomenal growth, the attitude of other churches was beginning to change from mere toleration to one of active interest. "What can we learn from the pentecostal churches" seemed to summarize Protestant thinking.

[4] Moberg, *The Church as a Social Institution*, pp. 118-125. According to Moberg there are five stages of denominational development: (1) incipient organization, (2) formal organization, (3) maximum efficiency, (4) institutional stage, (5) disintegration. It is the author's opinion that the second stage ended by 1930. By the middle of the century the pentecostal denominations were well into the "maximum efficiency" stage.

[5] Bishop Lesslie Newbigin, quoted in J. S. Murray, "What We Can Learn from the Pentecostal Churches," *Christianity Today*, June 9, 1967, p. 10.

This attitude indicated that the era of passive toleration which began in the middle-twenties was ending and that a new era of acceptance and cooperation was beginning. At any rate, the far-reaching holiness and pentecostal movements, which began in 1867, had developed into a great worldwide movement by 1967. As this movement entered its second century, it was possible only to conjecture as to how extensive it would eventually become.

BIBLIOGRAPHY

Collections

Archives of the Church of God. This collection is housed in the headquarters of the denomination in Cleveland, Tennessee. This is the best source for documents pertaining to the family of churches known as The Church of God.

Archives of the Church of the Nazarene. Located in Kansas City, Missouri, this constitutes an extensive source for manuscripts, periodicals, and general accounts relating to the National Holiness Movement and the holiness denominations which issued from it.

Archives of the Pentecostal Holiness Church. Located in Franklin Springs, Georgia, this collection is the best source for materials on the Pentecostal Holiness Church and the groups in the Southeast associated with that church.

Oral Roberts University Pentecostal Collection. This collection, in Tulsa, Oklahoma, is the most complete grouping of materials relating to the pentecostal movement in the world. An excellent file of manuscripts and periodicals as well as rare publications pertaining to the modern pentecostal denominations can also be found here.

The Pentecostal File of the Assemblies of God. This collection, relating to the history of the Assemblies of God group and others derived from this church, is located in the national headquarters in Springfield, Missouri.

Sources for the holiness movement in the Southern Methodist Church can be found in the libraries and archives of Emory University in Atlanta, Georgia, and Duke University in Durham, North Carolina.

Primary Sources

Asbury, Francis, *The Journal of the Rev. Francis Asbury*. 3 vols. New York: Bangs and Mason, 1821.

Bailey, S. Clyde, *Pioneer Marvels of Faith*. Morristown, Tennessee, n.d.

Bartleman, Frank, *How Pentecost Came to Los Angeles*. Los Angeles, 1925.

Britton, F. M., *Pentecostal Truth, or Sermons on Regeneration, Sanctification, the Baptism of the Holy Spirit, Divine Healing, the Second Coming of Jesus, etc.* Royston, Georgia: Publishing House of the Pentecostal Holiness Church, 1919.

Brumback, Carl, *God in Three Persons.* Cleveland, Tennessee: Pathway Press, 1959.

Buckalew, J. W., *Incidents in the Life of J. W. Buckalew.* Cleveland, Tennessee: Church of God Publishing House, 1920.

Carey, Thurman A., *Memoirs of Thurman A. Carey.* Columbia, South Carolina: A. E. Robinson, printer, 1907.

Cox, B. L., *My Life Story.* Greenwood, South Carolina: Congregational Holiness Publishing House, 1959.

Curnock, Nehemiah, ed., *The Journal of the Rev. John Wesley, A.M.* 8 vols. London: Robert Culley, 1910.

Etter, Mrs. M. B. Woodworth, *Marvels and Miracles; Signs and Wonders.* Indianapolis, 1922.

———, *Signs and Wonders God Wrought in the Ministry for Forty Years.* Indianapolis, 1916.

Ewart, Frank J., *The Phenomenon of Pentecost, A History of the Latter Rain.* St. Louis: Pentecostal Publishing House, 1947.

———, *The Revelation of Jesus Christ.* St. Louis: Pentecostal Publishing House, n.d.

Finney, C. G., *Memoirs of Reverend Charles G. Finney.* New York: Fleming H. Revell Company, 1876.

Fletcher, John, *The Works of the Reverend John Fletcher.* 4 vols. New York: Lane and Scott, 1851.

Ford, J. Massingberd, *The Pentecostal Experience.* New York: Paulist Press, 1970.

Godbey, W. B., *Commentary on the New Testament.* 7 vols. Cincinnati: M. W. Knapp, 1896.

Goff, Florence, *Tests and Triumphs.* Falcon, North Carolina, 1924.

Goss, Ethel A., *Winds of God.* New York: Comet Press Books, 1958.

Haygood, Atticus G., *Growth in Grace. A Sermon by Atticus G. Haygood, D.D., LL.D., Preached Before the District Conference of the Oxford District, North Georgia Conference, M. E. Church, South, Held at Covington, Ga., July 18th, 1885, and Published by Formal Request of the Conference.* Macon, 1885.

Haynes, B. F., *Tempest-Tossed on Methodist Seas.* Kansas City: Nazarene Publishing House, 1914.

Holmes, N. J., *Life Sketches and Sermons.* Franklin Springs, Ga.: Publishing House of the Pentecostal Holiness Church, 1920.

Hughes, George, *Days of Power in the Forest Temple.* Boston, 1874.

Ironside, H. A., *Holiness, The False and the True.* Neptune, New Jersey: Loizeaux Brothers, 1912.

Jackson, Thomas, ed., *The Works of John Wesley.* 14 vols. Grand Rapids, Michigan: Zondervan Publishing House, 1959.

Juillerat, L. Howard, ed., *Book of Minutes.* Cleveland, Tennessee: Church of God Publishing House, 1922.

Keen, S. A., *Pentecostal Papers or the Gift of the Holy Ghost.* Cincinnati: M. W. Knapp, 1896.

King, J. H., *From Passover to Pentecost.* Memphis, Tennessee: H. W. Dixon Printing Company, 1914.

———, and Blanche L., *Yet Speaketh, Memoirs of the Late Bishop Joseph H. King.* Franklin Springs, Georgia: Publishing House of the Pentecostal Holiness Church, 1949.

La Berge, Agnes N. O., *What God Hath Wrought—Life and Work of Mrs. Agnes N. O. La Berge, Nee Miss Agnes N. Ozman.* Chicago: Herald Publishing Company, 1921.

Lee, R. H., and G. H. Montgomery, eds., *Edward D. Reeves, His Life and Message.* Franklin Springs, Georgia: Publishing House of the Pentecostal Holiness Church, 1940.

McLean, A., and Joel W. Eaton, eds., *Penuel, or Face to Face with God.* New York, 1869.

McPherson, Aimee Semple, *In the Service of the King.* New York: Boni and Liveright, 1927.

———, *The Foursquare Gospel.* Los Angeles: Robertson Printing Company, 1946.

———, *The Story of My Life.* Los Angeles: Echo Park Evangelistic Association, 1951.

———, *This Is That, Personal Experiences, Sermons and Writings of Aimee Semple McPherson.* Los Angeles: Echo Park Evangelistic Association, 1923.

Officer, Sam E., *The Jesus Church.* Cleveland, Tennessee: Private Printing, n.d.

Parham, Charles Fox, *A Voice Crying in the Wilderness.* Joplin, Missouri: Joplin Printing Company, 1944.

Pickett, L. L., *God or the Guessers, Some Scriptures on Present Day Infidelity.* Louisville, Kentucky: Pentecostal Publishing Company, 1926.

———, *The Pickett-Smith Debate on Entire Sanctification, A Second Blessing.* Terrell, Texas: Private Printing, 1896.

Pierce, Lovick, *A Miscellaneous Essay on Entire Sanctification, How It Was Lost to the Church, and How It May and Must Be Regained.* Atlanta, Georgia: Private Printing, 1897.

Riggs, Ralph M., *The Spirit Himself.* Springfield, Missouri: Gospel Publishing House, 1949.

Robinson, A. E., *A Layman and The Book.* Franklin Springs, Georgia: Publishing House of the Pentecostal Holiness Church, 1936.

Shaw, S. B., *Echoes of the General Holiness Assembly.* Chicago: S. B. Shaw Publisher, 1901.

Simpson, A. B., *Emblems of the Holy Spirit.* Nyack, New York: Christian Alliance Publishing Company, 1901.

Smith, Joseph, *History of the Church of Jesus Christ of Latter-Day Saints.* Salt Lake City: Deseret News, 1902.

Sorrow, Watson, *Some of My Experiences.* Franklin Springs, Georgia: Publishing House of the Pentecostal Holiness Church, 1954.

Stolee, Haakon J., *Speaking in Tongues.* Revised Edition. Minneapolis: Augsburg Publishing House, 1963.

Sugden, E. A., ed., *Wesley's Standard Sermons.* 2 vols. Nashville: Lamar and Barton, 1920.

Synan, J. A., *Christian Life in Depth.* Franklin Springs, Georgia: Advocate Press, 1964.
Taylor, G. F., *The Spirit and the Bride.* Dunn, North Carolina: Private Printing, 1907.
Telford, John, ed., *The Letters of the Rev. John Wesley.* 8 vols. London: Epworth Press, 1931.
Tomlinson, A. J., *Answering the Call of God.* Cleveland, Tennessee: White Wing Publishing House, n.d.
———, *God's Twentieth Century Pioneer.* Vol. I. Cleveland, Tennessee: White Wing Publishing House, 1962.
———, "Journal of Happenings," Manuscript Diary of A. J. Tomlinson in the Archives of the Church of God. Cleveland, Tennessee, 1901-1923.
———, *The Last Great Conflict.* Cleveland, Tennessee: Walter E. Rodgers Press, 1913.
Tomlinson, Homer A., ed., *Diary of A. J. Tomlinson.* 3 vols. New York: The Church of God, World Headquarters, 1949-1955.
———, *The Shout of a King.* New York: The Church of God, World Headquarters, 1965.
Tomlinson, M. A., *Basic Bible Beliefs.* Cleveland, Tennessee: White Wing Publishing House, 1961.
White, Alma, *Demons and Tongues.* 4th Edition. Zeraphath, New Jersey: The Pillar of Fire, 1949.
Wilson, George W., *Methodist Theology vs. Methodist Theologians.* Cincinnati: Jennings and Pye, 1904.
Wood, J. A., *Auto-Biography of Rev. J. A. Wood.* Chicago: The Christian Witness Company, 1904.

Minutes, Yearbooks, and Handbooks

Annual Revision of the Compilation of the Local Churches. The Pentecostal Church of God of America. Joplin, Missouri: Messenger Publishing House, 1966.
Ashworth, C. A., *Yearbook of the Church of God in Christ.* Memphis, 1961.
Clark, Elmer T., *The Small Sects in America.* Revised Edition. Nashville: Abingdon Press, 1959.
Constitution and General Rules of the Fire-Baptized Holiness Church. Royston, Georgia: Live Coals Press, 1905, 1910.
Crayne, Richard, *Pentecostal Handbook.* Morristown, Tennessee: Private Printing, 1963.
Directory, The Assemblies of God. Springfield, Missouri: The Gospel Publishing House, 1962.
Discipline of the Evangelical United Brethren Church. Harrisburg, Pennsylvania: The Evangelical Press, 1951.
Discipline of the Fire-Baptized Holiness Church. Pembroke, North Carolina, 1916.
Discipline of the Fire-Baptized Holiness Church of God of the Americas. Atlanta, 1962.

Discipline of the Pentecostal Free-Will Baptist Church, Inc. Dunn, North Carolina, n.d.

Doctrines and Discipline of the Methodist Episcopal Church, South. Nashville: Southern Methodist Publishing House, 1866, 1878.

Holy Convocation, Church of God in Christ, Souvenir Book and Official Program (59th). Memphis, 1966.

Journal, General Conference of the Methodist Episcopal Church, South. Nashville: Southern Methodist Publishing House, 1866, 1870, 1878.

Landis, Benson Y., and Constant H. Jacquet, Jr., *Yearbook of American Churches.* New York: National Council of Churches, 1964-1970.

Mayer, F. E., *The Religious Bodies of America.* St. Louis: Concordia Publishing House, 1961.

Mead, Frank S., *Handbook of Denominations in the United States.* 4th Edition. New York: Abingdon Press, 1965.

Minutes, Church of God of the Mountain Assembly, Inc. Jellico, Tennessee, 1965.

Minutes of the Beulah Pentecostal Holiness Church. Franklin Springs, Georgia, 1896-1956.

Minutes of the Emmanuel Holiness Church Annual Assemblies of Alabama, Florida, Georgia, North Carolina, and South Carolina. Franklin Springs, Georgia, 1959, 1965.

Minutes of the General Assemblies of the Church of God (Cleveland, Tennessee). Cleveland: The Pathway Press, 1906-1966.

Minutes of the General Conferences of the Pentecostal Holiness Church. Franklin Springs, Georgia, 1910-1965.

Minutes of the Holiness Church of North Carolina. Kinston, North Carolina, 1908, 1909, 1910.

Minutes of the 1963 Sessions of the Conferences of the Congregational Holiness Church. Greenwood, South Carolina: Publishing House of the Congregational Holiness Church, 1963.

Minutes of the 60th Annual Assembly of the Church of God of Prophecy. Cleveland, Tennessee: White Wing Publishing House, 1965.

Tomlinson, M. A., ed., *Cyclopedic Index of Assembly Minutes (1906-1940) of the Church of God Over Which A. J. Tomlinson Was General Overseer and M. A. Tomlinson Is Now General Overseer* (Church of God of Prophecy). Cleveland, Tennessee: White Wing Publishing House, 1950.

Twentieth Anniversary of the Garr Auditorium. Charlotte, 1950.

U. S. Bureau of the Census, *Historical Statistics of the United States, Colonial Times to 1957.* Washington: Government Printing Office, 1961.

——, *Religious Bodies: 1926.* 2 vols. Washington: Government Printing Office, 1929.

——, *Religious Bodies: 1936.* 2 vols. Washington: Government Printing Office, 1941.

Yearbook of the Church of God in Christ. Memphis, 1960-1961.

Periodicals

Abundant Life (Tulsa, Oklahoma), 1967.
Altamont Witness (Greenville, South Carolina), 1911-1915.
Apostolic Evangel (Falcon, North Carolina), 1908-1926.
Apostolic Faith (Baxter Springs, Kansas), 1900-1925.
Apostolic Faith (Los Angeles), 1906-1909.
Beulah Christian (Providence, Rhode Island), 1895-1900.
Bridal Call, Foursquare (Los Angeles), 1921-1924.
Bridegroom's Messenger (Atlanta), 1965.
Bridegroom's Messenger (Dunn, North Carolina), 1907.
Christian Evangel, The. 1914-1919.
Church of God, The (Queen's Village, New York), 1966.
Church of God Evangel (Cleveland, Tennessee), 1910-1970.
Evangelist Speaks, The (Chester, Pennsylvania), 1966.
International Outlook (Los Angeles), 1963, 1964.
Life Magazine (New York), 1944, 1958.
Live Coals of Fire (Royston, Georgia), 1900-1907.
Living Words (Pittsburgh, Pennsylvania), 1903.
Los Angeles Times, 1906, 1907.
Pentecostal Evangel (Springfield, Missouri), 1919-1970.
Pentecostal Herald (St. Louis), 1967.
Pentecostal Holiness Advocate (Franklin Springs, Georgia), 1917-1970.
Presbyterian Survey (Atlanta, Georgia), 1964.
Saturday Evening Post (Philadelphia), 1964.
Sent of God (Tabor, Iowa), 1896-1920.
Voice of Holmes (Greenville, South Carolina), 1948.
Way of Faith (Columbia, South Carolina), 1901-1908.
White-Wing Messenger (Cleveland, Tennessee), 1910-1924.
Williamsburg Gazette (Williamsburg, Virginia), 1739-1772.
Word and Witness (Malvern, Arkansas), 1913-1916.

Articles

Aikman, Duncan, "The Holy Rollers," *American Mercury*, XV (October 1928), 180-181.

Boisen, A. T., "Religion and Hard Times," *Social Action* (March 1939).

Boland, J. M., "A Psychological View of Sin and Holiness," *Quarterly Review of the M. E. Church, South*, XII (July 1892), 342-354.

Buck, Marvin, "When the Holy Spirit Came to a Methodist Church," *Christian Life* (January 1962), 34-36.

Carter, Herbert, and Ruth K. Moore, "History of the Pentecostal Free Will Baptist Church," *The Bridegroom's Messenger* (October 1965), 4-16.

Corvin, R. O., "The Pentecostal Fellowship of North America," *Pentecost* (December 1949), 2.

Farrell, Frank, "Outburst of Tongues: The New Penetration," *Christianity Today* (September 13, 1963), 3-7.

Fidler, R. L., "Historical Review of the Pentecostal Outpouring in Los Angeles at the Azusa Street Mission in 1906," *The International Outlook* (January-March 1963), 3-14.

Flower, J. R., "Birth of the Pentecostal Movement," *Pentecostal Evangel*, XXXVIII (November 26, 1950), 3.

Griffis, Guion, "Camp Meetings in Ante-Bellum, North Carolina," *North Carolina Historical Review* (April 1933).

Hollenweger, Walter, "Pentecostalism and the Third World," *Pulse, Evangelical Committee on Latin America,* IV, 6 (December 1969), 11-13.

Holt, John B., "Holiness Religion: Cultural Shock and Social Reorganization," *American Sociological Review,* V (1940), 740-747.

King, J. H., "History of the Fire-Baptized Holiness Church," *The Pentecostal Holiness Advocate* (March-April 1921), a series of four articles.

Lapsley, James N., and John H. Simpson, "Speaking in Tongues," *The Princeton Seminary Bulletin,* LVIII (February 1965), 6, 7.

Mattke, Robert A., "The Baptism of the Holy Spirit as Related to the Work of Entire Sanctification," *Wesleyan Theological Journal* (Spring 1970), 22-32.

McIntire, Carl, Editorial, *Christian Beacon,* IX (April 27, 1944), 1-8.

Montgomery, G. H., "Christianity, the South, and Race Agitation," *The Pentecostal Holiness Advocate* (September 6, 1946), 3.

Murray, J. S., "What We Can Learn from Pentecostal Churches," *Christianity Today,* XI (June 9, 1967), 10-12.

O'Conner, Edward, "A Catholic Pentecostal Movement," *Ave Maria, A National Catholic Weekly* (June 3, 1967), 7-30.

Parham, Charles F., "A Critical Analysis of the Tongues Question," *The Apostolic Faith* (June 1925), 2-6.

——, "Sermon by Charles F. Parham," *The Apostolic Faith* (April 1925), 9-14.

Phillips, McCandlish, "And There Appeared Unto Them Tongues of Fire," *Saturday Evening Post* (May 16, 1964), 30-40.

Pinson, M. M., "The Finished Work of Calvary," *Pentecostal Evangel* (April 5, 1964), 7, 26-27.

Ralston, Thomas N., "Holiness and Sin—New Theory Noticed," *Quarterly Review of the M. E. Church, South,* XIV (July 1881), 441-451.

Riggs, Ralph M., "Those Store-front Churches," *United Evangelical Action,* IV (August 1, 1945), 4-5.

Roberts, Oral, "The Firstfruits of Our Labors," *Oral Roberts University Outreach* (Winter 1967), 1-24.

Stevenson, Janet, "A Family Divided," *American Heritage,* XVIII (April 1967), 4-24.

Sumner, Allene M., "The Holy Rollers on Shin Bone Ridge," *The Nation,* CXXI (July 29, 1925), 138.

Sydnor, Charles S., Jr., "The Pentecostals," *Presbyterian Survey* (May 1964), 30-32; (June 1964), 36-39.

Taylor, G. F., "Our Church History," *The Pentecostal Holiness Advocate* (January 20, 1921—April 14, 1921), a series of twelve articles.

Tinney, James S., "A Wesleyan-Pentecostal Appraisal of the Charismatic Movement," *The Pentecostal Holiness Advocate* (January 7, 1967), 4-10.

Van Dusen, Henry P., "Third Force in Christendom," *Life* (June 9, 1958), 113-124.

Wolff, M. J., "We Are Not Unitarians," *The Pentecostal Herald* (March 1967), 5.

Unpublished Materials

Beacham, Paul F., "Historical Narrative, A Bible School," Unpublished manuscript in the Library of Holmes Theological Seminary, Greenville, South Carolina. Written in March 1917.

Corvin, R. O., "A History of Education in the Pentecostal Holiness Church." Unpublished DRE dissertation, Southwestern Theological Seminary, Dallas, Texas, 1957.

Flower, J. Roswell, "History of the Assemblies of God" (n.p., n.d.), a short summary by one of the participants.

Gaddis, M. E., "Christian Perfectionism in America." Unpublished Ph.D. dissertation, University of Chicago, 1929.

Gilley, Billy Hawkins, "Social Trends as Reflected in American Fiction, 1870-1901." Unpublished Ph.D. dissertation, The University of Georgia, 1966.

Goodrum, C. L., "Some Studies in the Life and Times of John Wesley," Unpublished Master's thesis, The University of Georgia, 1939.

Hollenweger, Walter J., "Handbuch Der Pfingstbewegung, II. Haupteil, Nordamerika." Unpublished Doctoral dissertation, University of Zurich, 1965.

Hoover, Mario G., "Origin and Structural Development of the Assemblies of God." Unpublished Master's thesis, Southwest Missouri State College, 1968.

Menzies, William W., "The Assemblies of God: 1941-1967, The Consolidation of a Revival Movement." Unpublished Ph.D. dissertation, The University of Iowa, 1968.

Moore, Everett Leroy, "Handbook of Pentecostal Denominations in the United States." Unpublished Master's thesis, Pasadena College, Pasadena, California, 1954.

Paul, Harold, "The Religious Frontier in Oklahoma." Unpublished Ph.D. dissertation, The University of Oklahoma, Norman, 1966.

Ray, Mauldin A., "A Study of the History of Lee College, Cleveland, Tennessee." Unpublished Ed.D. dissertation, University of Houston, Texas, 1964.

Sala, Harold J., "An Investigation of the Baptizing and Filling Work of the Holy Spirit in the New Testament Related to the Pentecostal Doctrines of Initial Evidence." Unpublished Ph.D. dissertation, Bob Jones University, Greenville, South Carolina, 1966.

Turner, W. H., "The 'Tongues Movement': A Brief History." Unpublished Master's thesis, The University of Georgia, 1948.

Vivier, Lincoln Morse, "Glossolalia." Unpublished Doctoral dissertation, University of Witwatersrand, Johannesburg, South Africa, 1960.

Personal Interviews with Author

R. O. Corvin, Santiago, Chile, April 1967.

J. Roswell Flower, Springfield, Missouri, July 1969.

L. R. Graham, Memphis, Tennessee, November 1966.

Mrs. Nina Holmes, Greenville, South Carolina, January 1967.

H. T. Spence, Memphis, Tennessee, November 1966.

J. A. Synan, Franklin Springs, Georgia, May 1967.

Mrs. Bertha Teasley, Royston, Georgia, September 1963.

J. Floyd Williams, Franklin Springs, Georgia, May 1967.

Secondary Sources

Alexander, Gross, *History of the Methodist Episcopal Church, South*. New York: The Christian Literature Company, 1894.

Arthur, William, *The Tongue of Fire, Or the True Power of Christianity*. Columbia, South Carolina: L. L. Pickett, 1891.

Atter, Gordon, *The Third Force*. Peterborough, Ontario: The College Press, 1962.

Bach, Marcus, *They Have Found a Faith*. New York: The Bobbs-Merrill Company, 1946.

Barratt, Thomas Ball, *When the Fire Fell*. Oslo: Alfons, Housen & Soner, 1927.

Bates, Arlo, *The Philistines*. Boston: Ticknor & Company, 1888.

Bloch-Hoell, Nils, *The Pentecostal Movement, Its Origin, Development, and Distinctive Character*. Oslo, Norway: Universitetsforlaget, 1964.

Boland, J. M., *The Problem of Methodism: Being a Review of the Residue Theory of Sanctification and the Philosophy of Christian Perfection*. Nashville: Southern Methodist Publishing House, 1888.

Braden, Charles S., *Protestantism: A Symposium*. Nashville: Abingdon Press, 1944.

Brengle, Colonel S. L., *When the Holy Ghost Is Come*. New York: The Salvation Army Printing and Publishing House, 1914.

Brockett, Henry E., *The Riches of Holiness*. Kansas City: Beacon Hill Press, 1951.

Bucke, Emory Stevens, *et al.*, *The History of American Methodism*. 3 vols. Nashville: Abingdon Press, 1964.

Burnett, C. C., *In the Last Days, A History of the Assemblies of God*. Springfield, Missouri: Gospel Publishing House, 1962.

Burr, Nelson R., *A Critical Bibliography of Religion in America*. Princeton, New Jersey: Princeton University Press, 1961.

Campbell, Joseph E., *The Pentecostal Holiness Church, 1898-1948.* Franklin Springs, Georgia: Publishing House of the Pentecostal Holiness Church, 1951.

Candler, Warren A., *On with the Revolution: By One of the Revolutionaries.* Atlanta: Private Printing, 1887.

——, *Christus Auctor, A Manual of Christian Evidences.* Nashville: Publishing House of the Southern Methodist Church, 1900.

——, *Theater-Going and Dancing Incompatible with Church Membership.* Nashville: 1904.

Carradine, Beverly, *The Better Way.* Cincinnati: God's Revivalist Office, 1896.

——, *Golden Sheaves.* Boston: Joshua Gill, 1901.

Cash, W. J., *The Mind of the South.* New York: Alfred A. Knopf, 1941.

Chapman, J. F., *A History of the Church of the Nazarene.* Kansas City: Nazarene Publishing House, 1926.

Clark, Elmer T., *The Psychology of Religious Awakening.* New York: The Macmillan Company, 1929.

——, *The Small Sects in America.* Revised Edition. New York: Abingdon Press, 1949.

Conn, Charles W., *The Evangel Reader, Selections from the Church of God Evangel, 1910-1958.* Cleveland, Tennessee: Pathway Press, 1958.

——, *Like a Mighty Army, Moves the Church of God.* Cleveland, Tennessee: Church of God Publishing House, 1955.

Conwell, Russell, *Acres of Diamonds.* New York: Harper & Brothers, 1915.

Coulter, E. Merton, *College Life in the Old South.* New York: The Macmillan Company, 1928.

Cox, B. L., *History and Doctrine of the Congregational Holiness Church.* Greenwood, South Carolina: Publishing House of the Congregational Holiness Church, 1959.

Crawford, R. R., *A Historical Account of the Apostolic Faith.* Portland, Oregon, 1965.

Cross, Robert D., ed., *The Church and the City, 1865-1910.* New York: The Bobbs-Merrill Company, 1967.

Cross, Whitney R., *The Burned-Over District, The Social and Intellectual History of Enthusiastic Religion in Western New York.* New York: Harper & Row, 1965.

Curti, Merle, *The Growth of American Thought.* 2nd Edition. New York: Harper & Row, 1964.

Cutten, George Barton, *Speaking with Tongues.* New Haven: Yale University Press, 1927.

Davenport, Frederick Morgan, *Primitive Traits in Religious Revivals, A Study in Mental and Social Evolution.* New York: The Macmillan Company, 1905.

De Forest, John W., *The Wetherel Affair.* New York: Sheldon and Company, 1873.

Degler, Carl N., *Out of Our Past, The Forces That Shaped Modern America.* New York: Harper & Row, 1959.

Demerath, N. J. III, *Social Class in American Protestantism.* Chicago: Rand McNally & Company, 1965.

Duggar, Lillie, *A. J. Tomlinson, Former General Overseer of the Church of God.* Cleveland, Tennessee: White Wing Publishing House, 1964.

Eggleston, Edward, *The Circuit Rider: A Tale of the Heroic Age.* New York: Charles Scribner's Sons, 1909.

Evans, Avery D., *A. J. Tomlinson.* Cleveland, Tennessee: White Wing Publishing House, 1943.

Farish, Hunter D., *The Circuit Rider Dismounts, A Social History of Southern Methodism, 1865-1900.* Richmond, 1938.

Fisher, H. L., *History of the United Holy Church of America* (n.p., n.d.).

Flew, Newton R., *The Idea of Perfection in Christian Theology.* London: Oxford University Press, 1934.

Foster, Fred J., *Think It Not Strange, A History of the Oneness Movement.* St. Louis: Pentecostal Publishing House, 1965.

Frederick, Harold, *The Damnation of Theron Ware.* Cambridge: Belknap Press of Harvard University Press, 1960.

Frodsham, Stanley H., *With Signs Following.* Springfield, Missouri: Gospel Publishing House, 1946.

Gause, R. H., *Church of God Polity.* Cleveland, Tennessee: Pathway Press, 1958.

Gee, Donald, *All with One Accord.* Springfield, Missouri: Gospel Publishing House, 1961.

——, *The Pentecostal Movement.* London: Victory Press, 1949.

——, *Upon All Flesh, A Pentecostal World Tour.* Springfield, Missouri: Gospel Publishing House, 1947.

Geiger, Kenneth, *et al.*, *The Word and the Doctrine: Studies in Contemporary Wesleyan-Arminian Theology.* Kansas City: Beacon Hill Press, 1965.

Gewehr, Wesley M., *The Great Awakening in Virginia, 1740-1790.* Durham, North Carolina: Duke University Press, 1930.

Gibson, Luther, *History of the Church of God, Mountain Assembly.* n.p., 1954.

Girvin, E. A., *P. F. Bresee, A Prince in Israel.* Kansas City: Nazarene Publishing House, 1916.

Goff, Florence, *Life of Rev. J. A. Hodges.* Benson, North Carolina: Private Printing, 1903.

Harper, Michael, *As at the Beginning, The Twentieth Century Pentecostal Revival.* London: Hodder and Stoughton, 1965.

Hazeltine, Rachel C., *Aimee Semple McPherson's Kidnapping.* New York: Carleton Press, 1965.

Hofstadter, Richard, *Social Darwinism in American Thought.* Philadelphia: University of Pennsylvania Press, 1945.

Horton, Wade H., ed., *The Glossolalia Phenomenon.* Cleveland, Tennessee: Pathway Press, 1966.

Hudson, Hilary T., *The Methodist Armor, or a Popular Exposition of the Doctrines, Peculiar Usages, and Ecclesiastical Machinery of the*

Methodist Episcopal Church, South. Nashville: Publishing House of the Southern Methodist Church, 1919.

Hurst, J. F., *The History of Methodism.* 7 vols. New York: Eaton & Mains, 1902.

James, William, *The Varieties of Religious Experience.* New York: Longmans, Green & Company, 1902.

Johnson, Charles A., *The Frontier Camp Meeting; Religious Harvest Time.* Dallas: Southern Methodist University Press, 1955.

Johnson, Ruby F., *The Development of Negro Religion.* New York: The Philosophical Library, 1954.

———, *The Religion of Negro Protestants.* New York: The Philosophical Library, 1956.

Jones, W. M. D., *The Doctrine of Entire Sanctification Scripturally and Psychologically Examined.* Philadelphia: International Holiness Publishing House, 1890.

Kendrick, Klaud, *The Promise Fulfilled: A History of the American Pentecostal Movement.* Springfield, Missouri: Gospel Publishing House, 1961.

Knapp, Martin Wells, *Christ Crowned Within.* Cincinnati: God's Revivalist Office, 1886.

———, *Lightning Bolts From Pentecostal Skies, or Devices of the Devil Unmasked.* Cincinnati: The Pentecostal Holiness Library, 1898.

Law, William, *A Serious Call to a Devout and Holy Life.* New York: E. P. Dutton & Company, 1955.

Lawrence, B. F., *The Apostolic Faith Restored.* Springfield, Missouri: Gospel Publishing House, 1916.

Lindsay, Gordon, *The Life of John Alexander Dowie.* Dallas: The Voice of Healing Publishing Company, 1951.

Lindstrom, Harold, *Wesley and Sanctification.* Translated by H. S. Harvey. London: Epworth Press, 1946.

Lemons, Frank W., *Our Pentecostal Heritage.* Cleveland, Tennessee: Pathway Press, 1963.

Mann, Harold W., *Atticus Greene Haygood.* Athens: University of Georgia Press, 1965.

Martin, Ira J., *Glossolalia in the Apostolic Church.* Berea, Kentucky: The Berea College Press, 1960.

Mason, Mary, *The History and Life Work of Bishop C. H. Mason, Chief Apostle, and His Co-Laborers.* Memphis: Private Printing, 1934.

Mavity, Nancy Barr, *Sister Aimee.* Garden City, New York: Doubleday, Doran, & Company, 1931.

May, Henry F., *Protestant Churches in Industrial America.* New York: Harper & Row, 1949.

McDonnell, Kilian, *Catholic Pentecostalism: Problems in Evaluation.* Pecos, N.M.; Dove Publications, 1970.

McCrossan, T. J., *Speaking with Other Tongues, Sign or Gift, Which?* Seattle: Christian Publications, Inc., 1927.

McKitrick, Eric, *Slavery Defended: The View of the Old South.* Inglewood Cliffs, New Jersey: Prentice-Hall, 1963.

McLoughlin, William G., *Modern Revivalism.* New York: The Ronald Press, 1959.

McTyeire, Holland N., *A History of Methodism.* Nashville: Publishing House of the Southern Methodist Church, 1885.

Moberg, David O., *The Church as a Social Institution.* Inglewood Cliffs, New Jersey: Prentice-Hall, 1962.

Moody, William R., *The Life of Dwight L. Moody.* New York: Fleming H. Revell, 1900.

Myland, David Wesley, *The Latter Rain Covenant and Pentecostal Power.* Chicago: Evangel Publishing House, 1910.

Nichols, John Thomas, *Pentecostalism.* New York: Harper & Row, 1966.

Niebuhr, H. Richard, *The Social Sources of Denominationalism.* Hamden, Connecticut: The Shoestring Press, 1929.

Officer, Sam, *Wise Master Builders, and The Wheel of Fortune.* Cleveland, Tennessee: The Jesus Church, n.d.

Parham, Sarah E., *The Life of Charles F. Parham, Founder of the Apostolic Faith Movement.* Joplin, Missouri: The Tri-State Printing Company, 1930.

Paulk, Earl P., Jr., *Your Pentecostal Neighbor.* Cleveland, Tennessee: Pathway Press, 1958.

Peters, John Leland, *Christian Perfection and American Methodism.* New York: Abingdon Press, 1956.

Pierce, Alfred M., *Giant Against the Sky.* New York: Abingdon Press, 1958.

Pope, Liston, *Millhands and Preachers, A Study of Gastonia.* New Haven: Yale University Press, 1946.

Prince, Derek, *Purposes of Pentecost.* n.p., n.d.

Rauschenbusch, Walter, *Christianity and the Social Crisis.* New York: The Macmillan Company, 1907.

Ranaghan, Kevin and Dorothy, *Catholic Pentecostals.* New York: Paulist Press, 1969.

Redford, M. E., *The Rise of the Church of the Nazarene.* Kansas City: Nazarene Publishing House, 1951.

Robertson, Archie, *That Old-Time Religion.* Boston: Houghton Mifflin Company, 1950.

Root, Jean Christie, *Edward Irving, Man, Preacher, Prophet.* Boston: Sherman, French & Company, 1912.

Rose, Delbert R., *A Theology of Christian Experience.* Minneapolis: Bethany Fellowship, Inc., 1965.

Salisbury, W. S., *Religion in American Culture, A Sociological Interpretation.* Homewood, Illinois: The Dorsey Press, 1964.

Schaff, Philip, *History of the Christian Church.* New York: Charles Scribner's Sons, 1910.

Schroeder, W. Widick, and Victor Obenhaus, *Religion in American Culture.* London: Collier-Macmillan, Ltd., 1964.

Seldes, Gilbert, *The Stammering Century.* New York: Harper & Row, 1965.

Shaw, S. B., *The Great Revival in Wales.* Toronto: A. Sims, Publisher, 1905.

Sheldon, Charles M., *In His Steps.* New York: Thompson and Thomas, n.d.

Sheldon, H. C., *History of Christian Doctrine*. 2 vols. 2nd Edition. New York: Harper & Brothers, 1895.

Sherrill, John L., *They Speak with Other Tongues*. New York: McGraw-Hill Book Company, 1964.

Simkins, Francis Butler, *The South Old and New: A History, 1820-1947*. New York: Alfred A. Knopf, 1947.

Simmons, E. L., *History of the Church of God*. Cleveland, Tennessee: Church of God Publishing House, 1938.

Smith, George G., *The History of Georgia Methodism from 1786 to 1866*. Atlanta, 1913.

Smith, Timothy L., *Called Unto Holiness*. Kansas City: Nazarene Publishing House, 1962.

———, *Revivalism and Social Reform in Mid-Nineteenth-Century America*. New York: Abingdon Press, 1957.

Southey, Robert, *The Life of John Wesley*. 2 vols. London: Longman Hurst and Company, 1820.

Steele, Daniel, *A Defense of Christian Perfection*. New York: Hunt and Eaton, 1896.

———, *Love Enthroned, Essays on Evangelical Perfection*. New York: Nelson and Phillips, 1877.

Stevenson, Herbert F., *Keswick's Authentic Voice*. Grand Rapids, Michigan: Zondervan Publishing House, 1959.

Stewart, I. D., *History of the Freewill Baptists*. Dover, New Hampshire: The Freewill Baptist Printing Establishment, 1943.

Sweet, William Warren, *Methodism in American History*. New York: Abingdon Press, 1933.

———, *Religion in Colonial America*. New York: Cooper Square Publishers, Inc., 1965.

———, *Religion on the American Frontier. IV, The Methodists*. Chicago: The University of Chicago Press, 1946.

———, *Revivalism in America*. New York: Charles Scribner's Sons, 1944.

———, *The Story of Religion in America*. New York: Harper & Brothers, 1950.

Synan, Vinson, *Emmanuel College—The First Fifty Years*. Washington, D. C.: The North Washington Press, 1968.

Thomas, Iva, *History of Holmes Theological Seminary*. Franklin Springs, Georgia, n.d.

Thomas, Lately, *The Vanishing Evangelist*. New York: The Viking Press, 1959.

Torrey, R. A., *The Holy Spirit*. New York: Fleming H. Revell, 1927.

Turner, George Allen, *The More Excellent Way: The Scriptural Basis of the Wesleyan Message*. Winona Lake, Indiana: Light and Life Press, 1951.

Turner, W. H., *The Difference Between Regeneration, Sanctification, and the Pentecostal Baptism*. Franklin Springs, Georgia: Publishing House of the Pentecostal Holiness Church, 1947.

———, *Pentecost and Tongues*. Shanghai: Shanghai Modern Publishing House, 1939.

Underwood, B. E., *Fiftieth Anniversary History of the Virginia Conference of the Pentecostal Holiness Church*. Dublin, Virginia, 1960.

Vulliamy, C. E., *John Wesley*. New York: Charles Scribner's Sons, 1932.

Warfield, Benjamin B., *Perfectionism*. 2 vols. New York: Oxford University Press, 1931.

Waugh, Thomas, *The Power of Pentecost*. Chicago: Bible Institute Colportage Association, n.d.

Weatherford, W. D., *The American Churches and the Negro*. Boston: The Christopher Publishing House, 1957.

Weisberger, Bernard, *They Gathered at the River*. New York: Little, Brown, 1958.

Wimberly, C. F., *Are You a Christian?* Louisville: Pentecostal Publishing Company, 1917.

Winchester, Charles Wesley, *The Wells of Salvation*. New York: Eaton & Mains Publishing Company, 1897.

Winehouse, Irwin, *The Assemblies of God, A Popular Survey*. New York: Vantage Press, 1959.

Wood, J. A., *Perfect Love, or Plain Things for Those Who Need Them*. Chicago: The Christian Witness Company, 1880.

Wood, William W., *Culture and Personality Aspects of the Pentecostal Holiness Religion*. The Hague: Mouton Company, 1965.

Woodward, C. Vann, *Origins of the New South*. Baton Rouge: Louisiana State Press, 1951.

Zenos, Andrew C., *The Elements of Higher Criticism*. New York: Funk & Wagnalls Company, 1895.

INDEX